Grammar and Vocabulary for the TOEIC® Test

with answers

Self-study grammar and vocabulary reference and practice

JOLENE GEAR and ROBERT GEAR

CAMBRIDGE UNIVERSITY PRESS

CAMBRIDGE
UNIVERSITY PRESS

University Printing House, Cambridge CB2 8BS, United Kingdom

Cambridge University Press is part of the University of Cambridge.

It furthers the University's mission by disseminating knowledge in the pursuit of education, learning and research at the highest international levels of excellence.

www.cambridge.org
Information on this title: www.cambridge.org/9780521120067

First published 2010
7th printing 2016

Printed in Italy by Rotolito Lombarda S.p.A.

A catalogue record for this publication is available from the British Library

ISBN 978-0-521-12006-7 Paperback with answers and audio CD
ISBN 978-0-511-58791-7 Online resources

Thanks and acknowledgements

We would like to thank those people who made the publication of Grammar and Vocabulary for the TOEIC® Test possible. Our appreciation goes to the editorial team, Nora McDonald and Helen Ambrosio, as well as Sylvia Renaudon, Lynn Townsend and Tom Allen and the production and marketing teams, particularly Jeanette Alfoldi and Jane Durkin, for their combined efforts and painstaking care in helping to bring this book into print. We would also like to thank our colleagues at the University of Oulu, Finland and Sultan Qaboos University, Oman for their support in our efforts, with a special thank-you to Katja-Maaria Kilponen and Halle Marshall Mehtälä, for their input and feedback.

The author and publishers are grateful for the permissions granted to reproduce materials in either the original or adapted form. While every effort has been made, it has not always been possible to identify the sources of all the materials used, or to trace all copyright holders. If any omissions are brought to our notice, we will be happy to include the appropriate acknowledgements on reprinting.

p. 21(tl) ©Phil Degginger/Alamy; p. 21(tcl) ©D. Hurst/Alamy; pp. 21(tcr), 105(bc),140(t), 234(tr) ©Image Source/Alamy; p. 21(tr) ©Jim West/Alamy; p. 21(bl) ©Arcticphoto/Alamy; p. 21(bc) ©Photogenix/Alamy; p. 21(br) ©Alex Segre/ Alamy; p. 48(t ?); p. 48(b) ©Blend Images/Alamy; p. 66(l) ©Kevin Britland/Alamy; p. 66(r) ©Colin Craig/Alamy; pp. 91(l), 97(c), 105(tl) ©imagebroker/Alamy; p. 91(r) ©Whisson/Jordan/Corbis; p. 94(bl) ©Eyecandy Images/Alamy; p. 94(t) ©Foto28/ Alamy; p. 94(c) ©Pixland/Photolibrary; p. 94(br) ©LondonPhotos - Homer Sykes/ Alamy; p. 95 ©Greg Balfour Evans/Alamy; p. 97(t) ©Cephas Picture library/ Alamy; p. 97(b) ©Butch Martin/Alamy; p. 98 ©Neil Emmerson/Robert Harding Travel/Photolibrary; p. 105(tc) ©NUAGE/Alamy; p. 105(tr) ©Andres Rodrigues/ Alamy; p. 105(bl) ©Mira/Alamy; pp. 105(br), 189(t) ©westend61 GmbH/Alamy; p. 113(tl) ©Peter Titmuss/Alamy; p. 113(tr) ©les polders/Alamy; p. 113(bl) ©Torbjörn Largerwall/Alamy; p113(br) ©Ryan McGinnis/Alamy; pp. 129(a), (b), (e) ©Glowimages - artbox/Alamy; p.129(c) ©Rui Saraiva/Alamy; pp. 129(d), (f) ©Fancy/Alamy; pp. 136l, 188 ©Ace stock limited/Alamy; p. 136(cl) ©Lisa F. Young/Alamy; p. 136(cr) ©avatra images/Alamy; p. 136(r) ©David Young -Wolff/ Alamy; p. 140(b) ©amana images inc./Alamy; p. 144 ©Design Pics Inc./Alamy; p. 176tl ©David R Frazier Photolibrary Inc./Alamy; p. 176(tr) ©Arco Images GmbH/ Alamy; p. 176(cl) ©Lucidio Studio Inc/Alamy; p. 176(cr) ©ICP/Alamy; p. 176(b) ©Martin Novak/Shutterstock; p. 184 ©Radius Images/Alamy; p. 189(b) ©Ingram Publishing/Alamy; p. 243(bl) ©Deco/Alamy; p. 234(cr) ©Paul Risdale Pictures/ Alamy; p. 234(br) ©Peter Casolino/Alamy

Key
t, b, l, r = top, bottom, left, right
letters in brackets indicate picture label on page

Contents

Introduction

Who is this book for?

This book is for students preparing for the Test of English for International Communication™ (TOEIC®) and covers vocabulary and grammar useful for the business environment. It can be used as part of a TOEIC test preparation course in the classroom or for extra practice or review at home. Students who are not preparing for the TOEIC tests but want to review grammar and extend their vocabulary will also find this book useful.

How are the units organized?

The book consists of 25 units and 5 practice tests. There is a practice test section after every 5 units. Each unit presents and practices both the grammar and vocabulary within the context of a work-related topic. The units are divided into 4 parts:

A Context listening

This section introduces the vocabulary and grammar of each unit in context. It will help you to understand the grammar and vocabulary more easily.

B Grammar

This section is a review of important grammar points. Read through this section before you do the exercises. You can also refer back to this section when you are doing the exercises.

C Grammar exercises

This section provides grammar practice. Write your answers to the exercises and check your work using the answer key.

D Vocabulary

This section introduces the vocabulary for the topic in a 'key vocabulary' paragraph. The paragraph is followed by exercises for vocabulary practice. You can check your answers using the answer key.

Test practice sections

At the end of every five units, there is a test practice section. The tests are in the format used in the TOEIC test. The combined test practice sections make up one complete TOEIC Listening test, one complete TOEIC Reading test, two complete TOEIC Speaking tests, and two complete TOEIC Writing tests.

Each test practice section is accompanied by a grammar focus task and a vocabulary focus task. These are designed to raise your awareness of the way grammar and vocabulary are used in the TOEIC test.

Using the speaking practice test sections

Use the speaking practice test questions to practice the kinds of questions presented on the TOEIC Speaking test. The questions give you the opportunity to practice your oral skills. Focus on speaking clearly and using vocabulary and grammar accurately. If possible, you should record your answers so that a friend or teacher can give you their comments.

Using the writing practice test sections

Use the writing practice test questions to practice the kinds of questions presented on the TOEIC Writing test. The questions give you the opportunity to practice your writing skills. Focus on organizing your ideas and using vocabulary and grammar accurately. If possible, you should have a friend or teacher read your work and give you their comments.

Recording Scripts

The recording scripts for all the context listening sections and the listening practice tests are included. Look at the scripts after you answer the questions. Practice your listening skills by playing the recording again while you read the script. Practice your speaking skills by listening to the recording and pausing it to repeat what you have heard.

ONLINE Practice Tests

In association with *Grammar and Vocabulary for the TOEIC® Test,* Cambridge University Press will make available two complete online practice TOEIC tests – The practice TOEIC Test for Listening and Reading and the Practice TOEIC Test for Speaking and Writing. These tests can be found at www.cambridge.org/elt/toeictest. A guide to the scoring for the TOEIC Speaking and Writing test is also included on the website.

Overview of the TOEIC Test

The Test of English for International Communication (TOEIC) test can be used to show your proficiency in English for the workplace or for entry into a study program. Depending on the requirements you need to meet, you will take either the TOEIC Listening and Reading test or the TOEIC Speaking and Writing test. For a complete assessment of all your language skills, you may be required to take both TOEIC tests. These tests can be taken at ETS-approved locations worldwide.

The TOEIC Listening and Reading test
This test is a paper and pencil test using a multiple choice format. It lasts approximately 2 hours with 45 minutes for Listening and 75 minutes for Reading. You will need another 30 minutes for completing forms containing needed biographical information. The format of the test is as follows:

Listening Comprehension: 100 items
Part 1: Photographs: 10 items
Part 2: Question-Response: 30 items
Part 3: Conversations: 30 items (10 conversations with 3 questions each)
Part 4: Short talks: 30 items (10 talks with 3 questions each)

Reading Comprehension: 100 items
Part 5: Incomplete Sentences: 40 items
Part 6: Text Completion: 12 items (4 texts with 3 items each)
Part 7: Simple Passages: 28 items (7–10 texts with 2–5 questions each)
Double Passages: 20 items (4 pairs of texts with 5 questions per pair)

The TOEIC Speaking and Writing test
This test is an internet-based test in which your responses to the tasks are recorded for scoring. You have approximately 20 minutes for the Speaking test and 60 minutes for the Writing test. The format of the test is as follows:

Speaking Test: 11 items
Questions 1 – 2: Read a text aloud
Question 3: Describe a picture
Questions 4 – 6: Respond to a question
Questions 7 – 9: Respond to questions using information provided
Question 10: Propose a solution
Question 11: Express an opinion

Writing Test: 8 items
Questions 1 – 5: Write a sentence based on a picture
Questions 6 – 7: Respond to a written request
Question 8: Write an opinion essay

1 Applying for a job

Word forms

Noun, verb, adjective, and adverb forms

A Context listening

1 **A temporary position is open at MacNulty's Chocolate Factory. You are going to hear two people at an interview. Before you listen, look at the picture and answer these questions.**

1 Which person in the picture is the interviewer? ____________________

2 Which person in the picture is the candidate? ____________________

3 What job is the candidate applying for? ____________________

2 **Listen and check if you were right.**

3 **Listen again and fill in the blanks.**

1 You're the ___applicant___ for the secretarial job, right?

2 Your résumé certainly is ____________________.

3 Your last employer was very ____________________ with you.

4 He says you are ____________________, hard working, and efficient.

5 I'm a little surprised you haven't ____________________ for a permanent job.

6 You see, my background and ____________________ are in theater.

7 It was called "The Over- ____________________ Graduate."

8 You played the part of the secretary with such ____________________.

TOEIC® TIP

Listen carefully to talks and conversations. Practice identifying who is speaking, where the conversation or talk is taking place, and what is being discussed.

4 **Compare the following pairs of answers from Exercise 3.**

a **Look at answers 1 and 5, 2 and 3, 4 and 8, and 6 and 7. What is similar about each pair?** ______________________

b **In each pair, what parts of speech are the two words?**

1 noun ______________ 5 verb ______________

2 ______________ 3 ______________

4 ______________ 8 ______________

6 ______________ 7 ______________

5 **Match the two parts of the common phrases you heard in the conversation. Listen again if you need to.**

1 permanent a qualified

2 employment b letter

3 cover c job

4 over d agency

B Grammar

1 Word forms

A word may have more than one form depending on what part of speech it is. Look at the different forms of the word *compete*.
*We **compete** with several companies.* (verb)
*Our **competition** in this field is growing.* (noun)
*We are in a **competitive** market.* (adjective)
*We must think **competitively**.* (adverb)

2 Noun forms

Nouns are words that refer to things, people, places, etc. We use them in sentences as subjects or as objects.
*My **qualifications** are in theater. (qualifications =* subject*)*
*Secretaries can make a good **salary** nowadays. (salary =* object*)*

We can often recognize nouns through their suffixes (the part at the end of the word). Some noun suffixes indicate a person. The most common suffix for a person is *-er / -or*. Other suffixes for people include *-ess*, *-ic*, *-ist*, and *-ian*. The suffix *-ess* indicates that the person is female.
manager, senator, princess, critic, pianist, politician

We use the suffixes *–ion / -ation* and *-ment* to make verbs into nouns.
promote / promotion, apply / application, govern / government

We use the suffixes *-ness* and *-ity* to make adjectives into nouns.
happy / happiness, tidy / tidiness, stupid / stupidity

Other noun suffixes include *-acy, -age, -ance, -ant, -dom, -hood, -an, -ism, -ary, -ship.*
***Accuracy** is important in accounting.*
*The **package** arrived damaged.*

3 Verb forms

Verbs are words that show states or actions. In English, we always use a subject with a verb.
*Our boss **is** always happy.*
*He **manages** the department very effectively.*
*I **enjoy** working as a secretary.*

The verb form changes to agree with the subject (*I*, *he*, *she*, etc.) and to agree with the tense (present, past simple, etc.). ► (See verbs, Units 2, 3, 4, and 5.)
*He **prepares** a weekly report. They **prepare** a weekly report.*
*I **begin** a new job today. I **began** a new job yesterday. **I've** recently **begun** a new job.*

We can recognize verbs through their suffixes. The most common verb suffix is *-ize*, which we can use to make adjectives and nouns into verbs.
*The government is planning to **modernize** the transport system.*
*I didn't **recognize** you.*

Other verb suffixes include *-ate, -en,* and *-ify*.
*We won't **duplicate** the process next year.*
*We want to **widen** participation in our training program.*
*Will we have to **justify** our decision to the board?*

4 Adjective forms

Adjectives are words that describe people and things. ► For more information on how we use them, see Unit 9.

We can often recognize adjectives through their suffixes. Some common adjective suffixes are *-able, -ful, -ish, -ive, -less, -ous,* and *-y*.
The training session was ***valuable*** *and I was very* ***grateful*** *for the chance to attend.*
I appreciated his ***generous*** *gesture.*
Our manager is ***worthy*** *of her position.*

We use some verbs that express feelings to make adjectives. These adjectives use an *-ed* ending to describe the feelings. They use the *-ing* ending to describe the person / thing that causes the feelings. Verbs that we often use to make these adjectives are:
amaze, annoy, astonish, bore, confuse, embarrass, excite, fascinate, frighten, interest, satisfy, worry
I watched a very ***interesting*** *presentation about quality control yesterday. But I don't think Mike was* ***interested*** *since he kept looking at his watch.*

5 Adverb forms

Adverbs are words that describe actions. ► For more information on how we use them, see Unit 9.

We can often recognize adverbs through their suffixes. The most common adverb suffix is *-ly*.
The ad campaign was run ***effectively.***
Your résumé ***certainly*** *is impressive.*

Other adverb suffixes include *-ward* and *-wise*.
He wants to keep moving ***upward*** *on the corporate ladder.*
Turn this knob ***clockwise.***

C Grammar exercises

1 **Label the words in the box V (verb), N (noun), Adj (adjective) or Adv (adverb). Some of these words can have the same form but be different parts of speech.**

application N___ beneficial ___ employment ___ enthusiastically ___
experienced ___ impressively ___ interview ___ manageable ___
qualify ___ require ___ successful ___ suitably ___

2 **Use the words in the box in 1 to complete the columns below. Not all words have all word forms and some words have more than one form.**

noun	verb	adjective	adverb
application	apply	applied	-

3 **Underline the adjective or adverb that completes the sentences.**

1 The decision was *enthusiastic* / *enthusiastically* welcomed by the development team.
2 Hiring more people is *economic* / *economically* impossible at this time.
3 Have you found a *suitable* / *suitably* candidate for the assistant manager job?
4 The person chosen for the position has not been *official* / *officially* informed yet.
5 The second interviewee was extremely *polite* / *politely*.
6 Our project has been completed *successful* / *successfully*.

4 **Fill in the blank with the correct adjective form of the given verb.**

1 The book gave a fascinating (*fascinate*) account of how to succeed in business.
2 If you are ________________ (*excite*) about the job, you should apply.
3 You will find working at Blink's a ________________ (*challenge*) experience.
4 The rise in sales is an ________________ (*encourage*) development.
5 I was ________________ (*amaze*) that our shopping cart was so successful.
6 The documentary program about business takeovers was very ________________ (*interesting*).
7 I will be very ________________ (*annoy*) if Henri arrives late for another meeting.

5 **Look at the following interview questions. Make a new question using the underlined word or phrase to form the verb.**

1 When have you found a solution to a difficult problem?
When have you solved a difficult problem?
2 What was your motivation to apply for this position?
What ________________?
3 When did you get your qualifications to become an accountant?
When ________________?
4 What do you consider a challenge?
What ________________?
5 What have some of your accomplishments been in your career so far?
What ________________?

6 **How would you reply to these interview questions? Write responses, including another form of the word in italics.**

1 Why did you *decide* to apply for this job?
Actually, it was a very easy decision for me. This is just the sort of job I was looking for, so I had to apply!
2 Give some examples of your *success* when working in a team.
____
3 What are your short-term and long-term *plans*?
____
4 Why should we *employ* you?
____
5 What *motivates* you in a job?
____

D Vocabulary

Key Vocabulary

Read this paragraph about applying for jobs and check your understanding of the meaning of the words in bold.

When **employers** want to **fill a permanent** or **short-term / temporary vacancy**, they usually advertise the **position** in a newspaper or on the Internet. If you want to **apply for the job**, you should send a well-written **cover letter** and **résumé** to the company or **recruitment agency**. You should give details of your **qualifications** and **references**. If they think you might be the right **candidate** for the job, they will call you in for **an interview**. As well as the right qualifications and relevant **work experience**, they might look for other qualities, including **people skills**, **communication skills**, and the ability to work well as a team member. After the interview the company will decide whether to **reject** or **hire** you.

Vocabulary note

Career is a countable noun. We use it to talk about a job regarded as a long-term activity or professional occupation.
Job is a countable noun. We use it to talk about a specific task or the regular work a person does to earn money.
Work is an uncountable noun or a verb. We use it to talk about an activity a person does, usually for money.
*I have a **job** as a delivery man for a pizza place. My **work** consists of taking pizzas to our customers. In the future, I would like a **career** in restaurant management.*

1 Replace the underlined word or phrase in each of the following sentences with a word from the box that has the same or a similar meaning.

vacancies	candidates	employment	hire	~~impressed~~	reject	temporary

1 Peter certainly made a positive impression on the audience with his lecture. impressed
2 We plan to employ three new people in the components department. ____________
3 How many applicants are we seeing this morning? ____________
4 Bentley's is advertising several openings for a sales representative. ____________
5 I've been contacted by the recruitment agency about your vacancy. ____________
6 He did several short-term jobs in different companies. ____________
7 We don't accept candidates who don't speak a foreign language. ____________

2 **Read this extract from an email and underline the correct word.**

Delete Reply Reply All Forward Print

Hi Faryal,

I have some great news! Do you remember helping me look for a job? Well, last month, I **1** *applied / impressed* for a job at a large marketing company. I wasn't sure if I had all the right **2** *requirements / qualifications*, but I've taken a marketing course, so I wrote to the company. I included the **3** *recruitment / résumé* you helped me write and some **4** *references / employer letters* from my last two bosses. Someone from the company phoned me last week and asked me to come for an **5** *interview / application* the next day. I was a bit nervous, but I knew that I really had to **6** *position / impress* the interviewers. So before I went I practiced answering the interview questions that you emailed me. The interview was quite long but it seemed to go quite well. And I've just heard that they are **7** *offering / opening* me the job. I am the successful **8** *hire / candidate*! So I just wanted to thank you for the help you gave me…

3 **Match the sentences in column A with those in column B.**

Column A

1 I don't feel too disappointed.
2 I need to earn some money this summer.
3 I have been with this company a long time.
4 I want to keep the same job until I retire.
5 I'm sure I'll get the job.

Column B

a I am looking for a temporary job.
b I would like a better position here.
c There are more vacancies than applicants.
d Lots of people were rejected for the job.
e I want a permanent job.

2 Business documents

Present tenses

Present simple, present continuous, imperatives, state verbs

A Context listening

1 **You are going to hear Emma talking to her boss, John Fleming. Before you listen, look at the pictures and answer these questions.**

1 Where is Emma? ____________________

2 Where is John? ____________________

3 Why do you think John is calling Emma? ____________________

2 **Listen and check if you were right.**

3 **Look at the words from the conversation and put them in the correct category.**

attachment   file   ~~memo~~   fax   report   folder

1 types of documents: memo ________________ ________________
2 ways to send a document: ________________ ________________
3 used to organize documents: ________________ ________________

4 **Write complete answers to these questions about the conversation.**

1 When does Emma usually have her coffee break? Emma usually has her coffee at 10:00.
2 What does John want? ________________
3 What does the fax machine guarantee cover? ________________
4 How is Emma sending her copy of the report to John? ________________
5 What equipment does John need? ________________
6 Where is Emma looking for the file? ________________

5 **Look at your answers to Exercise 4 and answer these questions.**

1 Which sentence is about a regular action? ________________
2 Which sentence is about a general truth? ________________
3 Which sentences are about actions at or around the time of speaking? ________________
4 Look at answers 1 and 3. What tense are they? ________________
5 Look at answers 4 and 6. What tense are they? ________________
6 Look at answers 2 and 5. Do they fit the pattern in questions 1–5? ________________

B Grammar

1 Present simple

+	verb (*I, you, we, they*) verb + *–s* (*he, she, it*)	*I **live** in New York City.* *Emma **works** with John.*
–	*do not / don't* + verb *does not / doesn't* + verb	*We **don't need** any more files.* *He **doesn't share** an office.*
?	*do*... verb? *does* ... verb?	*What **do** you **think** about the contract?* ***Does** John **have** a printer?*

We use the **present simple** when we talk about:

- things that happen regularly
  *Emma **has** her coffee break at 10 A.M.*
  ***Does** Christina often **work** overtime?*
- a permanent situation
  *The hotel **doesn't have** a printer.*
  *I **live** within walking distance of the office.*
- a general truth
  *Customers **expect** friendly service.*
  *Some businesses **don't keep** accurate records of their transactions.*

We use some words with the present simple to show how often the action happens.

always	usually	frequently	often	sometimes	seldom	rarely	never

*I **don't always read** the morning newspapers.*
*She **often brings** her lunch to work.*

2 Imperatives

When we give an order or tell someone to do something, we use the infinitive without *to* and no subject.
***Call** me back with the figures.*
***Put** these papers into the folder, please.*

To make a negative imperative, we use *do not / don't* and the infinitive without *to*.
***Don't use** the fax machine. It's broken.*

3 Present continuous

+	*am / are / is* + verb + *-ing*	*Emma **is taking** a coffee break.*
–	*am / are / is not* + verb + *-ing*	*They **aren't talking** on the phone.*
?	*am / are / is* ... + verb + *-ing* ... ?	***Is** John **waiting** for the email?*

We use the **present continuous** when we talk about:

- actions that are happening at the time of speaking
  *I'**m sending** you an electronic copy as an email attachment now.*
  *Jenny **isn't using** the fax machine at the moment.*

- actions that are temporary
  *This week we **are offering** a special discount on swimsuits.*
  ***Are** you **advertising** a position for an accountant?*
- changing situations or trends
  ***Are** share prices **rising**?*
  *The average workplace **is becoming** safer.*

We often use these words with the present continuous to show when the action is taking place.

now	at this moment	currently	today	this week	this month	this year

*Margot **isn't working** on the inventory report **today.***

4 State verbs

We often use some verbs in the present simple because their meaning indicates a general truth rather than something temporary. State verbs describe:

- senses: *hear, see, smell, taste*
  *The hotel buffet **smells** wonderful.*
  ***Do** you **hear** that noise?*
- feelings: *enjoy, feel, like, mind, need, want, prefer*
  *What **do** you **want** me to do with it when I find it?*
  *I **don't like** the new advertising campaign.*
- thoughts: *agree/disagree, believe, know, mean, realize, recognize, think, understand*
  *I **know** the original copy of those papers is in the office.*
  *They **don't recognize** the market potential.*
- possession: *have, own, belong*
  ***Do** you **have** a copy of the Newhaven report?*
  *Mr. Franck **owns** a chain of restaurants.*
- description: *appear, contain, look, seem, sound*
  *Janet's suggestion **sounds** very interesting.*
  *This advertisement **doesn't look** very attractive, in my opinion.*

Some state verbs can be used in the continuous form when the meaning is temporary. Look at the examples in the table. The meaning of the sentences in each column is different.

Temporary	State
*What **are** you **thinking** about now?* (= considering)	*I **think** it's a good plan.* (= in my opinion)
***I'm having** problems with this program. Can you help me?* (= experiencing)	*We **have** a photocopier in our office.* (= possession)
***I'm seeing** Fran Harkins this afternoon.* (= meeting)	*I **see** that the office renovation has started.* (= notice)
*We**'re feeling** pressure from the competition.* (= experiencing)	*I **feel** we made the right decision.* (= believe)

C Grammar exercises

1 Complete the sentences with the correct form of the words in parentheses.

1 Sally collects (*collect*) shipments from the airport on Mondays.
2 You're too late. Your plane ________ (*take off*) right now.
3 Today Amy ________ (*not work*) late because she's finished the report.
4 ________ (*you finish*) work at 5 P.M.?
5 They ________ (*currently take*) inventory of the storeroom.

2 Choose the best ending to complete the sentences.

1 Mr. Williams uses a company car
   a when he travels to conferences. ✓
   b because the bus drivers are on strike.
2 Chloe is preparing her presentation so
   a she closes her door.
   b she wants some privacy.
3 Does Mary input Jim's data
   a because he is too busy?
   b because he has a meeting later?
4 I am locking my desk drawer
   a when I put anything valuable in it.
   b because I have some money there.
5 Jacob clears the papers from his desk
   a before he goes home.
   b because he is on holiday next week.

3 Underline the correct form of the verb.

1 A: June *looks* / *is looking* for some new office furniture.
   B: I don't know why. Her furniture *looks* / *is looking* new to me.
2 A: I *don't have* / *'m not having* any success in getting this printer to work.
   B: Oh, that printer doesn't work when the paper supply is low. We *have* / *are having* some in the supply room.
3 A: Jim always *enjoys* / *is enjoying* trade fairs.
   B: Well, he really *enjoys* / *is enjoying* this year's fair.
4 A: I *think* / *am thinking* about quitting my job.
   B: Really? I *don't think* / *'m not thinking* that is a good idea.
5 A: I *see* / *am seeing* that we need to reserve a place in the exhibition hall.
   B: Yes, we do. I *see* / *am seeing* one of the trade fair organizers about a place today.

TOEIC® TIP

In Listening Part 2, choices that include the same words and same tense as those in the question are frequently *not* the correct choices.
Example: *Is Mr. Timms thinking about replacing our equipment?*
Correct Answer: *Yes, he found a good deal.*
Incorrect Answer: *No, he is just thinking about replacing it.*
Incorrect Answer: *Yes, he is replacing the equipment.*

4 **Use the instructions to write a command.**

1 Cars may be coming. You should look both ways at a stop sign.
Look both ways for traffic.

2 The company does not want you to smoke in this area.
____

3 The bike route is safer to ride on than the highway.
____

4 You should not trespass because of the wild animals.
____

5 It is important to watch for animals crossing the road.
____

6 The stairs are slippery. You should be careful.
____

7 You shouldn't go the wrong way down this street.
____

5 **Write six true sentences about yourself. Use the words in box A and a verb from box B or your own verb.**

A

at this moment | always | before bedtime | currently | every morning | every now and then | most holidays | this week

B

drive | enjoy | have | meet | see | shop | sleep | take | think | travel | work | visit

1 Every now and then I take the bus to the city and visit the Natural History Museum.
2 ____________________
3 ____________________
4 ____________________
5 ____________________
6 ____________________
7 ____________________

D Vocabulary

Key Vocabulary

Read this paragraph about documents that we use in business and check your understanding of the words in bold.

There are many different types of business **documents** and these days they can be either in paper or **electronic** form. If you work in business, you are likely to see a lot of **correspondence** in your **in-boxes**, including letters, **emails,** and **faxes**, as well as internal documents such as **memos**, **reports,** spreadsheets, and **inventories**. You can keep paper documents or **hard copies** of **electronic documents** in **files** or **folders** at your desk. However, if they are **confidential**, you might want to put them somewhere more secure. If you want extra copies, you can **photocopy** the original. On a computer, you can organize your documents, or files, into folders to make them easier to find. Then, if you want to send them to someone, you can email them as an **attachment**.

TOEIC® TIP

When you are preparing for the listening section, look out for words that have the same or similar pronunciation. These words can cause confusion in the exam.

*I sent you a **fax** so that you would have it immediately.*
*I included all the **facts** and figures in the report.*

While you are studying, make a list of words that sound the same but have different meanings. Use the context to know which word is being used.

1 **Choose the best definitions for the words in the box.**

attachment correspondence ~~email~~ fax file folder memo photocopy report

1 a message that is sent over the Internet *email*
2 a machine-made copy of a document ______
3 information that you store on a computer as one unit ______
4 a document with details of an event or situation ______
5 a place on a computer where you can store files or programs ______
6 a short message sent to the staff of a company ______
7 a computer file that is sent with an email message ______
8 letters written from one person to another ______
9 a document sent by electronic image through a telephone line ______

2 **Fill in the blanks with the correct word in the box.**

correspondence	inventory	copy	report	folder	in-box	~~memo~~

1 The manager sent around a ____memo____ about possible overtime hours.
2 Thank you for the ________________ of the memo I misplaced.
3 I'm looking for the ________________ that contains all the new customer files.
4 I have to take care of all these documents in my ________________ before leaving this evening.
5 These figures don't match the ones in the market research ________________.
6 The stock room is closed while they take ________________ of all the items in stock.

3 **Underline the correct word in the following email.**

File Edit View Insert Format Tools Message Help

Hi Sam,
Greg said he told you about the fire in our office last night. Luckily, no one was there but the fire destroyed or damaged almost all of our **1** *documents* / *attachments*, so we're trying to figure out what we have left! We have **2** *reports* / *copies* of most of the contracts and invoices in the warehouse, as well as all of the **3** *confidential* / *electronic* letters, so hopefully we haven't lost anything really important. One thing I need is the contact list of clients' phone numbers. Our office computers aren't working, so could you print out a **4** *hard copy* / *photocopy* of the list and fax it to me? I will let you know if I need any other **5** *memos* / *files*.
Thanks,
Tammy

3 Air travel

Past tenses

Past simple, past continuous, *used to* and *be used to*

A Context listening

1 **You are going to hear Bill and Jenny talking about his journey. Before you listen, look at the picture and answer these questions.**

1 Where are Bill and Jenny? ____________________

2 Who was traveling? ____________________

3 Who met the flight? ____________________

2 **Listen and check if you were right.**

> ***Vocabulary note***
>
> **Journey** is a countable *noun* that refers to the action of going from one place to another.
> *When they introduce the new high speed train, the* ***journey*** *to the airport will only take 25 minutes.*
> **Trip** is a countable *noun* that refers to a short journey taken for business or pleasure.
> *I have to make a* ***trip*** *into town to pick up some groceries.*
> **Travel** is a *verb* that means to take a journey or an uncountable *noun* that refers to the activity of traveling.
> *I keep a diary of my* ***travels****. Next week I'll* ***travel*** *to Rome.*

3 Listen again and fill in the blanks.

1 *Check-in* used to take ______ a long time.

2 A *security guard* ______ me aside when I ______ the alarms with the metal pin in my foot.

3 Yes, I was expecting it. I ______ alarms these days!

4 Bad weather ______ a lot of problems.

5 In the confusion, I ______ my *boarding pass*.

6 One of the *cabin crew* ______ at the *boarding gate*.

7 My luggage ______n't ______ on the *carousel* at the *baggage pick-up*.

8 And I bet a lot of people ______ at the *lost luggage counter*.

4 Look at your answers to Exercise 3 and answer these questions.

1 Which sentences talk about a completed action in the past? ______

2 Which sentences are about actions that were in progress in the past? ______

3 Which sentence indicates a past action that is no longer true? ______

4 Which sentence indicates that someone is familiar with doing something? ______

5 Which sentences use the past simple? ______

6 Which sentences use the past continuous? ______

5 Look at the words in italics in Exercise 3. Which ones refer to:

1 people? security guard ______

2 places in the airport? ______

3 other things at an airport? ______

B Grammar

1 Past simple and past continuous forms

	past simple	past continuous
+	verb + *-ed* *He **checked** my report.*	*was / were* + verb *-ing* *He **was checking** my report.*
-	*did / did not* + verb *I **didn't watch** the movie.*	*was / were not* + verb *-ing* *They **weren't watching** the movie.*
?	*did* ... + verb? ***Did** he **speak** to the boss?*	*was / were* ... + verb *-ing* ... ? ***Was** he **speaking** to the boss?*

Many commonly used verbs are irregular in the past simple:
go → went
buy → bought
spend → spent
(► See Appendix 2 for a more complete list.)

2 Past simple and past continuous uses

We use the **past simple** when we want to:

- talk about a completed action in the past

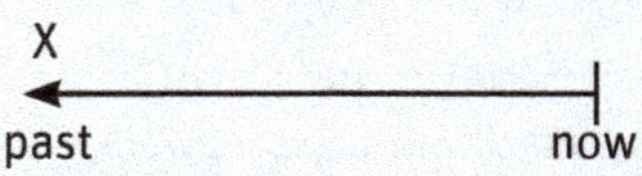

*I **looked** at a couple of magazines.*

- emphasize that an action is completed

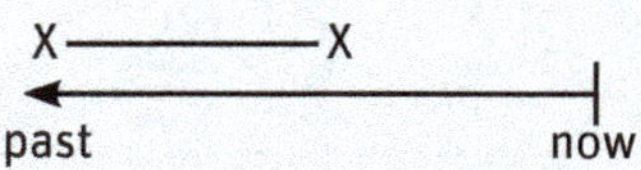

I ***worked*** for Blick Enterprises in the summer.
(= and then I stopped working for them.)

- talk about actions that follow other actions in the past

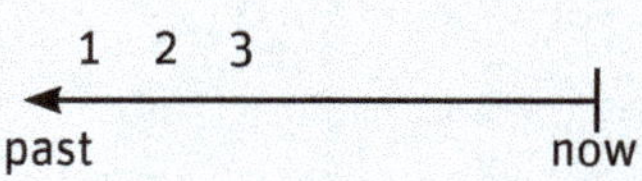

*When I finally **got** here and **went** to the baggage pick-up, my luggage **didn't turn up** on the carousel.*

- talk about an activity that took place regularly in the past

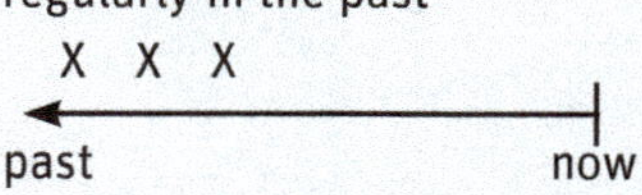

I ***brought*** my lunch every day last week.

We use the **past continuous** when we want to:

- talk about an action that was in progress at a certain point in the past, especially when another action interrupts it

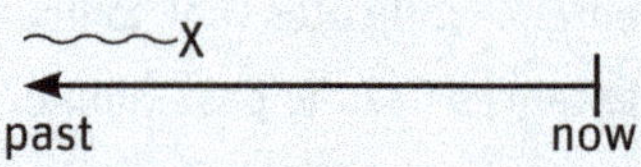

*I **was** just **catching up** on my email when your flight arrived.*

- emphasize the duration of the action

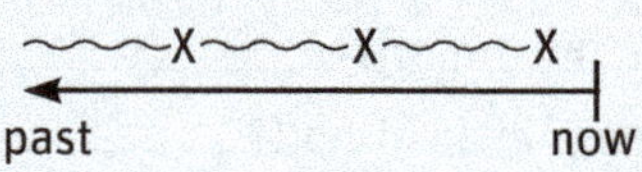

*I **was working** for Blick Enterprises all summer.*
(= it was a long time)

- talk about actions that continued at the same time in the past

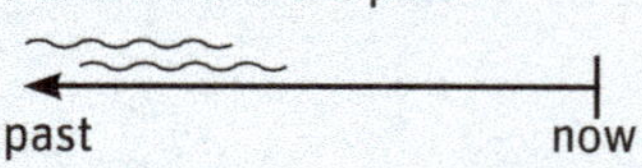

I ***was looking*** for my boarding pass while I ***was walking*** to the gate.

When and *while* both mean "during a period of time". We don't use *while* with the past simple.

3 *Used to* vs. *be / get used to + -ing*

It can be easy to confuse *used to* and *be / get used to*.

We use *used to* when we talk about past routines that we no longer follow and permanent situations that are no longer true.

+	*used to* + verb	*She **used to travel** with just one carry-on.*
-	*did not use to* + verb	*He **didn't use to** travel by plane.*
?	*did ... use to* + verb?	***Did** they **use to** inspect all the bags?*

*Betty **used to buy** a lot of duty free products.* (She doesn't buy a lot of duty free products anymore.)
*The boss **didn't use to take** so many flights.* (He now takes a lot of flights.)
***Did** Rahul **use to work** for an airline?* (Rahul may or may not work for an airline now.)

We use *be used to* + *-ing* when we talk about being familiar with doing something.

+	*am / are / is used to* + verb + *-ing* *was / were used to* + verb + *-ing*	*She **is used to working** under pressure.* *She **was used to working** under pressure.*
-	*am / are / is not used to* + verb + *-ing* *was / were not used to* + verb + *-ing*	*They **aren't used to giving** presentations.* *They **weren't used to giving** presentations.*
?	*am / are / is ... used to* + verb + *-ing ...?* *was / were ... used to* + verb + *-ing ...?*	***Are** you **used to taking** a coffee break?* ***Were** you **used to** taking a coffee break?*

*Jackie **is used to helping** customers find what they want.* (Jackie is familiar with this work and still does this.)
*I **wasn't used to dealing with** customer complaints.* (I wasn't familiar with this work in the past.)

We use *get* (or *become*) *used to* verb + *-ing* when we talk about becoming familiar with doing something.
*They **are getting used to living** in the city.* (They have moved to the city and are becoming familiar with living there.)
*Sue Wing **got used to working** at night and on the weekend.* (At first it was hard, but Sue became familiar with working at night and on the weekend.)

We can use *be* (or *get*) *used to* + noun.
*Jenny **is used to** the rain in Seattle.*
*Terry **isn't getting used to** the noise at the factory.*

C Grammar exercises

1 Look at Sara's schedule for yesterday.

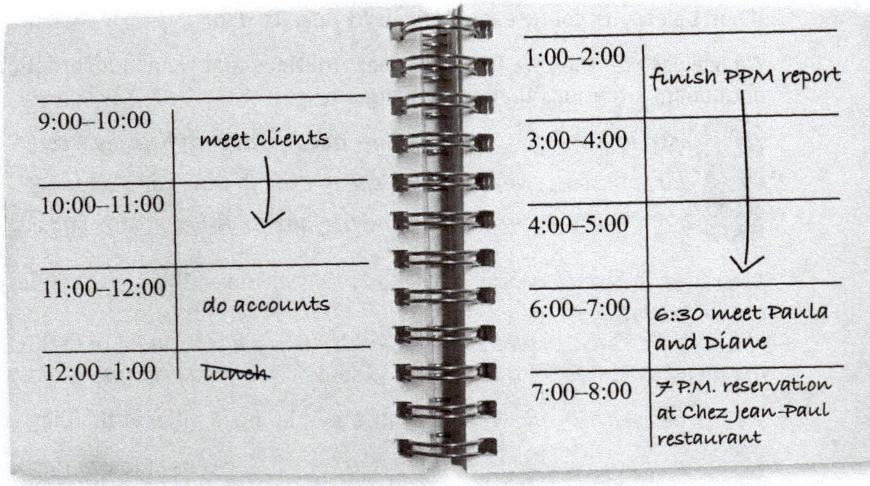

a **Complete the sentences with the words in parentheses. Use the past simple.**

1 (*do?*) What did you do yesterday? ________

2 (*meet / do*) Well, in the morning I ________.

3 (*not have*) I ________.

4 (*finish*) In the afternoon ________.

5 (*do / evening?*) What ________?

6 (*meet / go*) In the evening ________.

b **Complete the sentences with the words in parentheses. Use the past continuous.**

1 (*you / do / 10 A.M.*) What were you doing at 10 A.M. ________?

2 (*talk*) At 10 A.M. I ________.

3 (*finish*) At 3:15 I ________.

4 (*not drive / home*) At 6:45 I ________.

5 (*talk, while / wait*) At 6:45 I ________.

2 Fill in the blanks with the past simple or past continuous of the verbs in parentheses.

While I **1** was reading (*read*) the flight information board, I **2** ________ (*notice*) that my flight left from a different terminal. I **3** ________ (run) through the departure lounge to catch the airport shuttle bus when I **4** ________ (*trip*) over someone's luggage and **5** ________ (*drop*) my handbag. All the contents of my handbag **6** ________ (*fall*) out onto the floor. While I **7** ________ (*pick up*) my things, I **8** ________ (*see*) a passport under a chair in the lounge. I **9** ________ (*reach*) for the passport when I **10** ________ (*hear*) an upset passenger talking to an airport official. I quickly **11** ________ (*go*) over to them with the passport. But, while I **12** ________ (*talk*) to the airport official and the passenger, the shuttle bus **13** ________ (*leave*). The airport official **14** ________ (*arrange*) for me to ride with some pilots and flight attendants who **15** ________ (*go*) to the other terminal. And that is how I **16** ________ (*meet*) the pilot I **17** ________ (*marry*).

3 **Use some of the words in the box to write three sentences with your own ideas. Write about something you were doing when something else happened.**

call	drive	prepare	read	study	talk	TV	walk	watch	work

1 I was driving to work yesterday when I heard an ambulance behind me.
2 ______
3 ______
4 ______

4 **Underline the correct verbs.**

A: **1** *Did you use to / Used you to* have any problems with the job when you were a flight attendant?
B: Well, I **2** *used to find / am getting used to finding* it almost impossible to sleep in strange hotel rooms. That was a real problem for me.
A: Is that why you changed careers?
B: I suppose. Well, I **3** *was used to enjoying / used to enjoy* the traveling a lot but eventually I became a bit tired of the long haul flights. It was difficult to give up the regular trips to exotic locations, but now I **4** *used to stay / am used to staying* at home more.
A: Is there anything you miss?
B: Yes, I **5** *didn't use to pay / am not used to pay* very much for perfume and things like that because I bought them in the duty free stores during layovers, but now I have to pay normal prices again!

5 **Write three sentences about things you used to do but do not do anymore and three sentences about things that you are used to doing now. You can use the words in the box to give you some ideas.**

city	climb	go to sleep	home	jump	music	play	school	swim	work

1 When I was young, I used to take the bus to school in the morning.
2 ______
3 ______
4 ______
5 I am used to getting up early in the morning.
6 ______
7 ______
8 ______

D Vocabulary

Key Vocabulary

Read this paragraph about airplane travel and check your understanding of the words in bold.

When you arrive at the airport **terminal**, take your **baggage / luggage**, ticket, and identification to the **check-in desk. Passengers** who only have a **carry-on bag** can also check in online or on computers at the airport. Then proceed through **security** to the **boarding gate**. Check the information boards to see if your **flight** is **delayed** or how long of a **layover** you may have. As you **board your plane**, a member of the **cabin crew** will check your **boarding pass** and direct you to the correct **aisle** and seat. When you arrive at your destination, pick up your baggage from the **carousel**. If your flight was international, you will go through **customs** and **passport control**. If you have crossed several **time zones,** you may suffer from **jetlag** when you arrive.

1 Underline the correct word.

1 Even though I had nothing to declare, I was stopped and questioned at *boarding / customs*.

2 Sorry I'm late. The flight was *jetlagged / delayed* because of bad weather.

3 Erika flew across several *time zones / layovers* so she woke up at 4:00 A.M.

4 With these new e-tickets, *lost luggage / check-in* is much easier than it used to be.

5 Excuse me. Could you tell me which *carousel / boarding gate* the baggage from the Dubai flight will be on?

6 When I fly, I always choose the *aisle / carry-on* seat because it's easier to get up and walk around the plane.

7 The *security / cabin crew* helped me when I needed medical attention during my flight.

8 I've been waiting for half an hour for my *passport / baggage* to arrive. I hope they haven't lost it.

2 a Match the words with the definitions.

1 delays b____

2 flights ____

3 passengers ____

4 security ____

5 terminal ____

a People who travel in a vehicle without controlling or driving the vehicle.

b When you have to wait longer than expected for something to happen.

c The things that are done to keep someone or something safe.

d The building people go through before getting on or after getting off an airplane.

e Journeys in an airplane that carries passengers from one place to another.

b Use the words to fill in the blanks in the article on the next page.

New Employee at Airport Solves Bird Problem

When you think of a ___security___ risk at an airport, you don't usually think of animals! But an airport in Florida has had serious problems with birds. A lot of different bird species live near the ______ building and often fly over the airport. It's very dangerous for the ______ and can cause ______ and accidents. The airport was looking for a way to scare the birds away when they heard about the use of dogs at military airports. They bought a dog who has been very successful in scaring the birds, but not harming them. And of course he is also very popular – ______ on the planes always look out for him!

3 **Choose the word from the box that can fill all the blanks.**

boarding	flight	luggage	~~security~~	terminal

1 ___security___ guard, ___security___ check
2 lost ______ counter, ______ carousel, carry-on ______
3 ______ pass, ______ gate, ______ card
4 ______ number, ______ attendant, delayed ______
5 ______ building, airport ______, international ______

4 Shopping

Present perfect

Present perfect simple and continuous, *for* and *since*

A Context listening

1 **You are going to hear a conversation between Mary and Anita. Before you listen, look at the pictures and answer these questions.**

1 Where has Mary been? ______

2 What has Mary been doing? ______

3 Why has Mary come into work so early? ______

2 **Listen and check if you were right.**

3 **Read the following sentences and write T if the sentence is true and F if the sentence is false.**

1 Mary has just returned from a trip to the New York City book fair. ________

2 She has been going to this book fair *for five years*. ________

3 Mary has been wondering if there is a special occasion because there are so many people in the streets. ________

4 Mary has been at work *since 5 A.M.* ________

Listen to the conversation again to check your answers.

4 **Look at the sentences in Exercise 3. Which sentence shows an example of each of these?**

1 an action that happened at a time that is not specified ________

2 an action that happened recently ________

3 an action that began in the past and continues to the present ________

5 **You heard the words below in the conversation. Fill in the blanks.**

order	cash register	~~merchandise~~	counter	sale	display

The customer took some **1** merchandise ________ that was for **2** ________ from the **3** ________ case and brought it to the man working the **4** ________ at the check-out **5** ________ to pay for it. While paying, she asked him if she could place an **6** ________.

Vocabulary note

The words *sale* and *sell* can be confusing.
Sale is a noun. It has two meanings:
*I made a good **sale** today.* (*sale* = the act of selling)
*There is a **sale** on at the mall.* (*sale* = a time when a store sells goods at a lower price than usual)
Sell is a verb:
*He **sells** interior decorating supplies.*

B Grammar

We use the present perfect and the present perfect continuous to talk about actions or states that started in the past and continue to the present, or which finished recently.

1 Present perfect form

+	*has / have* + past participle	*He **has sold** his business.*
-	*has / have not* + past participle	*They **haven't sold** their business.*
?	*has / have* ... + past participle?	***Have** you **sold** your business?*

Many commonly used verbs have irregular past participles.
go → *gone* *fall* → *fallen* *write* → *written*
(See Appendix 2 for a more complete list.)

2 Present perfect continuous form

+	*has / have been* + verb *-ing*	*They **have been offering** a discount.*
-	*has / have not been* + verb *-ing*	*They **haven't been offering** any discounts.*
?	*has / have ... been* + verb *-ing*?	***Have** they **been offering** any discounts?*

3 Comparing present perfect and present perfect continuous

We use the present perfect or present perfect continuous when we talk about:

- an action that happened at a time that is not specified
  *Mr. Brockman**'s gone** to the bank. He **hasn't returned** yet.*
  *Oh, look! It**'s been snowing.***
  ***I've been wondering** why no one was on the streets.*
- an action that happened recently
  *I**'ve** just **returned** from my trip to the New York City book fair.*
  *It's getting cold in here. **Have** you **opened** the window?*
  *I'm very tired because **I've been working** at the check-out counter during the clearance sale.*
- an action that began in the past and continues to the present (often with *for* or *since*)
  *Mrs. Umar**'s been** the manager of a department store for 10 years.*
  ***I've been** here since 5 A.M.!*
  ***Haven't** you **been waiting** on customers all morning? Take a break.*
- an action that happened a number of times
  ***I've reorganized** the merchandise on the rack four times today already.*
  ***I've only been** to the Paris fashion market once.*
  *Mark**'s been stopping** for gas at the same station since he bought his first car.*

Use **present perfect** to talk about how often or how many times.
*I've **brought** my car to the mechanic four times this week.*

Use **present perfect** to focus on a completed activity.
*Min Ki **has fixed** my laptop problem.*

Use **present perfect continuous** to talk about how long.
*I've **been working** really hard all morning.*

Use **present perfect continuous** to focus on the activity.
*Min Ki **has been fixing** laptops during his time off.*

Both **present perfect** and **present perfect continuous** can be used with verbs that normally happen over a period of time. There is no difference in meaning.

*We **have lived** here for years.* | *We **have been living** here for years.*
*I **have waited** for Luke long enough.* | *I **have been waiting** for Luke long enough.*

C Grammar exercises

1 Fill in the blanks with the present perfect or present perfect continuous.

1 Carlo Merendino left five minutes ago. A sales representative calls wishing to speak to him. Ben says, "I'm afraid he ____has____ just ____left____ (*leave*)."

2 Carlo returns. Ben says, "A sales representative, Mr. Lee, ________ just ________ (*call*)."

3 Carlo asks Ben if Mr. Lee left a message. Ben says, "Mr. Lee ________ (*receive*) your order."

4 Carlo asks if Mr. Lee said anything else. Ben says, "Yes, he and his wife ________ (*invite*) you out for lunch tomorrow."

5 Carlo asks, "Are they in town?" Ben says, "Not yet, but they ________ (*reserve*) seats on an evening flight."

6 Carlo says, "It is a long flight from Hong Kong. They'll have jetlag." Ben says, "No, they ________ (*attend*) the American Gem Exposition in New York City this week."

7 Carlo says, "Really? I didn't know that Mr. Lee also dealt in jewelry." Ben says, "The company he works for ________ (*expand*) the business to include jewelry since January."

2 Write sentences about Martha's day using the present perfect or the present perfect continuous. Use your own ideas or the words in parentheses to help you.

1 Martha is folding up her umbrella. (*rain*)

It has been raining. / It has just stopped raining.

____

2 Martha is throwing away empty boxes. (*clean*)

____

____

3 Martha is putting new stock on the shelves. (*replace*)

____

____

4 Martha is putting away her cell phone. (*talk*)

____

____

5 There are lots of people in Martha's dress shop. (*sale*)

____

____

6 Martha looks happy. (*sell*)

____

____

3 **Read the article from a popular magazine and underline the best form of the verb.**

TOP STORIES

FASHION

Actor Robert Lee won last year's "Best Dressed Male" at the Screen Fashion awards. With this year's competition coming up, I am fortunate to have him take me along to his favorite clothing store to show me how he dresses so well. Robert **1** *has come* / *has been coming* here to buy clothes since he was 15. "They know me really well here," he tells me. "Silvio, the owner, **2** *has become* / *has been becoming* a good friend of mine." Robert **3** *has relied* / *has been relying* on Silvio to make him look fashionable since he became famous.

"This is where I come when I want to see the latest fashions," Lee tells me. "I **4** *have just placed* / *just been placing* an order for a new suit. I expect they **5** *have finished* / *have been finishing* it by now." Then Silvio comes out from a back room.

He **6** *has brought* / *has been bringing* with him the latest catalog for Robert to look at. Silvio tells me that Lee **7** *has always been* / *has always been being* a very loyal customer.

We recognize another customer who **8** *has waited* / *has been waiting*. She **9** *has sat* / *has been sitting* in a comfortable chair reading a magazine. It is Maria Garfield, the well-known TV announcer. She smiles at Robert, who waves back. Robert tells me that they **10** *have been* / *have been being* friends for many years. She tells us that Silvio **11** *has worked* / *has been working* on a dress for her to wear at the next Screen Fashion awards which she will be presenting.

4 **Write *for* or *since* in the spaces below.**

1 Ernie has been looking for the missing receipts __________ Tuesday.

2 Rachel has been ordering perfumes from the same supplier __________ 10 years.

3 The Browns have been selling antiques __________ 1951.

4 Mona has been working at the check-out counter in a department store __________ three months.

5 Business has been bad __________ that new shopping mall opened.

TOEIC® TIP

In Part 7 you will encounter many different types of reading materials, such as advertisements, brochures, business reports, etc. We have focused on many of these reading texts in this book. To become familiar with as many different kinds of material from the working world as possible, you should read English language newspapers, websites, flyers, etc.

D Vocabulary

Key Vocabulary

Read this paragraph about shopping. Check your understanding of the words in bold.

When a customer wants to buy something, they have to choose the type of **(retail) store** they want to go to. Some stores are **outlets** of large **chains** and some are small private businesses. When a customer enters a store they see the **display** of the **stock/ merchandise** that is **for sale**. All the merchandise has a **price tag** or a **label** with a **bar code**. If customers don't find what they are looking for, they can place an **order**. The **sales clerk** at the counter uses the bar code to enter the price of the product into the **cash register**. The customer pays for the purchases with cash or a credit card and any store **coupons** or special **gift certificates**. It is important for customers to keep their **receipts** in case there is a problem with the merchandise. If there is, the customer returns the **purchase** to the store with the receipt within a certain time period for a **refund**.

Vocabulary note

Some words have the same noun and verb form and are pronounced the same.
***Or**der* (noun/verb); ***an**swer* (noun/verb); ***pur**chase* (noun/verb)
Some words have the same noun and verb form but have a different pronunciation.
Re**cord* (noun), *re**cord (verb); ***in**crease* (noun), *in**crease*** (verb); ***re**fund* (noun), *re**fund*** (verb)

1 Read these email extracts and then complete the definitions with the correct word in italics.

I've just come back from the mall. I went with my brothers and sisters to try to buy birthday presents for Mom. Jessica had some *coupons* from the newspaper to get 10 cents off Mom's favorite brand of soap, so that's what she got. Matthew and Sarah decided to buy a *gift certificate* for Mom so she could choose her own birthday present.
I didn't get anything – I still haven't decided what to buy. Have you got any ideas?

Jeff is so ambitious. He used to be a *sales clerk* in a supermarket, and then he bought a small hardware store. He's determined to turn his small business into an international *chain* with *outlets* throughout the world. A new shopping mall with a lot of *retail stores* has just opened near his house, but he's not worried about the competition. And people do seem to be making a lot of *purchases* – his *cash register* was full last time I was there!

1 ____An outlet____ is a shop that sells one type of product or the products of one company.

2 ________ are things you buy.

3 ________ is a machine that is used in stores for keeping money in, and for recording everything that is sold.

4 ________ is a piece of paper that can be used instead of money to pay for goods or services.

5 ________ is a number of similar shops, restaurants, etc., owned by the same company.

6 ________ is a piece of printed paper that you can use to buy something at a cheaper price or to get something free.

7 ________ is a building or a place in a building where you can buy things.

8 ________ is a person who works in a store helping customers.

2 Use the words in the box to complete the sentences. Use each word twice, once as a verb and once as a noun. Put the word into the correct form.

display	order	purchase	stock	store

1 Stores ____display____ samples of their ____stock____ in their windows in order to attract customers.

2 This is Yun Son here. I'm calling to see if you have any of those new exercise machines in your ________. I'd like to place an ________ for one.

3 Tracy's Department Store ________ an interesting variety of convenience products, don't you think? And have you seen the wonderful ________ in their toy department?

4 Do we still ________ office chairs in the warehouse? We have a customer who would like to ________ one.

5 I would like my ________ gift-wrapped if possible. Oh, and by the way, I'd like to ________ some of those nice curtains that are in your catalog.

3 Underline the correct word.

1 Julia demanded a *refund* / *receipt* because the book she received was damaged.

2 When I took my purchases to the *chain* / *counter* to pay, I couldn't find my credit card.

3 Shoppers should carefully read the *labels* / *bar codes* on the back of the bottle.

4 We put in a large *order* / *gift certificate* for the coming season's greeting cards.

5 Pooja used a *coupon* / *purchase* for one of the items she bought.

6 We need to organize this new *display* / *merchandise* on the shelves.

7 These items don't seem to have a *price tag* / *stock* so I don't know the price.

5 Business trips

Future

Present continuous; present simple; *going to; will*

A Context listening

1 **Nan has taken care of the arrangements for Inez's business trip. She is telling Inez the plans she has made. Before you listen, look at the picture. What do you think her plans are? What will the weather be like?**

2 **Listen and check if you were right.**

3 Listen again and complete the sentences below.

1 What does Nan say about Inez's departure? "You ___leave___ Tuesday evening at 6:00."

2 What does Nan say about the Kivilinnan Guesthouse? "It ____________ for repairs."

3 What does Inez say about getting into Helsinki? "I ____________ just ____________ a taxi.

4 What does Nan say about Wednesday's transportation? "They ____________ someone to your hotel to pick you up at 9:30."

4 Look at your answers to Exercise 3 and answer the questions below.

1 Which sentence is a decision about future plans made at the moment of speaking? ________
What tense is used? ____________

2 Which sentence talks about timetables? ________
What tense is used? ____________

3 Which sentence talks about an action that has been planned for the future? ________
What tense is used? ____________

4 Which sentence talks about plans for the future made at sometime in the past? ________
What tense is used? ____________

5 Below are some words you heard in the conversation concerning Inez's trip to the trade fair in Helsinki. Group the words in the box in the categories below.

amenities	book	complimentary breakfast	~~guesthouse~~	reserve	hotel

1 place to stay ___guesthouse___

2 arrange to have a room, table, etc. ____________

3 services ____________

B Grammar

1 Present continuous

We can use the present continuous (▶ see Unit 2) when we talk about an event or action that we have planned for the future.

*We **are launching** our new line of office furniture at the trade show.*
*I'm **not returning** from the convention until Friday.*

2 Present simple

We can use the present simple (▶ see Unit 2):

- when talking about timetables and programs
  *You **leave** Tuesday evening at 6:00.*
  *When **does** the conference **begin?***
- when referring to a future time in a clause beginning with *after, as soon as, before, when, until*
  *Should I email them **as soon as I make** the booking?*
  ***When** we **arrive** in Helsinki, we will pick up the rental car that we booked.*

3 *Will*

+	*will ('ll)* + verb	*He**'ll come** to the conference.*
-	*will not (won't)* + verb	*I **won't come** to the conference.*
?	*will ...* + verb?	***Will** they **come** to the conference?*

We use ***will*** when we:

- make a decision about the future at the time of speaking
  *Let's see. It is 11:30 now. **I'll take** over the stand while you have lunch.*
  ***Will** it **take** long? No, it **won't take** more than 20 minutes.*
- indicate being prepared or willing to do something
  ***I'll let** you know what the options are.*
  ***Will you send** over some more brochures if we need them?*

4 *Going to*

+	*am / is / are going to* + verb	*She**'s going to come** to the conference.*
-	*am / is / are not going to* + verb	***I'm not going to come** to the conference.*
?	*am / is / are ... going to* + verb?	***Are** they **going to come** to the conference?*

We use ***going to*** when we:

- intend to do something in the future based on a decision made before now
  *I'll have to rethink what **I'm going to pack**.*
  ***Is** Lisa **going to be** in charge of product presentations at the show?*
- can see that something will happen in the very near future
  *Those brochures **are going to fall** off the counter.*

5 Comparing *will* and *going to*

Intentions

A: ***I'm going to look*** *at some of the other stands during my lunch break.* (A decision made before speaking.)

B: *That sounds like a good idea.* ***I'll join*** *you if you don't mind.* (A decision made at the moment of speaking.)

Predictions

A: *Move the display back a bit. It****'s going to get*** *knocked over.* (A prediction based on what the speaker can see.)

B: *No. It* ***won't fall****. I've attached it very securely.* (A prediction based on what the speaker believes.)

Sometimes we can use either *will* or *going to* with very little or no difference in meaning.

Tomorrow ***I'm going to*** */* ***I'll be*** *27 years old.*

*I think we****'re going to accomplish*** */ we****'ll accomplish*** *a lot at this trade show.*

C Grammar exercises

1 **Mr. Anderson wants to meet Mr. Brooke. Look at Mr. Brooke's schedule and complete his part of his conversation with Mr. Anderson.**

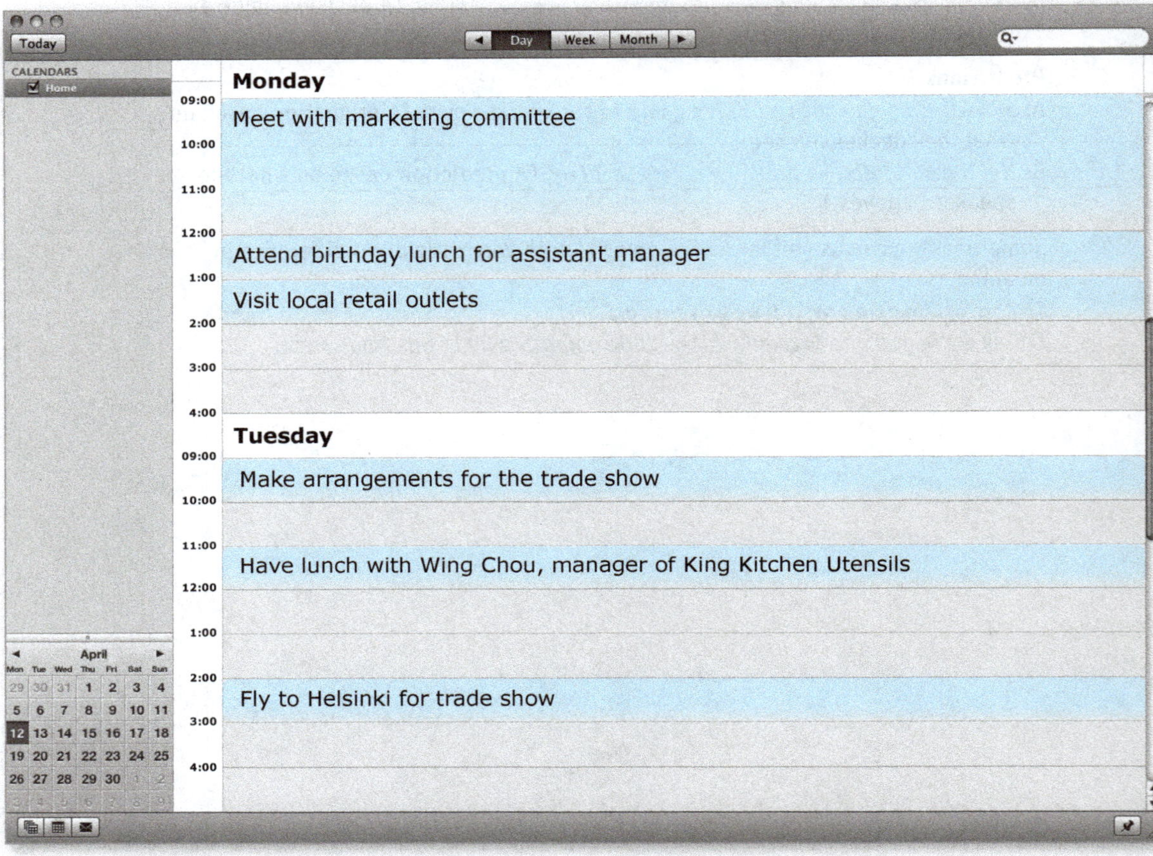

1 Mr. Anderson: Can we meet first thing on Monday morning?
Mr. Brooke: No, that's impossible. I'm meeting with my marketing committee.

2 Mr. Anderson: How about later for lunch?
Mr. Brooke: No, I can't do that either. ______

3 Mr. Anderson: What about Monday afternoon?
Mr. Brooke: That's not possible either. ______

4 Mr. Anderson: Are you free any time on Tuesday morning?
Mr. Brooke: Actually, ______

5 Mr. Anderson: Tuesday lunchtime then?
Mr. Brooke: I'm afraid not. ______

6 Mr. Anderson: What about Tuesday afternoon?
Mr. Brooke: I can't make it. ______

2 **Katrina and Juho are deciding how they will share their duties at a trade show. Fill in the blanks with *will* or the present simple of the verbs in parentheses.**

Katrina: OK, so, someone needs to set up the stand at 8 A.M.
Juho: **1** I'll do ________ (*do*) that if you like. I don't mind getting up early. **2** ________ you ________ (*make*) the coffee then?
Katrina: Of course! No problem. And **3** I ________ (*be*) at the stand from 9 A.M. to talk to customers.
Juho: Great. What **4** ________ I ________ (*do*) when I **5** ________ (*finish*) setting up the stand?
Katrina: You can hand out brochures and maybe go check out the competition.
Juho: Sounds good. **6** I ________ (*let*) you know if I see anything interesting. And then **7** I ________ (*give*) the product presentation at 12.
Katrina: Good idea. But before you **8** ________ (*do*) that, could you take my place at the stand for half an hour so I can take a break?
Juho: OK, **9** I ________ (*come*) back and be at the stand until the presentation **10** ________ (*start*). By the way, what time are we finished?
Katrina: Well, the public **11** ________ (leave) by 6 o'clock, but we **12** ________ (stay) until everything is packed away.

3 **Choose the most natural alternative.**

Graham: **1** *I'm going to go* / *I'll go* to the Food and Beverage Fair. Are you?
Clare: I didn't know it was on. Do you have a brochure?
Graham: Yes, it's right here in my bag. **2** *I'm going to get* / *I'll get* it for you. Here it is.
Clare: Thank you. Oh, this does look good. **3** *Are you going to attend* / *Will you attend*?
Graham: Yes, **4** *I'm going to go* / *I'll go* with Troy and Helen. **5** *We're going to get* / *We'll get* there early so we can taste the food samples. Do you want to come along?
Clare: Hmm, let me think. OK. Yes, thanks. **6** I *am going to come* / *will come*. What time **7** *are you going to go* / *will you go*?
Graham: Helen and Troy **8** *are going to pick* / *will pick* me up around 5 o'clock. I'm sure **9** *they are going to have* / *they'll have* room for you.
Clare: Oh, thank you. **10** *Are you going to call* / *Will you call* me and let me know for sure?
Graham: Of course. See you later.

D Vocabulary

Key Vocabulary

Read this paragraph about business trips and check your understanding of the words in bold.

Usually a business trip is less stressful if the traveler knows something about the **destination** before making the journey and has a well-planned **itinerary**. During periods when there are **exhibitions** or **conferences**, all kinds of **accommodation(s)**, from expensive hotels to lower-priced **guesthouses,** can fill up quickly. When there are not many **vacancies**, hotel **receptionists** will not accept **bookings** unless they get last-minute **cancellations**. So company representatives traveling on business trips should **reserve** their hotel rooms ahead of time. Fortunately, most hotels publish **brochures**, either online or in paper form, advertising the **facilities** and **amenities** available. These amenities may include such things as the availability of a gym or swimming pool, and **complimentary** meals. The hotel may provide **courtesy transportation.** In case it doesn't, a traveler should have some local currency available to pay for the taxi **fare**. Before **registering** at a hotel, travelers should pay attention to this information if they don't want to be disappointed.

Vocabulary note

The word *exhibit* can be a noun or a verb.
*We **exhibited** our new range of DVD players.*
The noun refers to an item in an *exhibition*.
*This **exhibit** is the most valuable in the museum.*

TOEIC® TIP

Words like *fare* and *fair* might be in answer choices in the exam because they are pronounced in the same way. A *fare* is the charge paid for transportation, such as a bus or train. A *trade fair* or *show* is an exhibition of products or services usually organized by or aimed at the business community.

1 Complete the sentences with the words in italics.

1. The Clive Hotel offers guests a complimentary breakfast and a courtesy bus to the airport. *courtesy / complimentary*
2. I am going to look for comfortable ________ at a small ________ within a few blocks of the station. *accommodations / guesthouse*
3. We can offer cheap and fast ________ to your next ________. *destination / transportation*
4. My ________ is planned so I can attend several ________ in the same region. *itinerary / conferences*
5. I have ________ at a hotel with excellent ________. *facilities / registered*
6. I'm sorry. We are fully ________ for next weekend, but we can put your name on a waiting list in case of an unexpected ________. *vacancy / booked*

2 Underline the word that completes the sentence.

1 Mr. Simms is making a *reserve* / *reservation* for those of us going to the conference.

2 The *reception* / *receptionist* at the desk in our hotel was very helpful.

3 If we are going to *cancel* / *cancellation* our trip, we will need to contact the hotel.

4 The *exhibit* / *exhibition* will last one week.

5 What time will *register* / *registration* take place at the conference?

3 Match the words with a word that has a similar meaning.

1 amenities	a cost
2 brochure	b courtesy
3 complimentary	c facilities
4 fare	d booklet

Practice test 1

TOEIC® TIP

Look at the answer choices for the missing words in Part 5 and Part 6 to identify whether you need to find the correct vocabulary word, the correct word form, or the correct grammatical structure. Then look at the sentence or paragraph to find the clues that will help you choose the answer.

Example: If the four answer choices are *go*, *goes*, *is going*, and *are going*, you should be looking for the subject of the verb to identify whether the correct answer choice should be plural or singular. You should look for the adverbs of time to identify whether the correct answer choice should be in the present simple or present continuous.

Listening

Part 1: Photographs

Directions: In this section, you will hear four statements about a photograph. The statements will not be printed on the test. As you listen, select the statement that best describes the photograph. You will hear the statements only once.

1 (A) (B) (C) (D)

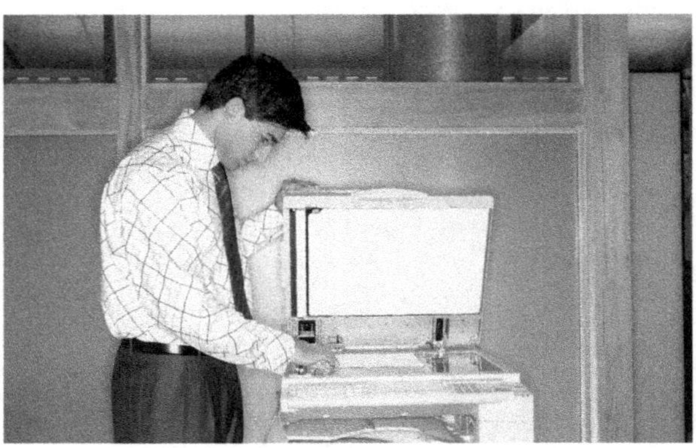

2 (A) (B) (C) (D)

Part 2: Question-Response

Directions: In this section, you will hear a question or statement followed by three responses. They will not be printed on the test. As you listen, select the best response. You will hear the question and statements only once.

3	(A)	(B)	(C)
4	(A)	(B)	(C)
5	(A)	(B)	(C)
6	(A)	(B)	(C)
7	(A)	(B)	(C)
8	(A)	(B)	(C)

Part 3: Conversations

Directions: In this section, you will hear two people having a conversation and will answer questions about what you heard. The conversations will not be printed on the test. Select the response that best answers the question. You will hear the conversation only once.

Questions **9–11** refer to the following conversation.

9 Where does this conversation take place?
(A) At a hotel
(B) In a secretary's office
(C) In a travel agency
(D) At an airport

10 What will the man do?
(A) Stay on the plane
(B) Change his itinerary
(C) Spend the night in Athens
(D) Catch a night flight to Copenhagen

11 What does the woman offer to do?
(A) Call the airport
(B) Print the schedule
(C) Change the itinerary
(D) Make a hotel reservation

Questions **12–14** refer to the following conversation.

12 Where does this conversation take place?
(A) In an office
(B) At a car factory
(C) In a repair shop
(D) At a rooftop restaurant

13 Where is the man going?
(A) To Paris
(B) On leave
(C) To the building next door
(D) To a different office

14 What does the woman offer to do?
(A) Close the window
(B) Transfer the man's calls
(C) Photocopy and file his reports
(D) Give him something for his headache

Part 4: Talks

Directions: In this section, you will hear a speaker giving a talk and will answer questions about the talk. The talks will not be printed on the test. Select the response that best answers the question. You will hear the talks only once.

Questions **15–17** refer to the following conversation.

15 Who is speaking?
(A) A representative of the airport
(B) A visitor to the hotel
(C) An IT expert
(D) A hotel employee

16 What does the speaker say about the business lounges?
(A) They sell food and drinks.
(B) They will have shower facilities.
(C) They will make trips more comfortable.
(D) They have telephones.

17 What is the purpose of this announcement?
(A) To tell passengers about changes to the airport
(B) To direct passengers to the business lounges
(C) To sell newspapers and magazines
(D) To tell passengers their flight times

Questions **18–20** refer to the following conversation.

18 Who is speaking?
(A) A dissatisfied employee
(B) A representative from a survey company
(C) A communications expert
(D) An office equipment sales manager

19 What is the speaker comparing?
(A) Workstations and lighting
(B) Shared facilities
(C) Staff duties
(D) Office layouts

20 Which piece of equipment is not mentioned?
(A) Computers
(B) Fax machines
(C) Photocopiers
(D) Printers

Reading

Part 5: Incomplete Sentences

Directions: In each sentence below, a word or phrase is missing. Select the best answer from the four choices to complete the sentence. Mark (A), (B), (C), or (D).

1 Fran received an ________ letter from that job she applied for.
(A) accept
(B) accepting
(C) accepted
(D) acceptance

2 Sue bought that suit on sale ________ I don't think she can get her money back.
(A) as
(B) so
(C) if
(D) but

3 The flight attendant went through the ________ and closed all the overhead compartments.
(A) cabin
(B) terminal
(C) boarding gate
(D) passport control

4 A vacancy will be opening ________ the spare parts department.
(A) of
(B) from
(C) in
(D) without

5 I ________ in the Andromeda project.
(A) participate
(B) participated
(C) participating
(D) participates

6 We need ________ the second point on the agenda.
(A) to talk
(B) to talk about
(C) talking
(D) talking about

7 Henderson's Jewelry is ________ a very good benefits package.
(A) having
(B) offering
(C) applying
(D) purchasing

8 I think ________ agree on Lucy's suitability for the job.
(A) we
(B) us
(C) our
(D) ours

9 Victor ________ to complete all the forms while waiting in the departure lounge.
(A) trying
(B) be trying
(C) was trying
(D) were trying

10 I'm afraid we'll have to ________ Mr. Jenkins for this job.
(A) reject
(B) rejecting
(C) rejected
(D) rejection

Part 6: Text Completion

Directions: Read the text below. Select the best word or phrase to complete the sentences. Mark (A), (B), (C), or (D).

Questions **11–13** refer to the following article.

When applying for a job, it is important to know about any company that invites you to an interview. By researching a company, you will be more ________ and interact more

11 (A) confidential
(B) confiding
(C) confident
(D) confidence

positively at the actual interview and are, therefore, more likely to be ________. To be

12 (A) recruit
(B) recruited
(C) recruiting
(D) recruitment

a successful ________, you should practice

13 (A) interviewer
(B) petitioner
(C) employee
(D) candidate

answering typical interview questions. This will help you to feel more relaxed and comfortable, especially when asked difficult questions. You should also plan what you are going to wear ahead of time and, of course, make sure you arrive punctually or ahead of the scheduled interview time.

Part 7: Reading Comprehension

Directions: In this section, you will read documents such as advertisements, email correspondence, newspaper articles, and letters. Select the best answer. Mark (A), (B), (C), or (D).

Questions **14–15** refer to the following newspaper report.

Cotton World, a popular fashion chain, was founded in 1990 when Samuel Twain opened his first store selling ready-to-wear clothing in a small shopping mall in Atlanta. In 1995 Twain went into partnership with a natural dye company and switched to cotton-only products. Demand for his cotton clothing with all natural colors became widespread and the company has made good profits since then. Twain has pointed out that his success has always depended on attention to consumer wants and social trends: He was quick to recognize the large potential demand for natural products and has promoted the health and natural aspects of his merchandise. Today, the Cotton World label has become a nationally known brand with a bright future.

14 What is Cotton World?
(A) A clothing store chain
(B) An international product
(C) A natural dye company
(D) A shopping mall

15 What has Twain's success depended on?
(A) Demanding natural colors
(B) Providing what customers ask for
(C) Recognizing a bright future
(D) Switching to cotton products

Questions **16–18** refers to the following message.

To: Ms. Mahoney

Date: 05/09 **Time:** 3:30 p.m.

WHILE YOU WERE OUT

Mr. Philip Douglas

Of: Interior Designs

Phone: 1-044 555-4637

- [x] telephoned
- [ ] please return call
- [ ] returned your call
- [ ] will call

Message: The chairs have not arrived. Mr. Jennings has been tracking down the shipment. Mr. Douglas will call when the chairs have been recovered.

Ms. Shaw

Reception

16 Who took the message?
(A) Ms. Mahoney
(B) Mr. Douglas
(C) Mr. Jennings
(D) Ms. Shaw

17 What does the message discuss?
(A) The recovery of Mr. Douglas
(B) Interior Design's track record
(C) A missing shipment
(D) A telephone call from Mr. Jennings

18 Who is trying to locate the chairs?
(A) Ms. Mahoney
(B) Mr. Douglas
(C) Mr. Jennings
(D) Ms. Shaw

Questions **19–23** refer to the following email and response.

Delete Reply Reply All Forward Print

From: Katherine Kanterin
Sent: November 12
To: Amelia Franklin

Dear Ms. Franklin,

We have just been informed that Target Air has canceled your original flight on December 11 from New York to London to Helsinki. They are offering a new routing: New York to London to Stockholm to Helsinki. See attached copy of the new booking REF 2FUSSH.

Please confirm if this is suitable for you as soon as possible so we can change your e-ticket and send you new documents. You can email us your confirmation at travel@LVT.com. Also, could you please inform us of a current contact number? Thank you.

Best Regards,

Katherine Kanterin
LeVonne Travels
1205 7th Ave.
New York, NY 10027

Delete Reply Reply All Forward Print

From: Amelia Franklin
Sent: 18 November
To: Katherine Kanterin

Dear Ms. Kanterin,

Thank you for letting me know about this cancellation. I have looked over the routing that Target Air has offered to replace the canceled flight and agree that it is suitable.

My cell phone is 1 (212) 555-3810.

Sincerely,
Amelia Franklin
Tiny Tot T-Shirts
24 Broadway
New York, NY 10064

19 Why did Katherine Kanterin write to Amelia Franklin?
(A) To sell her a ticket on Target Air
(B) To advise her of a change in her flights
(C) To offer her an extra destination
(D) To ask her to study the itinerary

20 In the first paragraph of the letter to Amelia Franklin, the word "routing" in line 4 is closest in meaning to
(A) Travel plan
(B) Road
(C) Destination
(D) Target

21 What does Katherine Kanterin want Amelia Franklin to do?
(A) Travel to Stockholm
(B) Send her documents
(C) Approve the change
(D) Buy an e-ticket

22 What has Katherine attached to her letter?
(A) A copy of the new booking
(B) A printout of the tickets
(C) A flight confirmation
(D) A paper copy of the REF 2FUSSH

23 Where does Amelia most likely work?
(A) At a travel agency
(B) At a clothing shop
(C) At a day care
(D) At an airport

Grammar Focus Task

Underline the correct form of the words in the following sentences.

1 I *participation / participated* in the Andromeda project.
2 He's *work / working* in Paris this week.
3 Sue *bought / buy* that suit on sale.
4 Twain's success *has / have* always *depending / depended* on attention to consumer wants and trends.
5 A vacancy *will be opening / will be to open* in the spare parts department.

Vocabulary Focus Task

Complete these sentences with words from the box.

chain	complimentary	file	flight	interview

1 It is important to know about any company that invites you to an ________________.
2 Which box does the ________________ go into?
3 We have just been informed that Target Air has canceled your original ________________.
4 Cotton World, a popular fashion ________________, was founded in 1990.
5 We will offer ________________ snacks and drinks.

6 Customer service

Questions

Question forms; *yes/no* questions and short answers; *wh-* questions; tag questions

A Context listening

1 **You are going to hear a woman complaining at the customer service desk. Before you listen, look at the pictures and answer these questions.**

1 What was the woman's problem? ______

2 Was her problem solved? ______

2 **Listen and check if you were right.**

3 **Listen again and answer these questions.**

1 Where was the woman?

2 Did the woman want to return a product?

3 Why was she at the customer service desk?

4 She brought her guarantee, didn't she?

5 The woman isn't satisfied with the product, is she?

6 Can she complain to the phone company online?

4 **Look at your answers in Exercise 3 and answer these questions.**

1 Which questions can you answer with a *yes* or *no*? ____________

2 Which questions ask for information? ____________

3 In what way are questions 2 and 6 different from 4 and 5? ____________

5 **All the words below are about customer service. Listen and underline the words you heard in the conversation.**

complaint courteous guarantee expectations defective quality reliability

B Grammar

The way to form questions depends on what information you want. The three common types of questions are *yes / no questions, information questions,* and *tag questions.*

1 *Yes / no* questions and short answers

You can answer these question forms with *yes* or *no.*
With *to be,* the verb goes at the beginning of the question.

verb	subject	
Is	*Julie*	*an accountant?*
Are	*yachts*	*expensive?*

When the verb is not *be* and consists of only one word, we use a form of the word *do* and the infinitive without *to.*

do	subject	verb	
Does	*Jack*	***work***	*in marketing?*
Did	*profits*	***drop***	*this quarter?*

When the verb contains an auxiliary or modal verb and a main verb, the auxiliary or modal verb goes at the beginning of the question.

aux verb	subject	verb	
Is	*Thomas*	***driving***	*today?*
Can	*Greta*	***make***	*copies of the report?*
Has	*Federico*	***worked***	*in sales?*

We also use negative questions to check information we think is correct. When the question is negative, the word *not* is used with the first verb.

Doesn't *Fatma* ***drive****?*
Isn't *it a beautiful day?*
Didn't *the newspaper* ***come*** *this morning?*
Can't *the workman* ***finish*** *today?*

The answer to a *yes / no* question can be a simple *yes* or *no*, or it can be a complete sentence. Often it is a short answer that repeats the verb that begins the question.

Is *Brenda coming in today? Yes, she* ***is****. / No, she* ***isn't****.*
Does *the bus stop in front of the hotel? Yes, it* ***does****. / No, it* ***doesn't****.*

Didn't *the shipment arrive yesterday? Yes, it* ***did****. / No, it* ***didn't****.*
Can't *Avani contact the head office? Yes, she* ***can****. / No, she* ***can't****.*

2 *Wh-* questions

Questions that ask for information begin with a question word (*who, what, why, where, how, when*).
When the question asks for the subject of the sentence, the word order is the same as in the statement.
***Liam** attended the meeting.* → *"**Who** attended the meeting?"* *"Liam."*
***This suitcase** was left in the hallway.* → *"**What** was left in the hallway?"* *"This suitcase."*

When the question requires other information (not the subject), the question uses a question word + the *yes / no* question form.

***When** was the contract signed?*	*It was signed **last week.***
***Where** is the mirror?*	*It's **in the women's department.***
***How many boxes** arrived in the shipment?*	*There were **20**.*
***How often** does he work overtime?*	*He works overtime **once a week.***

3 Tag questions

We can make questions by adding a tag question to the end of a statement. In the tag question, the verb goes before the subject, like in a *yes / no* question.

To make a tag question, we use an auxiliary verb (e.g. *have, do*), modal verb (e.g. *can, should*) or the verb *to be*, and a pronoun (e.g. *he, she*). The auxiliary verb and pronoun match the statement. When the statement is positive, the verb in the tag question is negative. When the statement is negative, the verb in the tag question is positive.

+	–
*Amy **is** representing us at the trade fair,*	***isn't** she?*
*Joseph **works** in our Houston branch,*	***doesn't** he?*
*The books **have** been delivered,*	***haven't** they?*

–	+
*Joseph **hasn't** left yet,*	***has** he?*
*Amy **can't** pick up the package,*	***can** she?*
*The invoice **didn't go** out yesterday,*	***did** it?*

When the tag is negative and the subject is *I*, we use the auxiliary *are* in place of *am*.
***I'm** late, **aren't I**?*

When the speaker uses a tag question to confirm an opinion, the speaker's voice goes down.
I don't have to write up the report, do I? (The speaker expects the answer to be *no.*)

It is difficult work, isn't it? (The speaker expects the answer to be *yes.*)

When the speaker uses a tag question to ask something, the speaker's voice rises.

I don't have to write up the report, do I? (The speaker doesn't know and is asking for this information.)

C Grammar exercises

1 **Write *yes / no* questions for these answers.**

1 Does the training program start tomorrow?

Yes, the training program starts tomorrow.

2 ______

No, we haven't had any complaints about our opening hours.

3 ______

Yes, maybe we should postpone the meeting.

4 ______

No, the sales representative is coming tomorrow.

5 ______

Yes, the committee decided on the new sales campaign.

2 **Read the conversation and fill in the blanks with a short answer.**

	Mary	**Eric**
1	Eric, do you know where my briefcase is?	No, I don't.
2	Did you see me carrying it when I came into the office?	No, ______.
3	Could it be in my car?	Yes, ______.
4	Perhaps I left it at the front desk.	Maybe ______.
5	Can you call the desk for me?	No, ______.
6	Why not? Is there a problem?	No, ______.
7	Will you tell me what's going on?	Yes, ______.
	Well?	Happy Birthday.
8	A new briefcase! Thank you. You remembered.	Yes, ______.

3 **Put the words in the correct order to make the questions and choose the correct answer.**

1 this / report / typed / who — *Who typed this report?* — *c*
2 Carlos / hired / was / when ______ ______
3 can / I / return / suit / this / where ______ ______
4 been / department / has / how / in / long / Ms. Wong / the / sports / working ______ ______
5 Anita / did / early / retire / so / why ______ ______
6 do / do / in / plan / Paris / to / what / you ______ ______

a Try customer service.
b I think she's ill.
c I did. Why? Is there a problem?
d I have a meeting with a fashion designer.
e I'd say about ten years.
f If I remember correctly, 2004.

4 **Complete the conversation with tag questions.**

James: You were at the staff meeting yesterday, **1** *weren't you?* ?
Eva: Yes, you didn't go, **2** ______ ?
James: No, I was out of town. What was it about?
Eva: You read the email about the customer service problems, **3** ______ ?
James: No, I didn't, but someone told me about it. We've had a few complaints, **4** ______ ?
Eva: Yes, about 20, I think.
James: They were mostly about defective products, **5** ______ ?
Eva: Yes, and there were also complaints about discourteous staff.
James: Really? That can't be a big problem, **6** ______ ?
Eva: I'm afraid so. You remember when Phil shouted at a customer, **7** ______ ?
James: Oh, yes, of course. But he was fired, **8** ______ ?
Eva: Yes, he was. But, I think the management is just worried. They don't want that to happen again, **9** ______ ?

D Vocabulary

Key Vocabulary

Read this paragraph about customer service and check your understanding of the words in bold.

Every business that wants to be successful must support the products or services that they offer with **courteous**, helpful, and friendly **customer service**. Customer service involves **building a relationship** with your customers or **clients**, where you **guarantee** to repair or replace **defective** products and listen to their **feedback**. In fact, one of the most important parts of customer service is **dealing with complaints**. Complaints are an opportunity to learn about mistakes, and if you deal with them carefully, you have the chance to **regain the trust** of that customer. Customers whose **expectations** are **satisfied** and who understand your **commitment** to **quality** and **reliability** are more likely to return and do business with you in the future.

Vocabulary note

A **deal** can be an agreement between two parties.

*The shipping company made a **deal** with the farmers to send a truck to pick up goods two days a week.*

A **deal** can also be something that costs less than you expected.

*I got a good **deal** on the car because it used to be a company car.*

1 Complete the definitions with the words in italics.

1 The customer comes into a store to make a purchase, but a client is dependent on the advice and service of a business. *client / customer*

2 A ________ on a product is an agreement that the buyer can get money back or a replacement if the product is defective. Buyers feel better knowing that if the ________ of the product is not up to a high standard, they can get their money back. *guarantee / quality*

3 Companies that are ________ to providing good service look at complaints as important ________ that help them improve their products or service. *feedback / committed*

4 Customer ________ is important to all companies because if they don't meet the customers' ________, they will lose business. *expectations / satisfaction*

5 A company that provides good ________ gets the reputation of being a ________ company. *service / reliable*

2 **A market researcher asked Monica to write answers to some questions. Read Monica's responses to the questions. Fill in the blanks with the words from the box.**

complaint courteous deal with ~~defective~~ expectations guarantee relationships satisfaction trust unreliable

1 What have you recently complained to a company about?

Not too long ago, a new store opened at the mall with a big promotion. I bought a coffee maker, but when I got home I discovered that the product was **1** defective ______. The heating plate did not heat up, so my coffee became cold very quickly. Fortunately, the coffee maker had a **2** ______.

2 How would you say your complaint was handled?

I had to wait for a while. But when the woman came to the customer service desk, she was very **3** ______ and helpful. She listened to my **4** ______ very calmly and she handled the problem very well. She took the coffee maker and gave me a new one.

3 How important is the way a complaint is handled?

I think that if a business doesn't **5** ______ a complaint quickly then it will lose the **6** ______ of the customer. We all have **7** ______ about the quality of service and products and if a business doesn't give us **8** ______ we will think of that business as **9** ______. We probably won't buy from that company again. On the other hand, if a business deals with complaints courteously and quickly, then it will build good **10** ______ with its customers.

7 Property

Embedded questions

Wh- questions; *yes / no* questions; questions with an infinitive

A Context listening

1 **You are going to hear three people talk to Frank Jacobs, a real estate agent. What do you think Frank's three clients want?**

1 Lydia ______________________

2 Robert ______________________

3 Alex ______________________

2 **Listen and check if you were right.**

3 Look at these questions. Listen to the conversations again and change the questions using the form that Frank and his clients used. Stop the recording when you need to.

Frank's and Lydia's questions

1 ~~Where can I~~ find Mr. Jacobs?
Could you tell me where I can find Mr. Jacobs?

2 Are you looking for a place to buy or to rent?

Frank's and Robert's questions

3 Where is your residence?

4 How quickly do you need to sell it?

Frank's and Alex's questions

5 How much renovation will the owner allow me to do?

6 Would the owner consider a lease that gives me the option to buy the building later?

4 Look at your answers in Exercise 3 and underline the correct words in italics.

1 In answers 1, 3, 4, and 6 the *first* / *second* verb comes before its subject.
2 In answers 2 and 5 the word order is *the same as* / *different from* the other answers.
3 In the conversation, Alex says, "I'm not sure what to do." This statement uses the *infinitive* / *past participle*.

5 Match the word you heard in the conversations with its meaning.

1 mortgage	a to make changes to improve a piece of property
2 realtor	b a piece of property to live in
3 renovate	c the bank loan a person gets in order to buy property
4 residence	d a person who helps people buy, sell, or rent property

B Grammar

Sometimes a question is within a sentence or another question. This is called an embedded question. We often use embedded questions as a polite way of asking a question.
I haven't found out ***whether the bank will give me a mortgage or not.***
Could you tell me ***what changes you have in mind****?*

1 Embedded *Wh-* questions

An embedded *Wh-* question uses the same word order as a statement, not a question. This means that the subject goes before the verb.

Question	Embedded question
What ***did*** *the customer* ***want****?*	*I wonder what the customer* ***wanted.***
When ***does*** *Jackie's flight* ***arrive****?*	*Do you know when Jackie's flight* ***arrives****?*
Where ***will*** *the conference* ***be held****?*	*I don't know where the conference* ***will be held.***
Why ***hasn't*** *Ina* ***locked*** *the door?*	*Can you tell me why Ina* ***hasn't locked*** *the door?*
Who ***is*** *Alfredo* ***inviting****?*	*I wonder who Alfredo* ***is inviting.***
How many books ***did*** *you* ***sell****?*	*I don't remember how many books you* ***sold.***
How much ***is*** *the rent?*	*Could you tell me how much the rent* ***is****?*
How ***should*** *we* ***handle*** *this?*	*Do you have any idea how we* ***should handle*** *this?*
Whose car ***can*** *I* ***take****?*	*I would like to know whose car I* ***can take.***

2 Embedded *yes / no* questions

An embedded *yes / no* question also uses the same word order as a statement, so the subject goes before the verb. We use *whether* and *if* in these questions, although each has a slightly different meaning. *Whether* indicates one of two possibilities and *if* indicates a condition. In some sentences we can use both.

Should *I* ***bring*** *my sweater or a jacket?* — *I don't know* ***whether*** *I* ***should bring*** *my sweater or a jacket.*

Are *you* ***coming*** *tonight?* — *Let me know* ***if*** *you* ***are coming*** *tonight.*

3 Embedded questions with an infinitive

An infinitive can replace the subject and verb after a *wh-* word or *whether* in the embedded question.

How can I solve *this problem?* — *I don't know* ***how to solve*** *this problem.*

Should I drive *or take the bus?* — *I wonder* ***whether to drive*** *or* ***take*** *the bus.*

There can be a difference in meaning.
Do you know ***where to buy*** *ink cartridges?* (= Where can a person buy ink cartridges?)
Do you know ***where I can buy*** *ink cartridges?* (= Where can I buy ink cartridges?)

C Grammar exercises

1 **Complete the conversations. Some sentences may have more than one possible answer.**

1 "I'd like to know ____where____ Laurence Baker is giving his speech." "In the Hawking room."

2 "Do you have any idea ________________ the flight from Boston is due to arrive?" "At 12:34 P.M."

3 "He couldn't tell me ________________ the property taxes might be." "Maybe you could ask your accountant."

4 "Do you know ________________ I can pay with a credit card?" "Yes, I think you can."

5 "I wonder ________________ is going to present the awards." "Apparently it's someone quite famous."

6 "I didn't know ________________ that noise was." "I think there was a problem with the heating system."

7 "Before the merger, I knew ________________ people worked in our company." "I know what you mean. There are so many new employees that I can't count them all."

8 "She asked us ________________ car was blocking the entrance." "Did you tell her it was mine?"

2 **Lydia is looking around an apartment with Frank, the real estate agent. Complete the conversation with embedded questions, using the words in parentheses.**

Lydia: OK, first I'd like to know **1** __how much the rent is__ (*be / how much / rent*) for this apartment.

Frank: Well, it's quite expensive. It's $1,300 a month.

Lydia: Oh, OK. But it is a really nice place. Could you tell me **2** ________________ (*available / be / when*)?

Frank: It will be ready to move into at the beginning of next week. Let me know **3** ________________ (*if / want / accept*) it.

Lydia: I have a few more questions before I make up my mind. First, do you know **4** ________________ (*cost / how much / electricity*) every month?

Frank: I will have to check with the utilities company to find out **5** ________________ (*pay / how much / the last tenants*).

Lydia: Also, I'd like to know **6** ________________ (*if / good school / be*) nearby.

Frank: Yes, there is a good school a few blocks from here.

Lydia: Oh, good. Do you know **7** ________________ (*start / the school year / if*) yet?

Frank: Yes, it started this week.

Lydia: Oh dear. I wonder **8** ________________ (*if / can / my children / start late*).

Frank: Oh yes, I'm sure that won't be a problem.

Lydia: Good. I think I will take the apartment. Let me know **9** ________________ (*can / the contract / when / sign*).

3 **Rewrite the following embedded questions as direct questions.**

1 Do you know what time to lock the front door? (*should*)
What time should I lock the front door?

2 I wonder whether to bring a coat or not. (*should*)

3 Can you tell me where to get a lunch voucher? (*can*)

4 I need to know who to include on the guest list. (*should*)

5 I don't know when to bring the files over to the main office. (*should*)

6 Let me know which color to paint the garage doors. (*want*)

4 **Use words in the box and the given phrase to write about a property you would like to rent, buy, or sell.**

if	what	how much	where	who
when	why	which	whose	how many

1 Could you tell me how many rooms the house has ?

2 I would like to know ________ .

3 I need to know ________ .

4 Would you know ________ ?

5 Do you have any idea ________ ?

6 I wonder ________ .

D Vocabulary

Key Vocabulary

Read this paragraph about property and check your understanding of the words in bold.

For most people, buying a **residence** is the most important purchase they will make. Because it is so expensive to buy a single-family house or just an apartment within a **building**, buyers usually finance their purchase by making a **down payment** on a percentage of the agreed price and taking out a **mortgage** on the remaining balance. Most people arrange the buying and selling through a **real estate agent**, or **realtor**, who **receives a fee** or **commission**. Usually a prospective buyer **makes an offer** for a property and if they make a deal with the **owner**, he or she **accepts the offer**. Some people buy property as an investment. Typically they will **renovate** and then **rent out** or **lease** the property, either **furnished** or unfurnished, through a realtor. These include **commercial spaces** as well as residential housing, both downtown and in the **suburbs**. The **landlord** signs a contract with the tenant(s), which includes details about the rights and responsibilities of each party.

Vocabulary note

The word *commercial* can be a noun or an adjective.
The noun means an advertisement on the television or radio.
*I thought the new **commercial** for Pizza Plaza was very funny.*
The adjective means intended to make money, or related to a business intended to make money.
*We sell both residential and **commercial** properties.*

1 **Use the words in the box to complete Nancy's comments about moving.**

~~apartment~~	commission	down payment	landlord	
mortgage	offer	owner	realtor	suburb	tenant

I've been living in a one bedroom **1** ___apartment___ downtown for a couple of years now, but I've decided to move. As a **2** __________ in the center of town, I have to pay a lot of rent and I've also had problems with the **3** __________. Last month I went to see a **4** __________ about buying my own house in a nice **5** __________ outside of downtown Austin . In the window of the real estate agency, I saw the house of my dreams and I have just enough money saved for a **6** __________, but I will have to get a **7** __________. I have made an **8** __________ to buy this property, and now I am waiting to hear if the **9** __________ will accept it. There are many costs when buying a house, but at least the **10** __________ the agent will get for selling this house will be paid by the seller.

2 **Underline the correct word.**

1 I want to rent office space in a <u>*building*</u> / *builder* / *build* near the business district.

2 We don't provide soft *furnished* / *furnishings* / *furniture* in our apartments.

3 The real estate agent has many *rents* / *renters* / *rentals* on his website that we could consider.

4 They were wondering if we had any houses that needed *renovate* / *renovation* / *renovator*.

5 My landlord *owns* / *owner* / *ownership* and rents out several buildings in this area.

6 Do you have any *residents* / *residential* / *residences* for sale in the La Paloma district?

3 **Choose the correct words or phrases to complete the sentences.**

1 I don't want to sell my property through a real estate agent because I don't want to pay the fee for this service. (*real estate agent* / *fee*)

2 Our rental business finds ________________ for ________________ who live overseas. (*tenants* / *landlords*)

3 We didn't have enough money for a ________________ , so they rejected our application for a ________________ . (*mortgage* / *down payment*)

4 We rent out both ________________ for businesses as well as family ________________ . (*commercial spaces* / *residences*)

5 I grew up in the ________________ of a large city, but now I like living downtown, so I rented an ________________ in a large building near city hall. (*apartment* / *suburbs*)

6 I've decided to sign a ________________ on a rental property for six months until I have the money to make an ________________ on a place of my own. (*lease* / *offer*)

8 Banking

Reported Speech

Reporting statements and questions; reporting verbs

A Context listening

1 **You are going to hear three of Mike's conversations. Before you listen, look at the pictures. Who do you think Mike is talking to and what do you think the conversation is about?**

1 ______________________________

2 ______________________________

3 ______________________________

2 **Listen and check if you were right.**

3 **Underline the word used in the conversation. Use your dictionary if you don't know the words.**

1 Mike went to the bank to make a *withdrawal* / *deposit*.
2 Mike saw a brochure about *interest rates* / *business loans*.
3 The *bank teller* / *loan officer* wanted to know about Mike and his wife's work experience.
4 Mike and Wilma are thinking about *borrowing* / *lending* money.
5 The bank will check Mike and Wilma's *credit rating* / *savings account*.
6 Mike didn't look at their *balance* / *debt*.

4 **Listen to the first two conversations again and complete the sentences in column A. Then listen to the third conversation and complete the sentences in column B.**

Column A

1 Would you like me to see if a loan officer ____is____ available ...
2 My wife and I ________________ to invest ...
3 Do you ________________ experience ...
4 ... we ________________ both managers of Oskari's ...
5 How much ________________ you ________________ about as a down payment?

Column B

6 The teller offered to see if a loan officer ________________ available ...
7 I told the loan officer that we ________________ to invest ...
8 She asked if we ________________ any experience ...
9 I said that we ________________ both managers at Oskari's ...
10 ... and she asked how much we ________________ about as a down payment?

5 **Look at the sentences in Exercise 4 and answer these questions.**

1 Which sentence(s) in Column A ...
  a are statements? __________
  b are questions? __________
  c make an offer? __________

2 Which sentence(s) in Column B ...
  a report what someone stated? __________
  b report what someone asked? __________
  c reports what someone offered? __________

6 **Look at the verb tenses in Exercise 4. In what way are the verbs in A and B different?**

____

B Grammar

Reported speech is the language we use when we are describing what someone said. We can report someone's speech in several ways.

1 Use of reporting statements and questions

The most common verbs that introduce a reported statement are *tell* or *say*. A reported question is introduced with the word *ask*. When we report statements and questions, we may need to make changes in the verb tense, pronoun, and time phrases.

*I **told** the loan officer that **we wanted** to invest in a franchise.*
*She **asked** if **we had** any experience in the business we were looking into.*

Statements
Yesterday, the manager's exact words to her personal assistant were,
"I want you to type this report by tomorrow."

Today, the personal assistant reports the manager's statement as
My manager said (that) she wanted me to type that report by today.
My manager told me (that) she wanted me to type that report by today.

Questions
Yesterday, the manager's exact words to her personal assistant were,
"Can you type this report by tomorrow?"
"When can you type the report?"

Today, the personal assistant reports the manager's question as
My manager asked me if I could type that report by today.
My manager asked me when I could type the report.

2 Forms of reporting statements and questions

Changes may occur in verb tense, time, place, demonstratives (e.g., *this*), and pronouns (e.g., *they*).

- Changes in verb tense:

present simple *I **work** in Miami.*	→	past simple *She said she **worked** in Miami.*
present continuous *I'm **buying** the green jacket.*	→	past continuous *She said she **was buying** the green jacket.*
be going to *Muna **is going to come** at 7 P.M.*	→	*was / were going to* *She said Muna **was going to come** at 7 P.M.*
will *I'**ll get** there first.*	→	*would* *She said she **would get** there first.*
can *I **can help** you.*	→	*could* *She said she **could help** me.*
May / might *I **may** not **get** there on time.*	→	*might* *He said he **might** not **get** there on time.*
must *I **must go**.*	→	*had to* *He said he **had to go**.*
past *I **signed** the form.*	→	past perfect *He said he **had signed** the form.*
present perfect *I'**ve spoken** to our CEO.*	→	past perfect *She said she **had spoken** to our CEO.*

- Changes may occur in time and place:

today	→	*yesterday or that day*
yesterday	→	*the day before*
now	→	*then*
tomorrow	→	*today / the following day / the next day*

If the reported speech occurs on the same day as the actual speech, the time may not change.

Monday: *"I'll send the refund **tomorrow**."*
Monday: *He said he would send the refund **tomorrow**.*
Thursday: *He said he would send the refund **the following day**.*

here	→	*there*

If the place has not changed, there is no change in the reported speech.

In the office: *"I'll meet you **here** tomorrow."*
In the office: *He said he would meet me **here** today.*
In a café: *He said he would meet me **there** today.*

- Changes may occur in demonstratives:

this → *that*	*that* → *this*
these → *those*	*those* → *these*

*"I need **those** files."*
*She told me that she needed **those** files.* (reported at a distance from the mentioned files)
*She told me that she needed **these** files.* (reported near the mentioned files)

- Changes may occur in pronouns. These changes depend on who is referred to in the original speech.

Kate talking to Nick: *I'll give **you** the key.*
Nick: *She said she would give **me** the key.*
Bella: *She said she would give **him** the key.*

Rajit talking to Sue and Si: ***I'll give you** the key.*
Sue: *He said he'd give **us** the key.*
Jo: *He said he'd give **them** the key.*

3 Reporting verbs

Instead of reporting the speaker's exact words, we can use different verbs to show the attitude of the speaker. Reporting verbs can be followed by *that*, a *to*-infinitive, a preposition + *-ing* / noun, or pronoun / noun.

Verb + someone + *that: assure, inform, persuade, remind*
*The manager **informed the staff that** the store would close later during the summer.*

Verb + *that: agree, announce, believe, claim, complain, deny, explain, insist, promise, propose, reply, request, suggest, think*
*Jeff **denied that** the accident was his fault.*

Verb + *someone* + *to*-infinitive: *advise, ask, encourage, invite, remind, urge, want, warn*
*She **invited me to take** a seat.*

Verb + *to*-infinitive: *agree, ask, claim, offer, propose*
*The teller **offered to see** if a loan officer was available to talk to me.*

Verb + *someone* + *a preposition* + *-ing* / noun: *advise about / on / against, remind about, congratulate on, thank for*
*She **advised me against renting** an apartment in that area of town.*

Verb + a preposition + *-ing* / noun: *complain about / to, apologize for, insist on*
*She **apologized for leaving** the lights on.*

Verb + someone + noun: *offer, promise*
*Lisa **offered Anna a ride** to work.*

Verb + *-ing* + noun: *accept, admit, suggest*
*Lee Wong **suggested selling** the stocks.*

C Grammar exercises

1 **Brian has a problem at the bank. Read what the bank teller told him.**

"There isn't enough money in your account to cover your check, so now you have a negative balance in your checking account. That charge on your statement is the overdrawn balance charge. Your deposit only covers the amount of the last check. The deposit doesn't cover the overdrawn balance charge. Your balance is still in the red. You'll be charged each day until the balance is in the black."

After Brian left the bank he told a friend what the bank teller said. Complete the sentences with the correct verb.

The teller said there **1** wasn't enough money in my account to cover my check. He said now I **2** __________ a negative balance in my checking account. He told me that the charge on my statement **3** __________ the overdrawn balance charge. He said my deposit only **4** __________ the amount of the last check. He said the deposit **5** __________ the overdrawn balance charge. He told me my balance **6** __________ still in the red. He said I **7** __________ be charged each day until the balance is in the black.

2 **Look at the phone messages for Rachel Bradley. What did the callers say?**

1 Mr. Canton said that his delayed shipment had arrived. b

- **a** "His delayed shipment had arrived."
- **b** "My delayed shipment has arrived."

2 Alfred Bertolini asked if you could send him the contract immediately. __

- **a** "Can you send me the contract immediately?"
- **b** "You could send me the contract immediately."

3 Janet Bocsh said that she couldn't get to this afternoon's meeting. __

- **a** "I can't get to this afternoon's meeting."
- **b** "Can you get to this afternoon's meeting?"

4 Mrs. Kowinski complained that she had been overcharged. __

- **a** "Have you overcharged me?"
- **b** "You have charged me too much."

5 Tony said that he was going to bring the proposal tomorrow. __

- **a** "You could send the proposal tomorrow."
- **b** "I'll bring the proposal tomorrow."

6 The safety inspector wanted to inform you that the safety inspections would take place as planned. __

- **a** "The safety inspections will take place as planned."
- **b** "The safety inspections have taken place as planned."

7 Ms. Anderson asked if she should confirm the flight. __

- **a** "You should confirm the flight."
- **b** "Should I confirm the flight?"

3 **Read the following sentences. Complete the reported statements using one of the words in the box.**

advised	congratulated	insisted	offered	~~reminded~~	suggested	thanked

1 Don't forget to back up the files.
He *reminded* me to back up the files.

2 We could look for someone more experienced.
She ________________ looking for someone more experienced.

3 Jim, you've done a nice job on the ad campaign.
She ________________ Jim on the nice job done on the ad campaign.

4 Would you like me to call a taxi for you?
He ________________ to call a taxi for me.

5 You shouldn't miss the budget meeting.
He ________________ me not to miss the budget meeting.

6 I appreciated your booking the tickets for me, Lily.
She ________________ Lily for booking the tickets for her.

7 You must finish the report today.
He ________________ that I finish the report today.

4 **Last week, you were in a meeting with Mimi. Report what she said using the verbs in the box.**

apologize	~~ask~~	congratulate	offer	remind	suggest

1 Thomas, can you fax this report this afternoon?
Mimi asked Thomas if he could fax that report that afternoon. / Mimi asked Thomas to fax that report that afternoon.

2 Ajay and Hae-Won, don't forget to send the schedule for the trade fair to the Paris branch.
____

3 Linda, well done on last week's promotion.
____

4 I'm sorry that I sent the agenda to everyone so late.
____

5 Why don't we ask Nathan what he thinks of the proposal?
____

6 Everyone, please have some of these chocolate brownies.
____

5 **Report advice that someone has given you or that you have given someone else.**

1 *My father told me not to get into credit card debt.*
2 ________________
3 ________________
4 ________________
5 ________________

D Vocabulary

Key Vocabulary

Read this paragraph about banking and check your understanding of the meaning of the words in bold.

The easiest way to get **cash** from your **savings** or **checking account** is to use your **debit card** and **PIN number** at an **ATM machine**, but you can also complete a variety of **transactions** inside a bank. If you want to **deposit a check** or **withdraw money**, the **bank teller** can do that for you. While you are at the bank, you might want to **check your balance** or perhaps talk to a **financial advisor** to discuss different ways you can **invest your money** to get a better **interest rate**. Or you might want to **borrow money** to buy a house or set up a business. The bank will **approve the loan** if you have a good **credit rating**. Of course, nowadays, you can also pay your bills, **transfer funds,** and even apply for loans online.

Vocabulary note

The words *loan*, *lend,* and *borrow* can be confused.
I need a ***loan***. (= a sum of money that needs to be paid back)
Can you ***loan*** */* ***lend*** *me some money?* (= let me have some money temporarily)
Can I ***borrow*** *your car?* (= use your car temporarily)
The borrower receives something and the lender gives something.
A person who takes out a loan **borrows** money.
The person or financial institution that provides the loan **lends** the money.

1 **Use the words to complete the sentences. Use each word twice, once as a verb and once as a noun.**

balance cash check credit deposit loan

1 I have a personal ____check____ that I want to ____deposit____ in my savings account.
2 The ________ I made was enough to cover the payment of my ________.
3 My ________ is good because I always ________ my accounts carefully.
4 Could you ________ me some ________ until payday?
5 I have to ________ my ________ to see if my salary is now in the bank.
6 I have two checks. I want to ________ this one, and would you ________ that one to my savings account?

2 **Choose the correct answer / word.**

1 My mechanic won't accept a credit card or check, so I have to go to an ATM machine to make a cash *transaction* / *withdrawal.*

2 I wrote a check on my *savings* / *checking* account, but there weren't enough funds left.

3 I suggest you put your savings in this account where it will earn a higher *credit* / *interest* rate.

4 I would like to *borrow* / *balance* money to set up a business.

5 Don't forget that the interest on your *cash* / *loan* is quite high.

6 Could I speak to a *bank teller* / *financial advisor* about investing my money?

7 I was looking for the nearest *PIN number* / *ATM machine* so that I could make a withdrawal.

8 Jimmy needed to *loan* / *transfer* money from his savings account to pay for his car.

3 **Complete this explanation by a business entrepreneur with the correct form of the words in the box.**

account	check	finance	fund	~~invest~~	debit	savings	withdraw

Some years ago, I made an **1** ___investment___ in a beauty salon. The business was going very well and I was putting cash into both my checking and my **2** ________________ accounts, but I was using my **3** ________________ card unwisely. I also took out a loan to make improvements to both my home and salon. I thought everything would continue smoothly, and I was **4** ________________ more money than I was depositing. Then there was a downturn in the economy and people were not spending as much money on beauty products and services. I didn't have the **5** ________________ in the bank to cover the payment of my loans. The balance in my **6** ________________ account was negative. I discussed the problem with a **7** ________________ advisor. Slowly, I am getting control of my spending habits and I am getting my bank **8** ________________ out of the red.

9 Commuting

Adjectives and Adverbs

Describing things; adding information about manner, place, time, frequency, and intensity

A Context listening

1 You are going to listen to four commuters talk about how they get to work. Listen and write the name of the commuter under the mode of transportation that he or she uses.

1 Ivana

2 ______

3 ______

4 ______

2 Listen to the first and second speakers again and fill in the blanks below.

1 My stop is not ___usually___ very crowded.
2 The station ... in the city can be ______ busy.
3 ... more people are ______ trying to get on.
4 The stop where I would have to change is ______ crowded.
5 ... sometimes the traffic jams cause ______ long delays.
6 The number 19 stop is ______ located around the corner ...

3 **Listen to the third and fourth speakers again and fill in the spaces below.**

1 I rent a ____tiny____ apartment … .

2 … place in the area is really ____________.

3 I don't have to wait in ____________ lines … .

4 I live in a ____________ suburb and … .

5 I could take the ____________ lane if I were in a carpool.

6 … carpool because I get ____________ being in the car alone … .

4 **Look at your answers to Exercise 2 and 3. Answer the following questions.**

1 What types of words have you written in 2 and 3?

The words in Exercise 2 are ____________

The words in Exercise 3 are ____________

2 What do the words in Exercise2 describe? ____________

3 What do the words in Exercise3 describe? ____________

5 **Match the words with the correct definition.**

1 carpool

2 rush hour

3 subway

4 traffic jams

5 commuter pass

a underground train system

b ticket for many trips over a set period of time

c share a vehicle and costs while commuting

d period of heavy traffic when people commute

e overcrowded roads causing slow moving traffic

B Grammar

1 Adjectives

Adjectives are words that describe people and things. (► See Unit 1, Word Forms for common adjective suffixes.)

We use adjectives before a noun or after certain verbs (*be, appear, look, seem, feel,* etc.).
*I could take the **fast lane** if I were in a carpool.*
*He **looks healthy**.*

We also use adjectives after *find / make / keep* + object.
***Keep** your car **clean** with our special car washing liquid.*

Adjectives have only one form that we use with both singular and plural nouns.
*In our office we have **small windows** and a **small bookshelf**.*

We can use adjectives together. When they are after the noun, they are joined with another adjective using *and*.
*We enjoyed the **long, cool** evenings of summer.*
*The trip was **short and productive**.*

2 Adverbs and adverb phrases

Adverbs are words that describe verbs, adjectives, and other adverbs. (► See Unit 1, Word Forms for common adverb suffixes.)

We use adverbs with verbs, adjectives, and adverbs.
*We worked **quickly**. We were **very** energetic. The day passed **incredibly** quickly.*

They can be one word or a phrase.
***This morning** the telephone was ringing **continuously**.*

Adverbs and adverb phrases have only one form that we use with both singular and plural verbs.
*He manages **effectively** and his staff members work **efficiently**.*

We use adverbs and adverb phrases to describe manner *(how)*, time *(when)*, place *(where)*, intensity *(how strong)*, and frequency *(how often)*.
*The boss **always** whistles **very loudly in his office during the morning**.*
How does the boss whistle? ***Loudly***
How loudly does he whistle? ***Very** loudly*
When does the boss whistle? ***During the morning***
Where does he whistle? ***In his office***
How often does he whistle? ***Always***

3 Comparing the forms of adjectives and adverbs

The most common ending for adverbs is *-ly*.
*The bus stops are **conveniently** located.*

Some adjectives that end in *-ly* have corresponding adverbs with the same form.
daily monthly weekly early

*The **daily** newspaper has arrived.* (adjective) *They deliver the newspaper **daily**.* (adverb)

Some adjectives that end in *-ly* do not have a corresponding adverb. We use an adverb phrase instead.
friendly likely lively lonely lovely silly ugly
*Dayna is a **friendly** person.* (adjective) *Dayna speaks **in a friendly way**.* (adverb phrase)

Some adjectives and adverbs have the same form.
deep fast hard high late little low much near
*Chris is a **hard** worker. Chris works **hard**.*

The adverb forms *warmly*, *hotly*, *coolly*, *coldly*, *lately*, *presently*, *shortly*, *scarcely*, and *barely* have different meanings from their adjective forms.

Adverb	Adjective
*We were greeted **warmly**.* (= in a friendly way)	*It was a **warm** day.* (= a comfortable temperature)
***Lately** I've been considering applying for a different job.* (= recently)	*Sorry I'm **late**. I was delayed by a traffic jam.* (= not punctual, not on time)
***Shortly** after noon I met the director.* (= soon)	*I'm going to take a **short** vacation next month.* (= not long)
*I **scarcely** left the room when the phone rang.* (= just / hardly)	*Good restaurants are **scarce** in this town.* (= rare)
*I **barely** sat down when the door opened.* (= just / hardly)	*The office floor is completely **bare**.* (= without covering)

The adverb forms *highly*, *lowly*, *deeply*, *nearly*, *hardly*, and *lately* have different meanings from the adverb form without *-ly* (*high*, *low*, *deep*, etc.).

Adverb without -ly	Adverb with -ly
*Our sales have soared **high** above expectations.* (= a long way up)	*Our customers have spoken **highly** of our product.* (= very positively)
*The country sank **deep** into a recession that lasted 10 years.* (= a long way down)	*We **deeply** regret that we were not able to reach an agreement.* (= strongly, extremely)
*I wished we lived **near** each other.* (= close to)	*I've **nearly** finished the report.* (= almost, but not quite)
*We fought **hard** to get the contract.* (= with a lot of effort)	*I **hardly** spent any time on it.* (=just a little)
*He stayed **late** on Tuesday.* (= after the usual time)	*She's been thinking **lately** about the new contracts.* (= recently)

C Grammar exercises

1 **Underline and label all the adverbs and adjectives in the following statements.**

1 The colorful (adj) brochures for the fair were promptly (adv) delivered to our main (adj) office.

2 A new shipment of electric cars will arrive soon.

3 We normally close the store at 6 P.M., but before the holiday season, we stay open late.

4 I leave my house for work early so I can take the long route on my bike through the quiet city park.

5 Ted has an expensive sports car that he sometimes drives to work even though the parking lot is not conveniently located.

2 **Change the adjective into an adverb. Some adjectives stay in the same form.**

1 Why is it called rush hour when the traffic moves so ___slowly___ (*slow*)?
2 The CEO spoke so ________________ (*quick*) that I couldn't understand him.
3 The newspaper is delivered ________________ (*daily*).
4 He drove really ________________ (*fast*) to get to work on time.
5 You typed this report very ________________ (*accurate*). Well done.
6 At first, we waited (*patient*) for the bus ________________.
7 It looks like we'll arrive ________________ (*late*).

3 **Read this extract from a letter and underline the correct word.**

Dear Paula,
I'm so tired! I've **1** *hard / hardly* been out of my office at all this week and have been **2** *late / lately* to almost all my meetings because **3** *near / nearly* every time I am ready to leave, I **4** *bare / barely* get to the door and my cell phone rings with something urgent that I have to deal with **5** *immediate / immediately*. I know that my colleagues have **6** *high / highly* expectations of me, but sometimes I feel I have become too **7** *deep / deeply* involved in the everyday running of the office. Maybe it's time for a vacation. I sure could use a rest on a **8** *warm / warmly* tropical island. Anyway, enough about work! How are you? ...

4 **Complete the sentences with one adjective and one adverb form of the words in parentheses.**

(considerable / considerably)

1 a The quality of cotton products has improved considerably.

b The improvement of cotton products has been considerable.

(rapid / rapidly)

2 a The cost of dining out has increased ________________ .

b There has been a ________________ increase in the cost of dining out.

(sharp / sharply)

3 a The price of gold has increased ________________ in recent days.

b News agencies have reported a ________________ increase in recent days.

(gradual / gradually)

4 a Demand for musical instruments has shown a ________________ rise in the last few months.

b The sale of musical instruments has risen ________________ in the last few months.

(steep / steeply)

5 a The stock exchange reported a ________________ rise in share prices today.

b Share prices have risen ________________ today.

(sudden / suddenly)

6 a Company policy has changed ________________ .

b There has been a ________________ change in company policy.

5 **Describe one of your favorite places using adverbs and adjectives. Explain where it is, what it is like, when and how often you go there.**

D Vocabulary

Key Vocabulary

Read this paragraph about commuting and check your understanding of the words in bold.

Most people commute to work along a regular **route**. In many **urban** areas, they have the choice between traveling by **public transportation** or by **private vehicle.** Commuters who drive may choose to **carpool** in **fuel-efficient** vehicles to save on the high cost of filling a **gas tank** and because of the difficulty of finding **parking spaces**. On public transportation systems, people can buy a **commuter pass** for the bus or **subway** to save on costs, but these **means of transportation** can also be **crowded** during **rush hour**. However, these commuters can avoid driving along **congested highways** or getting stuck in **traffic jams.** Sometimes the stress of these conditions causes **road rage.** People who live near their workplace can commute by foot or bike. Many cities provide **bike lanes**. If none of these means of transportation suit you, then a final option is to work from home.

1 **Match the definitions below with the following words.**

1 car pool ___e___
2 congestion ______
3 public transportation ______
4 road rage ______
5 rush hour ______
6 commuter pass ______
7 fuel efficient ______
8 urban ______

a operating with relatively little gas
b located in a city
c the condition when there is so much traffic that it makes movement difficult
d the time when traffic congestion and crowding on public transportation is at its worst
e ~~travel with a group of people, especially to work or school, in different members' cars~~
f vehicles such as buses and trains that operate at regular times for public use
g anger or violence between drivers, often caused by difficult driving conditions
h a ticket that can be used many times within a limited period and is cheaper than paying separately for each use

2 **Match a word from Column A with a word from Column B and use the two words to complete this newspaper article. You can combine some words in Column A with more than one word in column B, but in the article only one combination is correct in each blank.**

A	B
traffic	rage
public	lanes
bike	jams
rush	vehicles
commuter	spaces
road	passes
parking	transportation
private	hour

The city council has introduced a number of measures in an attempt to reduce the problem of **1** ___traffic jams___ . There have been many complaints that during **2** ______ (between 7 A.M. and 9 A.M. and after 4 P.M.) the roads are heavily congested and travel times are sometimes over an hour more than usual. There have even been reports of **3** ______ , with frustrated commuters fighting on the streets. A further complaint from those people who use **4** ______ is that there is a lack of **5** ______ near their workplaces. New measures include an improvement in **6** ______ so that there will be more buses running, the introduction of cheap **7** ______ for regular commuters, and the construction of a system of **8** ______ along the side of streets for commuters who don't want to use cars or buses.

3 **Below is part of Riitta's response to the TOEIC writing test opinion question. Use the words in the box to complete Riitta's response.**

bike lanes	carpool	highways	tank	traffic jams	road rage
subway	route	~~urban~~	public transportation		

There are many ways that people get to their place of work or study. What are some of the ways? Do you enjoy commuting? Give reasons or examples to support your opinion.

There are several ways to get to work and back home. I live in an **1** urban ______ area so I can take **2** ______ ; for me that is the bus or **3** ______ . I don't mind commuting since I don't have to travel a long distance. In fact, I enjoy commuting, especially when the weather is nice, since I can also walk or ride my bike along the new **4** ______ . When I walk or ride to work, I arrive feeling fresh and cheerful. It is also good exercise. But people who live farther out in the suburbs and drive along **5** ______ may not enjoy it very much. They often get caught in **6** ______ because there are so many cars during the morning and evening rush hours. I have several colleagues who **7** ______ to work from a long distance away. They live along the same **8** ______ so they can travel together and enjoy each other's company. By sharing the cost of filling the gas **9** ______ , they don't pay so much to commute. But they also have some trips that are very stressful. Last week, for instance, a friend told me of a **10** ______ incident that he saw. It sounded quite shocking.

4 **Look at Riitta's response in Exercise 3. Has Riitta answered the question? Has she given good reasons and examples to support her opinion?**

______

______

______

10 Advertising

Comparing

Comparative and superlative adjectives and adverbs; expressions of equality / inequality (*as … as*, *not as … as*, etc.); other ways of comparing

A Context listening

1 **You are going to hear Enzo and Clara. They work for an advertising agency and are discussing a new client. Before you listen, look at the pictures of Wrinkleless Wardrobes' products and match the picture with the name of the product and its target group.**

A	B	C
1 	1 personal steamer	1 retail stores
2 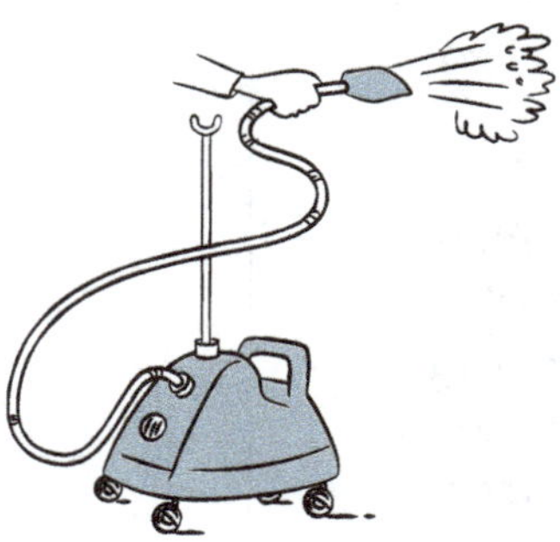	2 travel steamer	2 homemakers
3 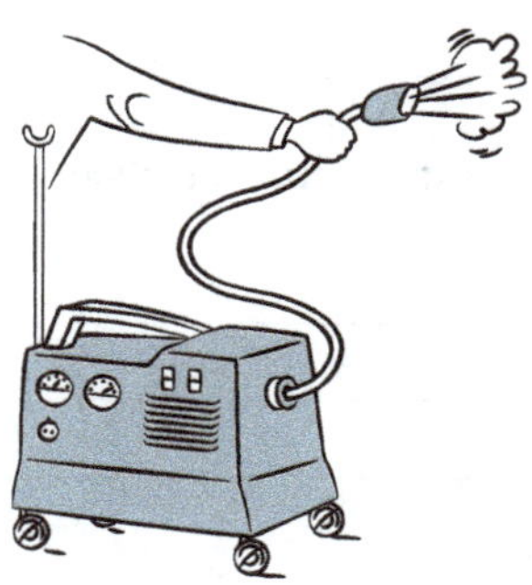	3 industrial steamer	3 people on trips

2 **Listen and check if you were right.**

3 Listen again and say whether these sentences are true or false. Correct the sentences that are false.

1 Wrinkleless Wardrobes want a promotional campaign for their ~~irons~~ steamers. false
2 The advertisements may be aimed at three target audiences. ______
3 Brochures and flyers will be handed out in a promotion taking place in a downtown store. ______
4 A jingle for a TV ad will be written. ______
5 A slogan is needed to drum up some publicity. ______

4 Underline the noun / noun phrases in Exercise 3 that refer to advertising.

5 Listen again and write a short answer to these questions.

1 Which steamer is the smallest? the traveler's steamer
2 Which is cheaper, using the hotel laundry services or a traveler's steamer? ______
3 Which steamer is the largest? ______
4 Is an iron as effective at removing wrinkles as a steamer? ______
5 Are steamers better than irons? ______

6 Look at the questions and your answers in Exercise 5. Answer these questions.

1 How many things do questions 1 and 3 compare? ______
2 How many things do questions 2 and 5 compare? ______
3 What structure does question 4 use? ______

B Grammar

1 Comparative and superlative adjectives and adverbs

We use comparatives to compare two people, things, or actions and superlatives to compare more than two. (► See Unit 1, Word Forms and Unit 9, Adjectives and Adverbs.)

Forming comparative and superlative adjectives and adverbs

adjective / adverb	comparative	superlative
One syllable:		
fast	+ *-er* *faster*	+ *-est* *the fastest*
ending in -e *fine*	+ *-r* *finer*	+ *-st* the finest
ending in one vowel + *-b*, *-d*, *-g*, *-n*, *-p*, or *-t* *sad*	double the last letter + *-er* *sadder*	double the last letter + *-est* *the saddest*
Two syllables:		
ending in -y *easy* *early*	change *-y* to *-i* and add *-er* *easier* *earlier*	change *-y* to *-i* and add *-est* *the easiest* *the earliest*
Two, three, or more syllables:		
serious *seriously*	+ *more* / + *less* *more / less serious* *more / less seriously*	+ the *most* / + *least* *the most / least serious* *the most / least seriously*

Using comparative adjectives and adverbs

We use comparative adjectives to compare two people, things, or places, or one thing, person, or place at two different times.

The Bridge Guesthouse is ***cheaper than*** *the Gable Lodge.*
My boss is ***more cheerful*** *today* ***than*** *he was yesterday.*

We use comparative adverbs to compare two actions, or one action at two different times.

Prices for food rose ***more rapidly than*** *those for clothing.*
We have promoted our products ***more successfully*** *this year* ***than*** *we did last year.*

We can use comparatives without the word *than* when the context makes the comparison clear.

The new desk chairs are ***more comfortable*** *(than the old chairs).*
It is supposed to be ***warmer*** *tomorrow (than it has been recently).*

Using superlative adjectives and adverbs

We use a superlative adjective to compare one thing, person, or place with all the others in a group.

The Rooftop isn't ***the cheapest*** *place to eat in the city.*

We use a superlative adverb to compare one action with other actions of a similar nature.

Of all my colleagues, I commute ***the farthest.***

We can also use superlative adjectives with *one of the / some of the*, ordinal numbers, or a possessive instead of the word *the*.
*Our manager is **one of the most cheerful** people I've ever met.*
*Matthew is **the second highest** earner on the team.*
*Interviewers always ask candidates about **their greatest** strengths.*

2 Irregular comparative and superlative adjectives and adverbs

Some adjectives and adverbs have the same comparative and superlative forms.
good / well → better→ best, bad / badly → worse → worst,
far / far → farther / further → farthest / furthest, late / late → later → latest

*This is a **better** product. It sells **better**. This is **the best** product. It sells **the best**.*

3 Comparing quantities

We can use comparatives and superlatives with adjectives to compare quantities.

quantifiers	comparative	superlative
a lot of / much / many	*more* (+ plural countable and uncountable nouns)	*the most* (+ plural countable and uncountable nouns)
a few	*fewer* (+ plural countable nouns)	*the fewest* (+ plural countable nouns)
a little	*less* (+ uncountable nouns)	*the least* (+uncountable nouns)

***More** people are buying **more** fruit and vegetables than ever before.*
*We had **fewer** errors in our calculations this year. In fact, we had **the fewest** errors ever.*
*We had **less** money to spend on advertising, but we managed to use **the least** money to create **the most** impact.*

Quantifiers can be used for emphasis.
*We have had **many** more sales this afternoon.*
*We have been **much** more successful.*

4 *As ... as*

Use the phrase *as ... as* when there is no difference between what is being compared and *not as ... as* when there is a difference.
Equality and inequality phrases can be used with adjectives, adverbs, and nouns.
*We were **as energetic as** the other team. They were **not as prepared as** we were.*
*We drove **as fast as** the speed limit allowed. We did **not drive as fast as** the car could go.*
*We made **as many sales as** our competitors, and we **didn't** spend **as much money as** we did last year.*

Equality and inequality phrases can be used with *just* to emphasize that there is no difference and with *almost, nearly, not quite* to show minor differences.
*This machine prints **just as fast as** that one.*
*This paper is **not quite as expensive as** that paper.*

C Grammar exercises

1 Underline the correct comparative or superlative adjective.

1 This is *the more exciting* / *<u>the most exciting</u>* advance in machine design in years.
2 Of the two hotels, I think you should stay at *the cheaper* / *the cheapest* one in order to keep costs down.
3 I think Tuesday would be *the less convenient* / *the least convenient* day of the week for a meeting.
4 That was *the more productive* / *the most productive* meeting we have had in a long time.
5 I prefer the *more flexible* / *the most flexible* working hours that I have in my job here at GTech.
6 We don't have much to talk about. This will be *a shorter* / *the shortest* meeting than last week's.
7 We have had *fewer* / *the fewest* complaints about noise since we put in carpets.
8 *The faster* / *The fastest* way to get downtown from here is to take the subway.

2 Use the adjectives in parentheses to make comparative or superlative adverbs and fill in the blanks.

1 Do you know which sales representative travels ___the farthest___ (*far*) each week?
2 Of all the designs we received, this one shows the product ________________ (*effective*).
3 I am trying to save money, so I am eating out ________________ (*frequent*) these days.
4 No machine operates ________________ (*noisy*) than the printer in my office.
5 Anita has been working ________________ (*hard*) to solve this problem.

3 Find the mistakes in the comparative or superlative adjectives and adverbs and correct them.

Before I announce the award for ~~more innovative~~ the most innovative TV ad of the year, I'd just like to say that this is the difficult decision the judges have ever had to make. We had to look at these ads the most carefully than ever. The entries this year were of much high quality than last year's and we were all extremely impressed. But in the end, we decided that one entry was innovative, not to mention funny than all the others. It is the most humor ad we have seen for a long time. It is also the one that most clear showed the use of new technology. The ads that were awarded second and third place were also excellent and the judges gave them only slightly few points than the winner. They were both as good as the winning ad in the quality of the acting, but in the end we thought the winning ad made greatest impact because it was the original, and we think the public will like it the better.

4 **Use *as* ... *as* to complete the following sentences.**

1 There was an emergency in the warehouse and the resident doctor arrived on the scene ___as fast as___ (*fast*) he could.

2 I love my new office even though it is ____________ (*big*) my previous one.

3 I was hoping for more humor in the office, but my new boss is ____________ (*serious*) the one who just left.

4 These chairs are ____________ (*comfortable*) the other ones. They hurt my back.

5 I'm having all kinds of trouble with my computer. I wish it were ____________ (*up-to-date*) yours.

6 The team members were suffering jetlag so they were ____________ (*enthusiastic*) the members on the other team.

5 **Look at the products below. Write two sentences using the comparative structure, two using the superlative structure, and two using *as* ... *as*.**

1 The larger car is more powerful than the smaller car.

2 ____________

3 ____________

4 ____________

5 ____________

6 ____________

D Vocabulary

Key Vocabulary

Read this paragraph about advertising and check your understanding of the words in bold.

> **Advertising** is an essential part of business. Businesses advertise in order to make potential customers aware of the products and services that they offer. Small companies may not be able to pay for **commercials** on television or other national or international **media**, but they can **place ads** in local media, such as in the **classified ad** sections of local newspapers, or they can buy **air time** on commercial radio stations. They can also produce **posters** or **flyers** relatively cheaply or even place ads on the internet. Large companies often have a special **budget** to pay **advertising agencies** that specialize in designing and producing ads. These agencies create commercials with **slogans** and **jingles** aimed at a particular **target** audience as part of a **promotional campaign** to **gain publicity** and **create brand recognition.**

1 **Match a word from column A with a word from column B and use the phrases to complete the sentences below.**

A	B
advertising	recognition
brand	audience
classified	time
target	agency
air	ads

1 He runs the largest _advertising agency_ in the town.

2 We saw a bicycle for sale in the ________________ .

3 The ________________ for our products is the 25 to 35 age group.

4 We have budgeted enough for 30 seconds of ________________ for ads during the televised football game.

5 This study shows that ________________ for our product is increasing.

2 **Read the comments on the next page from an online discussion about internet advertising and find the words to complete the definitions.**

Tues 14.53

Joe Bloggs
joined 03/05
Posts 18

The future of advertising is definitely online. For a start, advertising on the internet is not as expensive as advertising on TV. Also, you can choose your target audience more effectively by choosing your website carefully. Internet advertising is also less restricted by time. Your ad and slogan can be seen worldwide by internet users 24 hours a day. And don't forget that there are many more different ways to create a promotional campaign.

However, nothing can completely replace traditional ways of advertising, especially TV. Watching TV is one of the most common leisure-time activities all around the world. Because of this, TV commercials are still one of the most powerful ways to promote your product. TV ad writers can also be more creative, using catchy jingles, etc. to make their commercials really memorable.

Reply Contact

1 Advertising ________ is the business of trying to persuade people to buy products or services.
2 An ________ is a picture, short film, song, etc. that tries to persuade people to buy a product or service.
3 A ________ is an advertisement broadcast on radio or TV.
4 A ________ is a phrase that is repeated often and influences people to recognize a product or company.
5 A ________ is the main group of people that an ad campaign is aimed at.
6 A ________ is a short song used in a commercial.
7 When you ________ a product or service, you are making it known to the public through various techniques.
8 A ________ is a series of activities to make the public aware of a product.

3 Put the words from the box into the blanks.

advertising agency   air time   budget   commercial   flyers   media
~~promotional campaign~~   posters   publicity   slogan

Beth: So, are there any ideas for the new **1** promotional campaign ?
Angus: Well, actually, I was thinking that we could **2** ________ money to be sponsors in a fundraising activity.
Cindy: There's a marathon next month to raise money for cancer research. We could sponsor a local team.
Beth: Will the **3** ________ be at the event?
Angus: Yes, of course. A lot of people are expected to attend. It'd be good **4** ________ to sponsor an activity that helps people.
Beth: We could put up **5** ________ and hand out **6** ________ at the mall encouraging people to attend the event.
Cindy: Good idea. And what about buying some **7** ________ on local radio?
Angus: Yes, we can contact several **8** ________ stations in this region.
Beth: OK. Good. Let's contact our **9** ________ and have them create a clever **10** ________ .

Practice test 2

TOEIC® TIP
Many correct answers to questions in the Listening section Part 2 do not repeat the language of the questions. For example:
*What did Sara **want to talk** to you about?*
The report she is writing. (correct)
*She **wanted to talk** to me.* (incorrect)

TOEIC® TIP
Don't worry about not understanding every word in the conversation or talk. Use words you know to understand the basic ideas and help you answer the questions.

Listening

Part 1: Photographs

Directions: In this section, you will hear four statements about a photograph. The statements will not be printed on the test. As you listen, select the statement that best describes the photograph. You will hear the statements only once.

1 (A) (B) (C) (D)

2 (A) (B) (C) (D)

3 (A) (B) (C) (D)

4 (A) (B) (C) (D)

5 (A) (B) (C) (D)

Part 2: Question-Response

Directions: In this section, you will hear a question or statement followed by three responses. They will not be printed on the test. As you listen, select the best response. You will hear the question and statements only once.

6 (A) (B) (C)
7 (A) (B) (C)
8 (A) (B) (C)
9 (A) (B) (C)
10 (A) (B) (C)
11 (A) (B) (C)
12 (A) (B) (C)
13 (A) (B) (C)
14 (A) (B) (C)
15 (A) (B) (C)
16 (A) (B) (C)
17 (A) (B) (C)

Part 3: Conversations

Directions: In this section, you will hear two people having a conversation and will answer questions about what you heard. The conversations will not be printed on the test. Select the response that best answers the question. You will hear the conversations only once.

Questions **18–20** refer to the following conversation.

18 What product did the man purchase?
(A) A kind of pump
(B) A garden feature
(C) A swimming pool
(D) An instruction booklet

19 What is the man's problem?
(A) He cannot inflate his pool.
(B) The valve is broken.
(C) The pump doesn't attach properly.
(D) He can't assemble the pump.

20 What does the woman offer to do?
(A) Exchange the product
(B) Attach the pump correctly
(C) Send an instruction manual
(D) Send over a technician

Questions **21–23** refer to the following conversation.

21 Where does this conversation take place?
(A) In a cafeteria
(B) At a road construction site
(C) On a bicycle route
(D) In a meeting room

22 Why does the man apologize?
(A) He left his bicycle.
(B) He is late again.
(C) He doesn't want to ride a bicycle.
(D) He is unhappy about the new route.

23 What does the woman think?
(A) Commuting by bicycle is healthier than driving.
(B) Waiting for people is easier than complaining.
(C) Starting a meeting late is not a problem.
(D) Using a bicycle is safer these days.

Questions **24–26** refer to the following conversation.

24 What is the company "Greenaway Gadgets" planning?
(A) To improve its economic conditions
(B) To arrange a new period of consultation
(C) To borrow money for an expansion in production
(D) To solve their production problems

25 What do the speakers think about the "Greenaway Gadgets" plan?
(A) It is the wrong time to expand the company.
(B) It is not the best time to meet about it.
(C) It is the wrong goal for the company.
(D) It will cost too much money.

26 What will the man do by next week?
(A) See if the economic conditions are better
(B) Reject any unnecessary items
(C) Ask about increased sales
(D) Make a report

Questions **27–29** refer to the following conversation.

27 What was the man told about checks?
(A) The bank doesn't process checks any longer.
(B) You can process checks in the supermarket.
(C) They always clear after your salary is deposited.
(D) Checks written in red ink take longer to process.

28 Where did the woman work in the past?
(A) At a bank
(B) At a supermarket
(C) At a checkout counter
(D) At an electronics company

29 What advice does the woman give?
(A) Write checks in any color
(B) Believe everything you hear
(C) Buy only things you can pay for
(D) Find out who was telling the truth

Questions **30–32** refer to the following conversation.

30 What does the man want?
(A) Information on investments
(B) Several different rates
(C) A deposit form
(D) Money from his account

31 What does the man decide to do?
(A) Leave his money in his account
(B) Keep his money for a year
(C) Reinvest his money for six months
(D) Invest in the fund with the higher interest

32 When will the funds be transferred?
(A) After the man's salary comes in
(B) When the man goes to the bank
(C) After six months to a year
(D) When a better rate is offered

Part 4: Talks

Directions: In this section, you will hear a speaker giving a talk and will answer questions about the talk. The talks will not be printed on the test. Select the response that best answers the question. You will hear the talks only once.

Questions **33–35** refer to the following talk.

33 Who is Eduardo Gonzales?
(A) A property owner
(B) A prospective tenant
(C) A real estate agent
(D) An insurance dealer

34 Why is Eduardo giving this talk?
(A) To advise homeowners about tenants
(B) To inform visitors about transportation links
(C) To persuade people not to rent properties
(D) To inform tenants of potential problems

35 Where can interested people get the brochure?
(A) At the real estate agency
(B) At an insurance company
(C) From the sponsor
(D) From the landlord

Questions **36–38** refer to the following talk.

36 What is the main point of the talk?
(A) Complaints offer a good opportunity for a company.
(B) Do not complain unless it is really necessary.
(C) Companies prefer solving complaints.
(D) Some companies treat customers badly.

37 What may be true if customers do not complain?
(A) You have solved their problems successfully.
(B) They are probably loyal to your company.
(C) They do not think you are courteous.
(D) They go elsewhere without saying anything.

38 Who is the talk probably aimed at?
(A) Customers
(B) The competition
(C) Checkout cashiers
(D) Customer service personnel

Questions **39–41** refer to the following talk.

39 What is the main point of the talk?
(A) The importance of having a health check before you start work
(B) The necessity of reading an offer letter carefully
(C) The possibility of having a disagreement with your new employer
(D) The consequences of not understanding your new duties

40 Who is the talk directed at?
(A) Interviewers
(B) New officers
(C) Job candidates
(D) Employment agencies

41 What is NOT mentioned as a key piece of information to look for?
(A) The salary amount
(B) The required duties
(C) The need for a health checkup
(D) The length of time of the contract

Questions **42–44** refer to the following talk.

42 Who is speaking?
(A) A pedestrian
(B) A street cleaner
(C) An inventor
(D) A city official

43 What is the speaker comparing?
(A) New and old street cleaning devices
(B) Different kinds of chewing gum
(C) Public spaces and city streets
(D) Forms of environmental pollution

44 Where is the speaker?
(A) In an office
(B) At a factory
(C) On a sidewalk
(D) In a shopping mall

Questions **45–47** refer to the following talk.

45 What is being presented?
(A) Information on how to buy property
(B) Bank mortgage requirements
(C) How to negotiate a price for a house
(D) Estimating market conditions

46 Who wrote the document?
(A) A house buyer
(B) A property seller
(C) A professional negotiator
(D) A team of house buying experts

47 Who is the document aimed at?
(A) Guide publishers
(B) Real estate agents
(C) Bank loan officers
(D) New and experienced buyers

Writing

Questions 1–5: Write a sentence based on a picture.
Directions: In this section, you will be given two words or phrases and a photograph. You will be asked to write one sentence about the photograph, using the two given words or phrases. You can change the forms of the words and use them in any order.Your sentence will be scored on grammar and how relevant the sentence is to the photograph. You will have 8 minutes for this part.

Question 1:

phone / although

Question 2:

cyclist / because

Question 3:

money / out of

Question 4:

advertisement / busy

Questions 6 – 7: Respond to a written request
Directions: In this question, you will write a response to an e-mail. Your response will be scored on vocabulary, organization, and the quality and variety of your sentences. You will have 10 minutes to read and respond to each e-mail.

Directions: Read the email. In your email, ask TWO questions and make ONE suggestion.

From: R. Kumar
Subject: Arabian Car Sales Co.
Date: June 26th
To: James Kaiser

Dear Mr. Kaiser:

We would like to take this opportunity to introduce our new range of recreational vehicles. We are an acknowledged leader in the automobile business. Our network of 56 branches across the country can offer you unmatched sales, service, and parts facilities.

Please see the attachment for our full range of vehicles and their specifications and prices.

We hope you will find our rates competitive and in line with your requirements. We would be pleased to offer you a demonstration / test drive at your convenience.

Thank you.

R. Kumar

968 99260777

Directions: Read the email. In your email, ask ONE question and make TWO requests.

From: Sally Browning
To: Charles Lake
Subject: Reception at Grove Institute
Sent: February 12th

Dear Member:

Grove Institute 50th Anniversary Reception

You will be pleased to hear we plan to host a 50th Anniversary reception on the weekend of June 25–26, from 6:15 P.M., at the Grove Institute. Please let us know as soon as possible if you will be attending and if you plan to bring a guest.

We are looking forward to a successful anniversary event. Please let us know if you have any special requests that we need to address before your arrival.

We look forward to hearing from you soon.

Best regards,

Sally Browning

Question 8: Write an opinion essay
Directions: In this section, you will write an essay about a given issue. You will be asked to state your opinion and explain and support the opinion. A successful essay will usually contain a minimum of 300 words. Your essay will be scored on grammar, vocabulary, organization, and whether your opinion is supported with reasons and examples. You will have 30 minutes to complete your essay.

Essay question:
Do you think that people are exposed to too much advertising these days? Use specific reasons and examples to explain your answer.

Grammar Focus Task 1

Match the sentence with its description.

1 Are you sure it is broken? ____________
2 Why did the bank return the check?
____
3 You need the sales receipt to make an exchange, don't you? ____________
4 Could you tell me where we are supposed to meet? ____________
5 The supermarket cashier just told me that if you write a check in red ink, the bank will take longer to process the check. ____________

a An embedded question.
b A statement with a tag question.
c A *wh-* question.
d A *yes / no* question.
e A reporting statement.

Grammar Focus Task 2

Complete these sentences with words from the box.

as readable as	carefully	more quickly	successful	worse than

1 Before you sign a contract as a tenant, there are several things you should ____________ check.
2 We are looking forward to a ____________ anniversary event.
3 Believe me, red ink is ____________ any other color.
4 I tried to be on time today but the traffic jams were ____________ ever.
5 I think I could get here ____________ by bicycle.

Vocabulary Focus Task

Complete these sentences with a word that means the same as the definitions.

1 You can stay ahead of your competitors in the way you handle complaints____________ .
objections, criticisms
2 Did you ask him if the t____________ accepted the offer? *person who pays rent*
3 The f____________ can be transferred from my account tomorrow. *sum of money*
4 What is that a____________ agency called?
business that creates commercials
5 I'll definitely use the new bike r____________ for my daily commuting.
road for passage or travel

11 Company structure

Modals 1

Ability and possibility

A Context listening

1 **You are going to hear Alberto and Rosemarie Gomez talking about a problem facing their business. Before you listen, look at the picture.**

1 What is the Gomez's business? ____________________

2 What could be the problem they are facing? ____________________

3 What do you think they could do about the problem? ____________________

2 **Listen and check if you were right.**

3 **Listen and answer these questions.**

1 What does Rosemarie say is *necessary* for them to do to get a loan?

We ____must____ study the market, the costs, and the possible profits.

2 What does Rosemarie say she will *possibly do* when the sales representative from Wooden Toyz Company comes?

I just ____________ ask her about toys for older children.

3 According to Alberto, why is renting the empty store next door *not possible*?

We ____________ expand that much.

4 What reason does Rosemarie give when she is *unable to* reach the ceiling?

I ____________ reach that high.

5 What does Alberto say about *his ability* to help Rosemarie hang the balloons?

I ____________ do that for you.

6 What does Rosemarie say is *necessary* for them *not* to do?

We ____________ rush into anything.

4 **Compare the words in italics in Exercise 3 with your answers. What is the connection between them?** ____________

5 **Listen again and underline the words you hear in the conversation.**

logo income partner stockholders
expand profits earnings capital

B Grammar

1 Modals

Modals are the auxiliary verbs *can, could, may, might, will, would, shall, should, ought to,* and *must*. Modals give further meaning to the main verb.
*How **can** we **think** about expanding right now?*
*We **must** do something soon.*

Modals do not change their form.
*He **can travel** with me if he wants to.* (**not** ~~He cans travel ….~~)
*A partner **could bring** in the money needed for expansion.* (**not** ~~A partner could to bring …. .~~)

2 Ability

We use *can('t)* for present ability / inability and *could(n't)* for past ability / inability.
*Barbara **can speak** Korean, but she **can't speak** Arabic.*
*The previous manager **could state** the sales figures for the last 10 years, but he **couldn't remember** our names.*

When we are talking about one specific occasion in the past we use *couldn't, was(n't) / were(n't) able to.* We do **not** use *could.*
*He **was able to find** his suitcase.* (**not** ~~He could find ….~~)

We use *be able to* for ability / inability in all tenses.
*We **are / were / have been / will be able to** hire more employees.*

3 Possibility

We use *can / can't, could / couldn't, may / may not, might / might not,* and *must* to indicate the degree of possibility that the information is true.

Almost certain	*must*
Possible	*can, may, could, might*
Unlikely	*can't, couldn't*

When we are almost certain that something is true (often based on the evidence), we use *must.*
*I saw Jackie a few minutes ago. She **must be** here.*
*I hear you've been promoted. You **must be** very happy.*

When we are almost certain about something in the past, we use *must* + *have* + past participle.

*Jackie's coat is gone. She **must have left.***

*You **must have been** very happy when they told you about your promotion.*

When we think something is possible, we use *can, could, may,* or *might.*

*We **could rent** the empty store next door.*

*There **may not be** enough space on your computer for all the files.*

*We **might hire** a private bus if it's not too expensive.*

Use context to understand if *can* means possibility or ability.

*I **can** drive. My father taught me on country roads.* (ability)

*Don't worry if the taxi is late. I **can** drive you.* (possibility)

When we talk about possibility in the past, we use *could / may / might* + *have* + past participle.

*We **could have rented** that store, but we decided that it wasn't the best option.*

*He **may have been** in touch with someone.*

*He **might have contacted** them on his cell phone.*

When we think something is unlikely, we use *can't* or *couldn't.*

*You **can't be** hungry already. We just had a big lunch.* (**not** ~~You mustn't be ... .~~)

*He **couldn't have** the file. I just saw it.*

When we talk about something impossible in the past, we use *can't / couldn't* + *have* + past participle.

*You **can't have eaten** all those chocolates.*

*He **couldn't have taken** the file. I had it with me.*

C Grammar Exercises

1 Write *can('t)* or *could(n't)* in the blanks.

1 The shipment is late so we ___can't___ complete the order.

2 I preferred the old system of private offices to this open plan office. I ________ get a lot more work done before they changed it.

3 They didn't know how to run the fax machine, so they ________ send the fax.

4 Ms. Wong prefers to take the subway because she ________ find parking spaces near the office.

5 If you are having a problem with your computer, talk to Bill. He ________ fix anything.

6 Lucy was originally hired because she ________ speak French with the people at our Paris branch.

2 Read the following article and underline the word that completes the sentence.

File Edit View Favorites Tools Help

Back Search Favorites Media

Address Go Links

You **1** *may not / could* believe this, but one of the ways to increase milk production is to treat your cows like people. According to many dairy farmers, cows **2** *may / could not* feel happier and more relaxed if they are given a name. Cows with names like Daisy and Buttercup **3** *can / can't* produce more milk than their sisters without names. This belief **4** *might / must* now be proved after researchers test what many dairy farmers **5** *can / must* already know by experience. Naming a cow and talking to it like a person **6** *could / couldn't* make the cow feel like part of a family. One farmer noticed that when naming a cow, he interacts with her at a more individual level, and this **7** *can't / could* be the factor that reduces stress levels in the animal. The cow **8** *may / may not* have a better perception of humans and consequently, **9** *may / must* be more productive. That is the theory at least. Whatever the case, this surely **10** *mustn't / can't* be a bad thing for either cows or farmers.

3 **Choose the best ending to complete the sentences.**

1 I saw Mr. Williams in the office so — a he must be here.
b he might be here.

2 Mariam didn't look well so she
a couldn't have canceled the meeting and gone home.
b could have canceled the meeting and gone home.

3 I can't find my keys so
a I might have left them in the car.
b I might leave them in the car.

4 Tim said that he was very busy and
a he may not attend the office party.
b he may not have attended the office party.

5 Not many people came to the trade show.
a It couldn't be that it was at an inconvenient time.
b It could be that it was at an inconvenient time.

4 **Look at the pictures and write true or imaginary sentences about yourself. Use each of the words in the box.**

can	could	may	might	must	can't
couldn't	may not	might not	must not		

drive a car

snowboard

give a presentation

build a house

fix a computer

climb mountains

1 I can drive a car, but I couldn't be a taxi driver.
2 ______
3 ______
4 ______
5 ______
6 ______

D Vocabulary

Key Vocabulary

Read this paragraph about company structure and check your understanding of the words in bold.

Often a company is a business owned by one owner or **proprietor.** The owner receives the **profit** from the business, but also takes on the risks. When two or more individuals own the business it is called a **partnership.** Some companies **merge** with others or **expand** and **restructure** to become **corporations** that **raise capital** by offering **shares** to **stockholders**. The company can use the money from the shares to invest in its **products** or services and **make a profit**. The **management** of corporations is performed by **directors** who do not own the company but follow the instructions of the stockholders. Sometimes a company expands by making a successful **takeover bid** for another company through purchasing a majority of the shares. When a company does business, the earnings received are used to pay **overhead** (the cost of running the business) and the stockholders receive the remaining money in the form of **dividends.**

Vocabulary note

The word *produce* has two different pronunciations. ***Pro**duce* is the noun and *pro**duce*** is the verb.

The nouns *produce* and *product* have different, but related meanings.
Produce refers to the food that farmers grow.
*We can buy fresh **produce** at the farmer's market.*
Produce can be used as an adjective.
*We have fresh strawberries in the **produce** section.*
Product refers to goods that have been manufactured.
*Parts of many **products** are made in different countries.*

1 **Read the extract from a business podcast and fill in the blanks with a word from the box.**

corporation	directors	partnership	~~proprietor~~
stockholders	produce	expansion	

One of the most interesting news stories this week was that the **1** ___proprietor___ of ATC, Phillip Allen, has decided to enter into a **2** ________ with another well-known business person, Lucia Mendez, to set up a new IT company. It is understood that the partners will continue as **3** ________ of the new company, which will be called ATech. The plan is to become a major **4** ________ in the high tech sector. **5** ________ are eagerly awaiting a new share offering which will raise much needed capital for the **6** ________ plans. It is thought that ATech will **7** ________ a range of new high definition mobile communication devices.

2 **Choose the correct word to complete the sentences.**

1 If this ___partnership___ is going to be a success, communication between the ___partners___ must be a priority. *partners / partnership*

2 There has been a lot of talk recently about a ______________ between the Good Old Egg company and the Fancy Cake company. If these companies ______________, they will be able to put cake products on the market at a much lower price. *merge / merger*

3 Bonnie Floyd is on the new ______________ team. She used to ______________ HopScotch Bakeries. *management / manage*

4 The company would like to ______________ but the costs of the ______________ may be too high. *expansion / expand*

5 According to ______________ law, the individual stockholders are not responsible for the ______________'s liabilities. *corporation / corporate*

6 We are presently undergoing a complete ______________. Once we have fully ______________, we will be much more competitive. *restructured / restructuring*

3 **Some of the words in this email are in the wrong place. Find the wrong words and put them in the correct place.**

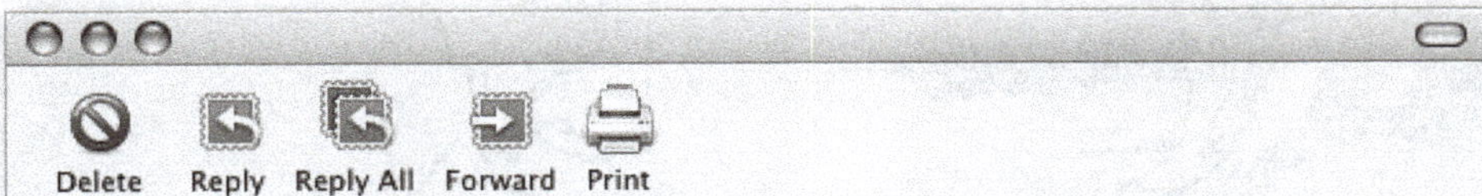

Hi Carol

It has been a very busy year. As you know, a few years ago we ~~takeover bid~~ merged with a soft drinks company and the whole business has been profits. When that happened, all employees were given the opportunity to buy directors in the company, so I became a management. Some employees sold their shares, but I kept mine. The restructured have made excellent decisions and the company has been making good shares despite very high stockholder. So, I have received some nice overheads. Now it seems that merged is planning to make a dividends for another company.

12 Employment contracts

Modals 2

Obligation and necessity; orders and advice

A Context listening

1 You are going to hear Maria, a personnel officer, answering Alex's questions about a contract for employment. Before you listen, look at the pictures. What questions do you think Alex has about the contract?

2 Listen and check if you were right.

3 Listen again and complete these sentences.

1 I need to clear up ______ some questions before I sign it.

2 After five years, the company ______ you an extra day of vacation time ...

3 But obviously you ______ your manager know if ...

4 During the first month ... you can leave at any time and you ______ us in advance.

5 After you have been with us one month, you ______ us at least three weeks in advance ...

6 However, if an employee is involved in any kind of misconduct, we ______ any notice to terminate a contract.

7 Employees ______ that this never happens.

8 I think you ______ away and read it though once more ...

4 Complete the table below with the first word or phrase of your answers in Exercise 3.

strong obligation or necessity	advice or suggestions	no obligation or necessity
need to		

5 Choose the word in column B that is often used with the word in column A.

Column A	Column B
1 doctor's	a leave
2 give	b conditions
3 lay someone	c a contract
4 sick	d note
5 terminate	e off
6 terms and	f notice

B Grammar

1 Obligation and necessity

We use the verbs *must, have to,* and *need to* to express obligation or a need to do something. All these verbs have a similar meaning.

*You **must** / **have to** / **need to bring** in a doctor's note if you are sick.*

Must* and *have to

Both of these verbs express obligation, but there are differences between them:

- opinion or statement of fact

  When it is our personal opinion that something is important, we use *must* more frequently.

  *My computer files are a mess. I **must organize** them better.*
  *My cousin is visiting me. You **must meet** her.*

  When we are stating a fact instead of giving a personal opinion, we use *have to* more frequently.

  *I work on the 9th floor. I **have to take** the elevator to get to my office.*
  *Do you **have to travel** a lot in your job?*

- written or spoken rules

  When we write rules or instructions, we usually use *must.*

  *Applications for the managerial position **must arrive** before 4:00 Friday afternoon.*

  When we discuss rules, we usually use *have to.*

  *We also **have to give** you three weeks notice if we decide to lay you off.*

- tense

  We can only use *must* to talk about obligation in the present tense.

  *I **must read** over the contract.*

  We can use *have to* in all tense forms.

  *I **had to read** over the contract.*
  *How many employees **have** you **had to fire**?*
  *I'll **have to finish** this email tomorrow.*

Mustn't* and *don't have to

The meaning of *mustn't* is different from the meaning of *don't have to.*

*You **mustn't** park in the staff parking lot.* (= Do not park in the staff parking lot. You are not allowed to park there.)

*You **don't have to** park in the staff parking lot.* (= It is not necessary for you to park in the staff parking lot. It is optional, so you can if you want to.)

*This chemical is very acidic. You **mustn't spill** it.*

The factory tour is optional. You ***don't have to go*** *on it.*

Need to

Need to indicates that it is necessary for someone to do something. The meaning is similar to *must*.

I ***need to pay*** *that bill by June 15th.*

When something needs to be done, we often use the verb + *-ing*.

The office needs redecorating.

We use the negative form to indicate that something is not necessary. The meaning is the same as *don't have to*.

You ***don't need to attend*** *the presentation. = You* ***don't have to attend*** *the presentation.*

2 Orders and advice

We use the verbs *must*, *had better* (*'d better*), *should*, *ought to*, and *could* to give orders or advice.

You ***must*** *finish this report before our annual meeting.* (= an order or very strong advice)

*You'****d better*** *read through the company regulations.* (= strong advice)

You ***should*** *fix that crack before you paint the wall.* (= advice)

You ***ought to*** *go through that form again. The numbers don't add up.* (= advice)

You ***could*** *call the maintenance person to remove that tree branch.* (= mild advice or a suggestion)

The negative forms *had better not, should not,* and *ought not to* are used to give advice against doing something.

*You'****d better not miss*** *your flight because you can't get a refund.*

You ***shouldn't go*** *to the clinic without an appointment.*

We use *should / ought to* + *have* + past participle to talk about a past action that was or was not a good thing to do.

I ***should have read*** *the contract.* (It was a good thing to do, but I didn't do it.)

I ***shouldn't have walked*** *around in the rain.* (It was not a good thing to do, but I did it.)

C Grammar exercises

1 **Neela and Troy are talking about some of their work colleagues. Match the situation with the advice or obligation and choose the right verb to complete the sentence.**

	Situation			Advice or obligation
1	Ahmed has been offered a job with a good salary.	e	a	She *should* / *shouldn't* have come to work on time.
2	Bill was off work for a whole week due to sickness.	______	b	He *must* / *mustn't* present a doctor's note.
3	Rajit has already completed his health and safety training.	______	c	She *should* / *doesn't need to* ask someone in personnel.
4	Jane's lost her job because she was late to work every day.	______	d	He *must* / *mustn't* give his notice three weeks in advance.
5	Lillian needs to find a job with a better salary.	______	e	He *must* / *shouldn't* sign the contract before he starts work.
6	Mary is not sure how much vacation time she is permitted.	______	f	She *has to* / *mustn't* let herself get too stressed.
7	Pete wants to leave the company.	______	g	He *must* / *won't* have to do it again for another two years.
8	Sang-mi gets ill when she is working under a lot of pressure.	______	h	She *should* / *shouldn't* wait any longer before applying at the employment agency.

2 **Fill in the correct form of *mustn't* or *don't have to*.**

1 You really ___mustn't___ sit so close to the computer. You will hurt your eyes.
2 I ______________ attend today's training session since it's the same as the one I went to yesterday.
3 You ______________ forget to read the small print on your contract.
4 We ______________ be late for the appointment.
5 I enjoy the weekends because I ______________ get up so early.
6 Oh good! We ______________ wait very long until payday.
7 The new company rule says we ______________ smoke inside the buildings.

3 **Read the email that Zoe sent to a friend about her lucky escape while on vacation. Choose the right verbs.**

Delete Reply Reply All Forward Print

Hi Lupe

I **1** *must* / *mustn't* tell you what happened at work this week. I was getting very stressed about the amount of work I had to do – and annoyed with my boss for giving me so much! Lucas said I **2** *should calm / should have calmed* down and, well, I **3** *should listen / should have listened* to him. But instead I started saying unkind things about my boss. I **4** *should keep / should have kept* my mouth shut. Unfortunately, the boss was walking past the office and I thought he **5** *must overhear / must have overheard* me talking about him because he called me into his office. I was very nervous and thought that I **6** *should apologize / should have apologized*. But before I could say anything he smiled and told me that he was very pleased with my work. He said that I **7** *must work / must have worked* all weekend to get the reports done in time and that he was thinking of recommending me for a promotion. I felt very lucky of course, and I have learned a lesson. In the future I **8** *had better / had better not* complain to my colleagues.

4 **Write sentences about each photo using the words in the box. You can use the words under the photos.**

should	had better	must	need to	have to	shouldn't
had better not	mustn't	don't need	don't have to		

1 cross street cars

They should be careful crossing the street.
They mustn't step out in front of cars.

2 sign contract read

____

____

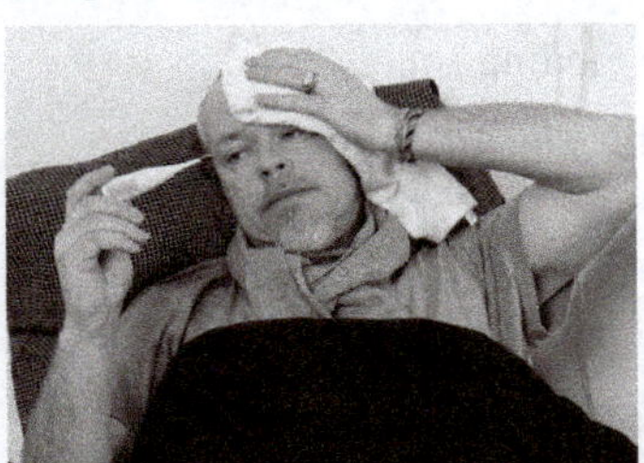

3 doctor ill home

____

____

4 traffic officer stop

____

____

D Vocabulary

Key Vocabulary

Read this paragraph about contracts and check your understanding of the words in bold.

Before you decide to **accept a job offer**, you should carefully read the contract of employment if the employer provides one. The contract is a legal agreement that defines various **terms and conditions** that both employer and employee must follow. These will include such things as the amount of **vacation time** you are **entitled to per annum** or how much paid **sick leave** you can take off of work. It may also state **regulations** concerning a leave of **absence** for events such as **maternity / paternity leave**. A very important condition concerns how much **notice** you have to give if you wish to **quit** your job, in other words **terminate your contract**. The contract will also mention how many days **notice** the employer has to give you if they are going to **lay** you **off** because they no longer need you, as well as state how your employer can **fire** you if you are guilty of **misconduct.** The contract will also state a number of other **company regulations** that you must understand and agree to when you **sign**.

1 Read this conversation between Clarissa and Tom. The words in italics are in the wrong place. Put them in the correct place.

Clarissa: I have been looking at the *terminate* of employment here. And I don't understand something. **1** ___terms___

Tom: What is that? Have you read it carefully?

Clarissa: Well, it says here that they can *per annum* my contract if I don't fulfill all the *sick leave*. **2** ________, **3** ________

Tom: Yes, that is right. They can fire you if you are guilty of *sign*, for example. **4** ________

Clarissa: Oh dear. And what about if I get sick?

Tom: Well, they allow you a certain number of days for *conditions*. **5** ________

Clarissa: And what does *misconduct* mean? **6** ________

Tom: Oh, that just means in one year.

Clarissa: Oh I didn't know that. Thank you. I guess I will *terms* the contract then. **7** ________

2 Underline the correct word form.

1. The *regulates* / *regulations* are very clear about parking in the loading zone.
2. Sandra will be *absent* / *absence* from the office for 10 days while she goes on a training course.
3. Mr. Henrick has received an *acceptance* / *accept* letter for the job that we offer to the best candidate.
4. Tim isn't going to *sign* / *signature* the contract until he has talked to his lawyer.
5. We have to *terminate* / *termination* the project because of a lack of funding.
6. It states here in your contract that your *entitled* / *entitlement* for paid vacation time is four weeks.

3 **Complete the sentences with one of the following words.**

fired	lay off	~~misconduct~~	notice
quit	sick leave	signature	vacation

1 He was fired from the company for misconduct.

2 Please add your ________________ at the bottom of the form.

3 If you decide to leave the company you must give at least one month's ________________ .

4 I was so angry that I shouted at our manager and then he ________________ me.

5 You will earn two days of paid ________________ time for every month you work here.

6 Did you hear that Marie ________________ her job? She got a better job offer.

7 Last month I was quite ill and took several days of ________________ .

8 With the downturn of the economy, the factory has had to ________________ a large number of employees.

13 Dining out

Modals 3

Permission; requests; offers; suggestions

A Context listening

1 **Lauren and Brandon are going out. Before you listen, look at the picture and answer the questions.**

1 Where are Lauren and Brandon? ____________________

2 What is Lauren going to have? ____________________

3 What is Brandon going to have? ____________________

2 **Listen and check if you were right.**

3 **Listen again and complete these sentences.**

Brandon: Oh, there isn't much of a view here. **1** ___Could___ we have that table ...
Waiter: And **2** ____________ I suggest today's special?
Waiter: And **3** ____________ I get you something to drink, madam?
Brandon: Umm, **4** ____________ you mind bringing ...
Waiter: OK. **5** ____________ I take your menus?

4 **Look at the completed sentences in Exercise 3 and answer these questions.**

1 In which sentence is the person asking for permission to do something? ____________

2 In which sentences is the person requesting something? ____________

3 In which sentence is the person offering to do something? ____________

4 In which sentence is the person making a suggestion? ____________

5 **Match the words you heard with a word or phrase that has the same meaning.**

appetizer	beverage
drink	main dish
entrée	meal choices
menu	starter

B Grammar

1 Asking for permission

When we ask for permission to do something, we use the modals *can, could, may,* and *might*. These words have different levels of formality.
Can *I join you for lunch?* (informal)
Could *I join you for lunch?* (less informal)
May *I join you for lunch?* (more formal)
Might *I join you for lunch?* (very formal)

We can also use *would / do you mind* to ask for permission.
Would *you* ***mind*** *my joining you for lunch?*
Do *you* ***mind*** *if I join you for lunch?*

2 Making a request

When we request someone else do something, we use the modals *can, could, will,* and *would*.
Can / Will *you take the minutes for the meeting?* (informal)
Could / Would *you close the door on your way out?* (more formal)

We can ask someone else to do something without using the modals. These are normally more formal and impersonal forms that we don't use in conversation.
We ***ask*** *the audience to turn off their cell phones.*
Please *fasten your seatbelts for takeoff.*

We can also use *would / do you mind* to make a request.
Would *you* ***mind*** *closing the window?*
Do *you* ***mind*** *not tapping on the desk?*

3 Making an offer

We can offer to do something in several ways using the modals *can* and *could*.
I ***can / could*** *make some refreshments for the meeting.*
Can / Could *I bring you a cup of coffee?*
How can *I help you?*

4 Making a suggestion

We can make a suggestion to do something in several ways using the modals *should*, *can*, and *could*.
Should *we go over the accounts together?*
We ***can / could*** *hire a part-time employee.*
Can't / Couldn't *you bring that point up with the manager?*

We can also make a suggestion to do something without using a modal.
Why don't *we take up a collection for the flood victims?*
Let's *buy some plants for the office.*
How about *having lunch at the new restaurant today?*
What about *taking on a new salesperson over the holiday season?*

C Grammar exercises

1 Complete these sentences with one of the phrases in the box.

a asking for permission	**c** making an offer
b making a request	**d** making a suggestion

1 "Why don't you take a break?" *The speaker is* ___d___.

2 "Could you bring two more glasses of water, please?" *The speaker is* ________.

3 "May I work at home this afternoon?" *The speaker is* ________.

4 "Can you get me on an early morning flight out of London tomorrow?" *The speaker is* ________.

5 "How about adding music to our advertisement?" *The speaker is* ________.

6 "Can I take a copy of this brochure?" *The speaker is* ________.

7 "I could fix that noise in your car engine for you." *The speaker is* ________.

2 Complete Mr. Lewis's part of a phone conversation with a customer using phrases from the box.

Can I book	~~Can I help~~	Could I suggest	Could you speak
Let me look	Would you like	Would you mind	

Good morning, Chandler's Bistro. **1** Can I help ________ you? ... **2** Hello, hello. **2** ________________ a little louder, please? Oh, hello Mr. Binger... . You can't make it? OK, I'm sorry to hear that. I'll cancel your booking then ... **3** ________________ another reservation for a different night? ... Yes, of course. **4** ________________ you a table on Friday night at 7:30 P.M.? Yes, good... . I'll make the reservation for four people... . Ah, I see. You would like a table for eight. **5** ________________ holding the line for a second? I'll just check the reservation book... . I'm sorry, Mr. Binger. I'm afraid I can't reserve a table for eight at that time. We're fully booked. **6** ________________ to be sure. Ah, here's a free table. **7** ________________ 8:30 P.M.? ... Good. That's excellent. I'll have a table ready for you at 8.30 on Friday, for a party of eight then.

3 Anita and Evelyn are discussing going out to eat. Their suggestions contain errors. Find the errors and correct them.

Anita: **1** Why do[n't] we go out for a meal and a movie after work today?

Evelyn: That's a good idea. **2** How about to going to that Chinese restaurant that everyone's talking about?

Anita: **3** Yes, let's can go there. It's within walking distance of the movie theater as well.

Evelyn: **4** Should we be look at the website to see what's playing?

Anita: **5** Couldn't we just to pass the movie theater on our way to the restaurant?

Evelyn: Yes, that sounds like a great idea. **6** What about invite the new trainee?

Anita: Sure. Why not? She seems really nice.

4 **Choose the correct word to complete the question and match it to the correct answer. Sometimes more than one verb is possible.**

1  *Could* / *Would* I take your picture? b

2  *Will* / *May* you take this folder over to the main office? ___

3  *May* / *Will* I open the window ___

4  *What* / *How* about changing the background color on our website? ___

5  Why *can't* / *don't* we drop the price on those shirts that aren't selling? ___

6  *Would* / *Do* you mind bringing me back a sandwich from the snack bar? ___

a Of course. Could you open the door as well? 

b Sure, should I sit like this? 

c Of course. How about a coffee as well? 

d Can I take it this afternoon? I'm busy with this report right now. 

e I think it is attractive. Would you mind if we left it as it is? 

f OK. How about a 50 percent discount? 

5 **Write four sentences that you might use at work. Write one to ask for permission, one to ask someone to do something, one to offer to do something, and one to make a suggestion.**

1 Can you take my calls while I'm out of the office?

2 ______________________________

3 ______________________________

4 ______________________________

5 ______________________________

D Vocabulary

Key vocabulary

Read this paragraph about dining and check your understanding of the words in bold.

Some business people dine out as part of their jobs to entertain clients and discuss projects. Sometimes they go for a **buffet lunch** or on a special occasion they might have a **three-course dinner** that includes an **appetizer** or **starter**, a **main course** or **entrée**, and a **dessert**. **Beverages** are served with the meal. The **menu** tells you the food that is offered and the price of each **dish**. Places to dine vary from **restaurants** where a **host / hostess** will greet you, to **self-service cafeterias.** However, all quality restaurants will provide **waiter** service. A good waiter or waitress will make **recommendations** about the choice of dishes and drinks. At the end of the meal, it is normal in many countries for diners to include a **tip** for the service, in addition to the amount of the check for the meal itself.

Vocabulary note

Dinner is one of the main meals of the day, whereas *a dinner* is a social event accompanied by a meal. A *diner* can be a person having a meal. A *diner* can also be a cheap, informal restaurant. *To dine* is a verb that means to eat. A person can *dine out*— eat at a restaurant or *dine in*—eat at home. *Dining* can be a noun, as in *Our restaurant offers fine dining.* or a compound noun, as in *Come this way to our dining room.*

1 **Put the words in the box into the correct group.**

~~appetizer~~ dinner cafeteria dessert waiter
bill / check restaurant entrée hostess tip

Places to eat	Food and drinks	People	Payment
	appetizer		

2 **Look at the underlined word in the sentences. Choose a word from the box that is similar in meaning.**

dishes	recommend	dessert	starter	~~beverages~~

1 Let's see if we can get the attention of the waiter to bring some drinks. *beverages*
2 May I suggest the Greek salad? ________
3 We have a range of meals to suit all tastes and appetites. ________
4 Would you like to finish your meal with a nice chocolate cake? ________
5 What would you like as an appetizer? ________

3 **Fill in the blanks in the conversation between Markku and the new employee, Sonja.**

buffet	cafeteria	course	dessert	dishes	~~lunch~~	menu	starter	waiter

Markku: This is our new executive dining room. Most of the managers come here to eat. They serve a buffet **1** *lunch* for a fixed price as well as a full **2** ________ with several choices.

Sonja: Oh, this is very nice. I see it has **3** ________ service.

Markku: Yes, it does. They offer a three **4** ________ meal consisting of a soup or salad for a **5** ________, usually two main **6** ________, and fruit pie for **7** ________. And they have an excellent beverage menu.

Sonja: How nice. And how long does the **8** ________ stay open?

Markku: Well, the waiters get off work at 2:30 and then there is just a **9** ________ selection. It stays open until about 9 P.M. for employees on the late shift.

Sonja: Oh, that is good news. I'm going to enjoy my promotion to junior executive.

14 Safety at work

Prepositions 1

Prepositions of time; prepositions of place; prepositions of movement

A Context listening

1 **You are going to hear Marie and Tony talking about safety issues at work. Before you listen, look at the picture and answer these questions.**

1 What safety precautions are there in the office? ______

2 What is still a problem? ______

2 **Listen and check if you were right.**

3 **Fill in the blanks below.**

1 ... the update we'll give everyone at the meeting ____on____ Wednesday morning.

2 But according to the new guidelines on hazards ________ work ...

3 ... hard hats and safety goggles for going ________ the factory area.

4 ... I put up a warning sign ________ the water cooler ...

5 The noise ________ machinery on the factory floor ...

6 All I hear ________ the moment is the sound of people talking ...

7 ... a lot of background noise ________ this office.

Listen to the conversation again and check your answers.

4 **Look at the completed sentences in Exercise 3 and answer these questions.**

1 Which sentences have prepositions that describe a point in time?

____

2 Which sentences have prepositions that describe a place or position?

____

3 Which sentences have prepositional phrases showing movement?

____

5 **Fill in the blanks with one of the words in the box to make phrases you heard in the conversation.**

slippery	~~fire~~	hard	safety	warning

1 ____fire____ doors

2 ________ goggles

3 ________ escape

4 ________ floors

5 ________ hats

6 ________ sign

7 ________ extinguisher

B Grammar

We use prepositions before a noun or a noun phrase.
***at** home* *__in__ the big, white house*

Some prepositions can have several meanings.
*I have a family photograph **on** my desk at work.* (= physical location)
*I saw the report **on** community services.* (= about)
*I made the power point presentation **on** my laptop.* (= using)
*I am **on** the advertising committee.* (= a member of)

1 Prepositions of time

At, in, on
The prepositions *at, in,* and *on* often show time.

at a specific time	*in* a period of time	*on* a day or date
***at** 10:00* ***at** noon* ***at** night*	***in** December* ***in** 2002* ***in** the summer*	***on** Wednesday* ***on** June 15th* ***on** my birthday*

By, until
The prepositions *by* and *until* indicate an end point in time.
By indicates an action that can continue up to a point in time, but not after that time. The action can end anytime before that point in time.
*We need to have the report ready **by** 10:00.* (The report can be completed at any time before 10:00, but not later than 10:00.)

Until indicates an action that continues up to a point in time, but not after that time.
*We will work on the project **until** 10:00.* (We will work continuously and at 10:00 we will stop working.)
*We can't work on the project **until** Jim arrives.* (We will not work now and when Jim arrives we will start working.)

In, for, during
In indicates how soon the action will take place.
*The meeting starts **in** ten minutes.*

For indicates how long the action lasts.
*We were at the conference **for** two days but left sometime during the last day.*

During indicates a period of time within which an action happens.
***During** the rainstorm we stood under the tree for two hours.*

2 Prepositions of place

We use some prepositions to show where something is.

In, at, on
We use *in* to describe when something is inside something else.
*I hear the sound of people talking **in** the background.*
*Do you work **in** a large office building?*

We use *at* for a specific location or event.
*The annual meeting will be **at** the Belcrest Hotel.*

We use *on* for a point on a surface or along a line.
*The noise from machinery **on** the factory floor doesn't reach up here.*
*The invoices are **on** the desk.*

Over, above
Over and *above* mean higher than something else.
*I put some tape **over** the tear in the paper.* (= directly on top of)
*The light **above** my desk has stopped working.* (= higher than, but not on top of)

In some cases *over* and *above* are the same.
*Please hang the picture on the wall **over / above** the piano.*

Under, below
Under and *below* mean lower than something else.
*My office is one floor **below** the manager's office.* (= in a lower position)
*The paper is **under** all those files.* (= covered or concealed)

Beside / by, between, among
Beside / *by*, *between* and *among* all indicate a position of one or more people or things in relation to other people or things.
The speaker was standing by / beside the president of the company. (= next to)
*What should you do if there is a fire **between** you and the escape route?* (= two things)
*My desk is **among** the ones on the south side of the building, near the fire escape.* (= more than two)

Behind, in front of, opposite
Behind, *in front of*, and *opposite* indicate a position of facing or not facing a person, place, or thing.
*The outlet is on the wall **behind** the desk.* (= in the back of)
*I parked **in front of** the building.*
*I parked on the **opposite** side of the street.* (= on the other side of the road)

3 Prepositions of movement or direction

Some prepositions show movement from one location to another.

From, to
From and *to* indicate movement in leaving and arriving at a place.
*We walked **from** the office **to** the restaurant.*

Into, out of
Into and *out of* indicate movement to or from an enclosed area.
*We went **into** the factory area.* (= move to the inside of an area)
*I took the files **out of** the filing cabinet.* (= move to the outside of an area)

Onto, off
Onto and *off* indicate movement to or from the outside or surface of an area.
*The CEO stepped **onto** the stage to make his speech.* (= move to the top of)
*Peter fell **off** the ladder while he was trying to change a light bulb.* (= move from a place)

Across, over
Across and *over* indicate movement from one side of an area to another side.
*We went **across** the street to a pizza place.* (= movement from one side to another)
*We saw the thief jump **over** the wall.* (= movement from one side to another by going above something)

Along, through
Along and *through* indicate movement following one point in a line to another point.
*We walked **along** the road.* (= movement following a line)
*We walked **through** the tunnel.* (= movement from one end to the other inside something)

Some of the words that are common prepositions can be used in other ways.
*We climbed **up** the ladder.* (preposition)
*We got **up** early this morning.* (phrasal verb, ► see Unit 25)

*I signed the contract **above** the dotted line.* (preposition)
*Look at the phrase **above**.* (adverb, ► see Unit 9)

C Grammar exercises

1 **Underline the correct preposition.**

Place

1 Is there enough office space *with / from / in* the building?

2 The supply room is *at / from / after* the far end of the building.

3 When I am *at / from / for* work, I usually eat in the staff cafeteria.

4 I would like to have a seat *between / on / beside* the window, please.

Time

5 Hina comes to work every day *at / for / on* 9:00 exactly.

6 Inventory will take place *in / at / on* Monday and Tuesday.

7 Julie is going to take her vacation time *in / at / on* August.

8 We have to turn this proposal in *until / by / in* 10:00.

Movement

9 The noise *along / from / about* the factory can be annoying.

10 I took the file *out of / towards / among* the filing cabinet for Mr. Simmons.

11 The firefighter had to break *onto / out / into* the building to put out the fire.

12 Every year many people are injured by falling *through / over / at* a household pet.

2 **Some of the prepositions in this memo are wrong. Find and correct them.**

From: Maria Johnson
To: All staff
Subject: Safety **1** ~~among~~ at work

The safety inspection team noticed the following safety hazards **2** during their recent inspection:

Sharp items are often left **3** above desks. You should keep equipment such as staplers, scissors, and letter openers **4** in a closed drawer when not in use.

Electrical and phone cords are lying **5** from the aisles **6** between desks. These could cause workers or visitors to trip.
Boxes and other equipment have been left **7** out the aisles. These obstruct movement **8** beside the offices and they also create a tripping hazard.
In one office, a photocopier machine was situated **9** in forward of the emergency exit.

3 **Read this email from Sara to her friend Alena about her accident at work. Fill in the blanks with a suitable preposition. Some blanks can have more than one answer.**

Delete Reply Reply All Forward Print

Hi Alena,
Today I had an accident **1** ___at___ work. Don't worry–I'm fine! Although it could easily have been much worse. Believe it or not, it happened **2** __________ "Safety at Work Week." Our head office sent around some posters all about various hazards that occur **3** __________ the office. I was trying to impress my boss so I volunteered to pin them up **4** __________ the wall. And guess what happened. I climbed **5** __________ a chair and then one of its legs broke and I fell **6** __________ the desk. I cut my forehead and there was a lot of blood. Jennifer got some bandages **7** __________ the first aid kit and wrapped up my head. Then she took me **8** __________ the emergency room **9** __________ the hospital to get treatment. I got five stitches **10** __________ my head, and, of course, I missed the rest of the session **11** __________ safety at work. They made me rest for a few hours **12** __________ the hospital and now I am home and feeling much better. By the way, the poster I was trying to pin up was one showing the dangers of balancing **13** __________ chairs to reach high places. According to the poster it is much safer to use a stepladder. I guess I have learned my lesson!
Always, Sarah

4 **Use the pictures to write sentences about hazards or safety precautions in these workplaces. Use prepositions in your sentences.**

1 If you listen to loud music at work, you should use headphones.
2 Yesterday I slipped on a wet floor and hurt my back.
3 ______________________
4 ______________________
5 ______________________
6 ______________________

D Vocabulary

Key Vocabulary

Read the paragraph about safety and check your understanding of the meaning of the words in bold.

In order to prevent **injuries** and **fatalities** at work, employers are required by law to provide a safe work environment. Government agencies set **guidelines** that regulate the number of **fire extinguishers**, **fire doors**, **fire escapes**, and **emergency exits** that must be available in a workplace. Workplaces should also **comply with** rules about the number of **first aid kits**, the use of **hard hats**, **safety goggles**, **ear plugs**, and other safety equipment and the quality of the **ventilation system**. If there are **flammable** or **hazardous materials** in the building, they should be in suitable containers. Management should inform their employees about the **safety risks** of **slippery floors** or **dangerous gases**.

1 **Match the words in column A with a word in column B to make a compound noun.**

Column A	Column B
1 fire	a aid
2 hard	b extinguisher
3 first	c goggles
4 safety	d exit
5 hazardous	e system
6 ventilation	f material
7 emergency	g hat

2 **Match one of the compound nouns from 1 with its meaning.**

1 *fire extinguisher* a piece of equipment used to put out flames
2 ______________ an escape route from a building
3 ______________ items that are dangerous
4 ______________ a way to bring fresh air into an area
5 ______________ protective head cover
6 ______________ immediate care for an injury or sudden illness
7 ______________ protective glasses

3 **Underline the correct word form.**

1 Even clean, brightly-lit offices contain <u>*hazards*</u> / *hazardous* that can lead to injury.

2 Small objects can't damage your eyes if you wear *safely* / *safety* goggles when working with certain tools.

3 A variety of materials can cause fires, so it is important to use the right kind of fire *extinguisher* / *extinguishes*.

4 There is no air conditioning in these offices. We keep the windows open for good *ventilate* / *ventilation*.

5 You should be careful when you use *flammable* / *inflamed* materials.

6 You must *compliance* / *comply* with the safety regulations on our premises.

7 The floors at the main entrance are wet. Be careful you don't *slippery* / *slip* and injure yourself.

4 **Cross out the word that does not belong in each list.**

1 ~~avoid~~ cut injure slip

2 danger emergency hazard fire escape

3 blue jeans hard hat safety goggles protective clothing

4 fire smoke dangerous gases ventilators

5 **Underline the correct word or phrase.**

1 An exit route should have <u>*fire doors*</u> / *extinguisher* to prevent the rapid spread of fires.

2 It is important that we are aware of the safety *work* / *risks* in our offices and know what to do in an emergency.

3 It is noisy in the factory so we have to wear *safety goggles* / *ear plugs*.

4 This area is a designated *hard hat* / *smoking* area because there is a danger from falling objects.

5 All work areas should have a *fire extinguisher* / *first aid kit* available in case of injury.

6 The ambulance rushed several workers to the hospital after the explosion, but fortunately there were no *injuries* / *fatalities*.

7 The manager handed out booklets on health and safety *gases* / *guidelines*.

15 Meetings

Prepositions 2

Verb + preposition; noun + preposition; adjective + preposition

A Context listening

1 **Look at the pictures. The people in picture 1 are at a meeting. What do you think they are discussing in the meeting? ______________________**

1

2

2 **Listen and check if you were right.**

3 **Listen and complete these sentences.**

1 Alberto wants to know if they did anything about the broken automatic gate.
2 John's ______ the situation is that the maintenance department has ordered the parts.
3 The members at the meeting have definitely ______ taking part in the city fundraising event.
4 Over the weekend, Andrea was ______ the idea of holding an auction.
5 Elisa wants Alberto to take ______ planning the auction.
6 Alberto says that he knows several people who might be ______ participating.

4 **Look at your answers in Exercise 3 and find examples of the following patterns.**

1 verb + preposition agreed on
2 adjective + preposition ______
3 noun + preposition ______

5 **Match the word you heard in the dialogue with its meaning.**

1 Let's get straight to the **items on the agenda.**
2 Can someone volunteer to take **minutes** today?
3 The vote was **unanimous.**
4 Well, let's put it to a **vote.**

a indicate your choice
b everyone in agreement
c points to discuss
d written record of the meeting

B Grammar

We use certain prepositions following specific nouns, adjectives, and verbs. Our choice of preposition is based on the noun, verb, or adjective that precedes it. Usually, there is only one option, although some words have two or three possible preposition options. The word + preposition selections in the following tables are the most common.

1 Nouns + prepositions

Noun	Preposition
information, nothing, anything, something, truth	about
demand, excuse, explanation, in return, in exchange, need, reason, reputation, responsibility	for
belief, change, increase / decrease, drop, rise / fall	in
advantage / disadvantage, cause, idea, indication, kind, knowledge, understanding, opinion, awareness	of
effect, influence, impact	on
agreement, contact, connection, contract, dealings, in association, involvement, meeting, negotiation	with

*I knew **nothing about** the matter.*
*What was the **reason for** that interruption?*
*The **change in** our strategy has produced good results.*
*We appreciate your **understanding of** the situation.*
*The immediate **effect on** the market will be a slowdown.*
*We have an **agreement with** the landlord that covers parking.*

2 Adjectives + prepositions

Adjective	Preposition
anxious, concerned, confused, enthusiastic, excited, happy, knowledgeable, optimistic / pessimistic, sorry, worried	about
astonished, awful, surprised, terrible, useless	at
amazed, annoyed, astonished, concerned, excited, impressed, inspired, shocked, surprised	by
appropriate, concerned, eligible, famous, ready, responsible, suitable	for
disappointed, involved, interested, specialized	in
aware, conscious, capable / incapable, certain, sure, frightened, full, short, proud, tired, sick, typical	of
based, dependent, insistent	on
annoyed, bored, disappointed, impressed, meet, pleased, satisfied	with

*They are **optimistic about** the marketing strategy.*
*We were **surprised at** his response.*
*The boss was **impressed by** our new web page.*
*We are **responsible for** locking the doors when we leave the office.*
*I was **disappointed in** the response to our ad.*
*He was **aware of** the time change.*
*The statistics are **based on** our research.*
*I was **satisfied with** our final product.*

3 Verbs + prepositions

Verb	Preposition
care, complain, forget, hear, joke, know, learn, read, talk, think, warn, wonder, worry, write	about
aim, laugh, look, shout, smile	at
choose, decide, differentiate	between
apologize, apply, check, forgive, hope, prepare, search, wait, wish, use	for
learn, prevent, stop, suffer, protect	from
believe, specialize, succeed	in
run, divide, cut, translate	into
assure, convince, accuse, suspect, approve / disapprove, consist	of
agree, concentrate, count, depend, insist, rely, congratulate, compliment, spend	on
apologize, describe, explain, listen, point, present, speak, talk, write, happen	to
play, fill, provide, supply	with

*I have been **thinking about** holding an auction.*
*Have you **looked at** the business section of the morning newspaper yet?*
*I haven't **decided between** flying or driving there.*
*I have been **searching for** a file that I'm sure I left on my desk.*
*I have **learned from** my mistakes.*
*His manager didn't **succeed in** getting the go-ahead on the project.*
*You'll never guess who I **ran into** at the mall.*
*I **apologized to** the customer. I **apologized for** the error on the invoice.*

The following verbs and prepositions are usually used with an object: *forgive*, *prevent*, *stop*, *protect*, *assure*, *convince*, *accuse*, *suspect*, *compliment*, *congratulate*, *provide*, *spend*, and *supply*.
*He **convinced** me **of** the importance of the project.*
*I **congratulated** him **on** the fine job he had done.*
*Management **provided** us **with** everything we needed to put on a successful show.*

C Grammar exercises

1 **In six of these sentences there is a noun followed by the wrong preposition. Find the sentences with the mistake and correct them.**

1 Demand ~~with~~ for our products has increased recently.
2 I don't know anything with the outcome of yesterday's meeting.
3 There was a sudden drop in orders last month.
4 The outbreak of the flu virus has had an impact of sales.
5 Could you get in contact on them this afternoon?
6 There has been no change for the demand for natural foods.
7 Caroline took responsibility for the mistakes in the catalog.
8 I'd like to ask your opinion over this proposal.

2 **Fill in the blanks in this conversation with the adjectives in the box.**

anxious	aware	annoyed	~~bored~~	enthusiastic	interested	pleased

Allen: I'm so **1** ____bored____ with going to meetings where people spend hours discussing things that don't affect me.

Yui: I know, me too! I'm really not **2** ________ in whose responsibility it is to organize a training course when I'm only there to discuss the latest sales figures. I guess we should try to be more **3** ________ about them.

Allen: Do you think that the management is **4** ________ of this problem? Maybe we should talk to someone about it.

Yui: Don't you think they will be **5** ________ by that?

Allen: Not necessarily. Management may be **6** ________ with the fact that someone is putting forward suggestions. If you are **7** ________ about talking to someone, I don't mind saying something.

3 **Read the statements and make sentences using the words in parentheses. Use a verb + preposition.**

1 I found a tear in the dress when I got home.
(She / complain / tear / dress)
She complained about a tear in the dress.

2 I am so sorry that your order was damaged.
(He / apologize / damaged order)
____

3 I can't find the file anywhere.
(I / search / everywhere / missing file)
____

4 I had difficulty in unlocking the door.
(I / finally / succeed / opening / door)
____

4 **Read this extract from the minutes of a meeting. Fill the blanks with the words in the boxes.**

agreement	~~demand~~	excited	impact
increase	meet	prepare	satisfied

about	~~for~~	for	in	on
with	with	with		

The chair presented the case for the construction of a new visitor's center to accommodate the increasing **1** demand for improved facilities by the public. It was agreed that we should **2** __________ ______ a team of architects to design a suitable building based on input from our panel. A committee was formed to look into the possible environmental **3** __________ ______ the wildlife of the area. In general, the committee members were **4** __________ ______ the project and expressed **5** __________ ______ the chair's recommendations.

A proposal was made to increase the entrance fee for day visitors during the summer months. The proposal was based on information indicating that an increased number of visitors will be visiting the area this summer. The proposal was voted on but was rejected since the board is currently **6** __________ ______ our financial status. However, a separate proposal for an **7** __________ ______ the overnight camping fee was accepted. Park attendants will need to **8** __________ ______ the expected increase in visitors.

5 **Read this short article from a website and underline the correct preposition.**

Megan Adler has an unusual job: knocking people over. You are probably wondering what the reason **1** *for / with* doing that is. In fact, Megan works as a research coordinator with the responsibility **2** *for / on* studying how people fall over. The research team is searching **3** *with / for* a way of preventing injuries in elderly people. The work mainly consists **4** *of / with* measuring the reaction times of people when they are made to fall over in a special room. The floor of the room moves unpredictably and various objects are placed on the walls and floor, so people can hold onto them or trip over them. The people being tested are loosely held in a harness so that they never actually make contact **5** *on / with* the floor. They never get hurt, and they don't complain **6** *about / of* it because they are paid for their time. The research has led to knowledge **7** *about / by* how to prevent falls, a serious cause of injury for the elderly. Megan is proud **8** *on / of* her work and enjoys telling people that she has a job knocking people over; but of course no one ever believes her.

D Vocabulary

Key Vocabulary

Read the paragraph about meetings and check your understanding of the meaning of the words in bold.

Formal meetings are **scheduled** for a particular time and place. Members receive an **agenda** and a list of **items** for discussion before the meeting. The **chair(person)** starts the meeting by asking for **approval of the minutes** and for **matters arising** from the minutes of the previous meeting. As members discuss the agenda items, they may **brainstorm ideas** and can **propose solutions** or **raise issues.** They may need to **vote** on a **motion** either by a **show of hands** or by a **(secret) ballot.** If all members agree, then the result is **unanimous.** The motion is passed if the vote is unanimous or has the majority of the votes. The final agenda point is "any other business" or **AOB.** When the members have discussed the agenda items, the meeting is over. If they haven't covered the items, the chairperson **adjourns** the meeting until a later date.

1 **Match the words in column A with the definitions in column B.**

A	B
1 AOB	a a written record of what was said at a meeting
2 minutes	b be in complete agreement
3 ballot	c subjects for discussion from the last meeting
4 unanimous	d the last thing to discuss on the agenda
5 matters arising	e the person who leads a committee, board, or meeting
6 chair	f voting on paper

2 **Match a word from the first box with a word or phrase from the second box and use the phrases to complete the sentences below.**

propose brainstorm agenda ~~secret~~ motion

passed a solution ~~ballot~~ ideas items

1 This is a sensitive issue, so I think we should vote on it by *secret ballot.*
2 Can anyone ________ to the parking problem? Any ideas at all?
3 I think we should ________ for a way to promote the new store.
4 I have several ________ to discuss so this may be a long meeting.
5 The ________ after a long discussion about the issue.

3 **Match the beginnings and endings of these questions from a meeting.**

1 Ron, didn't you want to propose	a the minutes from the previous meeting?
2 Rose, did you want to raise	b a possible solution to the parking problem?
3 Could I see a show	c the issue of the new pension plan?
4 Do we agree to approve	d of hands for all those in favor of the motion?

Practice test 3

Listening

Part 1: Photographs

Directions: In this section, you will hear four statements about a photograph. The statements will not be printed on the test. As you listen, select the statement that best describes the photograph. You will hear the statements only once.

1 (A) (B) (C) (D)

2 (A) (B) (C) (D)

Part 2: Question-Response

Directions: In this section, you will hear a question or statement followed by three responses. They will not be printed on the test. As you listen, select the best response. You will hear the question and statements only once.

3 (A) (B) (C)
4 (A) (B) (C)
5 (A) (B) (C)
6 (A) (B) (C)
7 (A) (B) (C)
8 (A) (B) (C)

Part 3: Conversations

Directions: In this section, you will hear two people having a conversation and will answer questions about what you heard. The conversations will not be printed on the test. Select the response that best answers the question. You will hear the conversations only once.

Questions **9–11** refer to the following conversation.

9 What is the woman expecting to receive?
(A) An interview
(B) A contract
(C) A vacation
(D) A better salary

10 What advice does the man give the woman?
(A) Be prepared for the interview
(B) Find out how much her salary will be
(C) Check the details of her contract
(D) Look for another job that has a better contract

11 Why is the man in the supermarket at this time of day?
(A) He is working there.
(B) He is attending an interview.
(C) He is waiting for his check.
(D) He is shopping for food.

Questions **12–14** refer to the following conversation.

12 Where did the people plan to go?
(A) To a taxi stand
(B) To a restaurant
(C) To a friend's house
(D) To the woman's office

13 What problem do the people have?
(A) The taxi has not arrived.
(B) The reservation was not confirmed.
(C) The restaurant does not do home deliveries.
(D) The apology was not accepted.

14 What do the people decide to do?
(A) Order another taxi
(B) Stay at home
(C) Ask for an apology
(D) Go to the Thai restaurant

Part 4: Talks

Directions: In this section, you will hear a speaker giving a talk and will answer questions about the talk. The talks will not be printed on the test. Select the response that best answers the question. You will hear the talks only once.

Questions **15–17** refer to the following talk.

15 Who is speaking?
(A) An office worker
(B) An office manager
(C) A nutrition specialist
(D) A television chef

16 What does the speaker say office workers should do?
(A) Eat smaller lunches
(B) Try to work in the afternoon
(C) Take a nap after lunch
(D) Eat less in general

17 According to the speaker, why do we feel sleepy in the afternoon?
(A) We eat too many snacks.
(B) We don't eat enough for breakfast.
(C) Our brains don't get enough oxygen.
(D) Our digestive systems are working inefficiently.

Questions **18–20** refer to the following talk.

18 Who is this talk for?
(A) Experienced sales staff
(B) Production personnel
(C) Market researchers
(D) People in business

19 What is the topic of the program?
(A) Starting your own business
(B) Helping your business grow
(C) Locating your customers
(D) Doing good market research

20 According to the speaker, how can you get people to return to your business?
(A) Have attractive product displays
(B) Build good customer relations
(C) Make selling a priority
(D) Sell in large quantities

Reading

Part 5: Incomplete Sentences

Directions: In each sentence below, a word or phrase is missing. Select the best answer from the four choices to complete the sentence. Mark (A), (B), (C), or (D).

1 The job requires an ________ team member.
(A) enthusiasm
(B) enthusiastically
(C) enthusiastic
(D) enthuse

2 There is a first aid ________ in the secretary's office.
(A) bag
(B) kit
(C) carton
(D) equipment

3 Suzuki San is an authority ________ marketing strategies.
(A) with
(B) of
(C) on
(D) by

4 Of the two parking lots, one was for customers and ________ was for staff.
(A) other
(B) others
(C) the others
(D) the other

5 The chairperson was ________ our response to the agenda item.
(A) surprising with
(B) surprised at
(C) surprised for
(D) surprise about

6 Ms. Wong was looking forward to purchasing some duty-free ________.
(A) bits
(B) pieces
(C) elements
(D) items

7 The noise in this cafeteria is ________ loud.
(A) much
(B) too much
(C) extreme
(D) extremely

8 Alberto Martinez checked ________ at the airport two hours before his flight.
(A) on
(B) off
(C) in
(D) at

9 Did you see that Sibley's has been ________ more staff?
(A) renting
(B) collecting
(C) hiring
(D) making

10 I propose that we ________ now and meet again at 2 P.M.
(A) adjourning
(B) to adjourn
(C) adjourned
(D) adjourn

Part 6: Text Completion

Directions: Read the text below. Select the best word or phrase to complete the sentences. Mark (A), (B), (C), or (D).

Questions **11–13** refer to the following memo.

To: All personnel
From: Jane Ross
Re: Travel expenses

It has become clear to management that some staff members abused their use of company credit and ________ for their business expenses

11 (A) overcharge
(B) overcharging
(C) overcharges
(D) overcharged

at the recent trade fair. This has ________ the

12 (A) paid
(B) improved
(C) cost
(D) estimated

company a lot of money. Because of this, the procedures for reporting and claiming expenses while on company business have had to be reviewed and updated. A special committee met over the weekend and has come ________ with

13 (A) up
(B) over
(C) above
(D) on top of

several recommendations. Management has decided to implement several of them effective next week.

Please read the enclosed new rules. I do hope all staff members will understand the importance of strictly following these rules. They are for the good of the company.

Part 7: Reading Comprehension

Directions: In this section, you will read documents such as advertisements, email correspondence, newspaper articles, and letters. Select the best answer. Mark (A), (B), (C), or (D).

Questions **14–16** refer to the following message.

To: Mr. Maher

Date: 09/05 **Time:** 12:35 A.M./P.M.

WHILE YOU WERE OUT

Ms. Susan Darren
Of: Micro Appliances
Phone: (968) 555-3216 ext. 2909

☐ telephoned ☒ please return call
☐ returned your call ☐ will call

Message: Tuesday's meeting time has been changed due to Mr. Gere's change of travel plans. New time set for 6 P.M.

Ms. Platini
Reception

14 Who made the phone call?
(A) Ms. Darren
(B) Ms. Platini
(C) Mr. Maher
(D) Mr. Gere

15 Why was the call made?
(A) To change Mr. Gere's travel plans
(B) To return a call to Ms. Darren
(C) To cancel a meeting at Micro Appliances
(D) To notify Mr. Maher of the new meeting time

16 What should Mr. Maher do?
(A) Meet Ms. Platini at Micro Appliances
(B) Attend the meeting at 6 P.M. on Tuesday
(C) Call Mr. Gere back
(D) Change the meeting time

Questions **17 – 18** refer to the following invoice.

Wattayah Automotive Co., Ltd.
P.O. Box 1223
Dubai

Branch: Central
Customer: Ari Luokala
Contact Number: 513192
Last Mileage:53,566 MI
Vehicle Description: PL590868 Jeep '08

Invoice Number:120666
Date: 04/03
Plate# 7739 HY
Promised Date 03/04
Charge to: Cash customer

Job description	Issued qty.	Unit Price	Amount
100,000 KM SERVICE	1		220.000
LABOR	5 hours	90.000/hr	450.000
OIL: Engine – 20W50	2 liters		45.000
FILTER, OIL	1	24.000	24.000
SPARK PLUG	6	12.000	72.000
BELT	1	110.000	110.000
GROSS TOTAL:			921.000
		LESS DISCOUNT 8%:	73.680
		NET TOTAL:	847.320

17 How many spark plugs did Ari Luokala buy?
(A) 1
(B) 2
(C) 5
(D) 6

18 How much did Ari pay Wattayah Automotive?
(A) 220.000
(B) 921.000
(C) 73.680
(D) 847.320

Questions **19–23** refer to the following two memos.

Memo

From: Peter Alvarez
To: All staff
Date: Monday, May 26
Subject: Fire drill

Please note that we will be holding a fire drill the day after tomorrow (May 28th) at 11 A.M. The fire alarm will be activated and all personnel are required to head for the nearest exit. Of course, the elevators must not be used during the drill.

As preparation for the drill, would all staff please examine the fire safety instructions that are posted in several places throughout the company premises? Please also make a note of the nearest fire exits. Staff members who are not on the first floor at the time the alarm is sounded are expected to use the emergency fire escape. Thank you for your cooperation.

Memo

From: Peter Alvarez
To: All staff
Date: May 27
Subject: Important change of time and instructions for fire drill

The fire drill planned for May 28th has been postponed for one day for technical reasons. The new date will be Thursday, May 29th. Please pass this message on so that word gets around in time. Note also that the time will change. We now plan to conduct the drill between 2 P.M. and 3 P.M.

It has come to our attention that because structural repairs are being made on the outside of the building above the second floor, use of the fire escape may interfere with the work being done. Therefore, staff members who are working above the second floor must take the inside staircase during the drill, and those who are on the second floor must use the fire escape.

19 On what day was the fire drill originally planned?
(A) Monday
(B) Tuesday
(C) Wednesday
(D) Thursday

20 Why was the drill postponed?
(A) Because repairs are being done to the outside of the building
(B) Because management was worried about the fire escape
(C) Because the original day chosen was not convenient
(D) Because of technical complications

21 What exit should a worker on the second floor use during the drill?
(A) The front entrance
(B) The inside staircase
(C) The fire escape
(D) The elevator

22 Why have the instructions for leaving the building been changed?
(A) A change of time has been made
(B) The fire escape will be blocked off
(C) Staff would get in the way of the repair work
(D) The restructuring of the building will be finished

23 What have staff members been asked to do before the drill?
(A) Avoid using the elevator
(B) Change the time of the drill
(C) Pass on the new information
(D) Be on the ground floor for the drill

Speaking

Questions 1–2: Read a text aloud

Directions: In this part of the test, you will read a text aloud. You will have 45 seconds of preparation time and then 45 seconds to read aloud.

Question 1:
Classic Eurodrive is the ideal car rental solution for traveling in Europe for a period from 2 weeks up to 6 months. The top of the line vehicle that awaits you is less than 3 years old. You benefit from unlimited mileage, a multi-risk insurance package valid in 25 European countries, and 24/7 roadside assistance. Classic Eurodrive has developed the winning formula for successful travel with complete peace of mind. Visit your local agent or call our toll free number at 1-800-555-222 for details of our competitive pricing.

Question 2:
Taking frequent business trips can be very stressful and tiring. After all, a business trip is not a vacation, so you probably won't get a chance to relax. You may be suffering from jetlag when you arrive for your business meeting. However, you can practice some relaxation techniques to reduce your stress level and help you cope with a busy schedule and important meetings. You will cope better and you will also be able to create a positive impression among both your colleagues and business clients. This website has a variety of different relaxation exercises to help you.

Question 3: Describe a picture

Directions: In this question, you will see a photograph. Describe it in as much detail as possible. You will have 30 seconds of preparation time and 45 seconds to talk about the photograph.

Questions 4–6: Respond to questions

Directions: In this section, you will hear and answer three questions. Begin speaking immediately after you hear a beep. You will not have any preparation time. You will have 15 seconds to answer Questions 4 and 5, and 30 seconds to answer Question 6.

Imagine that a newspaper reporter is interviewing you about a restaurant you have started. You agree to answer some questions about your company.

4 What made you decide to open up a restaurant?
5 Can you say why you think your restaurant is a success?
6 Tell us about the kind of food you serve and your customers.

Questions 7–9: Respond to questions using information provided

Directions: In this section, you will read information and then answer three questions based on what you have read. You will have 30 seconds to read the information. You will not have any additional preparation time. You will have 15 seconds to answer Questions 7 and 8, and 30 seconds to answer Question 9.

Mapleview, Incorporated
Annual Convention

May 26

Hurshel's Business Institute
Main Hall

Topic
Office of the Future

8:00 A.M.–9:00 A.M. Registration
(Registration Fee: Members of Technical Office Solutions Association $55, Nonmembers $100)

Morning Session

9:00 A.M.	The Opening Ceremony
10:00 A.M.	The Hi-tech Office of Tomorrow (Technical Office Consultants)
11:00 A.M.	The Comfortable Office, James Horowitz (Norwich Business Trends)
12:00	Noon Lunch in Edward C. Oakland restaurant

Afternoon Session

1:30 P.M.	Chairs of the Future, Simone Maxwell (Maxwell Associates)
3:00 P.M.	Current research in Ergonomics, Don Esterhazi (Esterhazi Enterpises)
4:30 P.M.	The Virtual Office Becomes Reality, Ben Fossett (Fossett and Das Associates)

Please Note: Mapleview, Inc reserves the right to make changes to the convention schedule without notice.

Question 10: Propose a solution

Directions: In this question, you will be told a problem. After 30 seconds preparation time, you should respond, showing you understand the problem and suggesting a solution. You will have 60 seconds to give your answer.

Now listen to the voice message.

Question 11: Express an opinion

Directions: In this question, you will be asked your opinion on a particular subject. You then have 15 seconds to prepare and 30 seconds to give your answer.

What are some important features of your ideal job?

Grammar Focus Task

There is one mistake in each sentence taken from the test. Underline the mistake and write the correct word or phrase.

1 Suzuki San is an authority to marketing strategies.
2 We called for it to come on 7 o'clock, didn't we?
3 Could you to fax Mr. Chang the corrected contract?
4 You can that increase the number of customers.
5 The elevators must not are used during the drill.

Vocabulary Focus Task

Complete these sentences with a word that means the same as the definitions.

1 There is a ___first aid kit___ in the secretary's office. *Set of articles to use in case someone is injured.*
2 I will give some instructions on how to e________ your business. *Increase the size of*
3 I propose that we a________ now. *Close*
4 Remember you need to check the contract carefully before you s________ it. *Write your name on*
5 I suggest that you eat smaller meals for l________ and eat healthy snacks in between meals. *Meal eaten around midday*

16 Import / export

Referring to nouns

Demonstratives; *one / ones*; *some / any*; quantifiers; *each / every*; *either / neither*

A Context listening

1 **You are going to hear journalist Anna Copeski in an online podcast, interviewing Harry Stubbs about his business. Look at the pictures. What do you think Harry's business is and what are some of the problems he faces?**

____

2 **Listen and see if you were right.**

3 **Here are some of Harry's statements. Choose the word that completes the sentence. Then listen again and check your answers.**

Well, you can't put a product in just **1** *any / some* box. You know, **2** *any / some* are just not strong enough. We deal with freight that has **3** *any / some* special requirements for containers and **4** *this / these* have to be specially made.

OK, well, **5** *this / these* is a small box that is suitable for very fragile items. **6** *Each / Both* the inside and the outside of the box are cushioned. As **7** *either / neither* cardboard **8** *nor / or* plastic offer enough protection, we use a material that was specially developed for **9** *this / these* type of packaging.

Well, **10** *every / all* manufacturer has a different requirement. **11** *One / Ones* may be exporting a product that is fragile and needs protective packaging, **12** *that / those* is, some type of cushioning, to prevent the cargo from breaking. **13** *That / Those* are very popular.

4 **Look at the italicized words in Exercise 3 and answer these questions.**

1 Which two words in 1–4 talk about an unknown amount of something? ______________

2 Which two words in 5–9 talk about something close to the speaker? ______________

3 Which three words in 10–13 do we use with, or to replace, singular nouns? ______________

5 **Look at the words in A that Harry used when talking about his business. Find a word in B that has the same meaning or a similar meaning.**

A 1 commodity 2 containers 3 cushioning 4 damaged 5 dimensions 6 reinforce

B a make stronger b size c ruined d product e protection f boxes

B Grammar

We can use different words to refer to nouns. We use some of them before a noun to give more information about it. Some of the words can replace the noun. We use these words when we do not want to repeat the noun.

1 Demonstratives: *this*, *that*, *these*, *those*

Demonstratives are adjectives or pronouns that show when or where something is in relation to the speaker.

Demonstratives as adjectives
We use *this* and *these* for a recent time or to show a position that is close.
*The traffic was bad **this** morning.* (= today)
*We need to replace **these** computers.* (= computers that are near to the speaker)

We use *that* and *those* for a distant time or to show a position that is away from the speaker.
*I had a bad cough **that** day.* (= a day in the past)
*I'll stop by your house to pick up **those** plants after work.* (= plants that are far from the speaker)

Demonstratives as pronouns
We also use *this* / *that* / *these* / *those* to replace a noun.
*You like chocolates, don't you? Try some of **these**.*

We use *this* / *that* to refer to another part of the sentence or to refer to a whole sentence.
*We are planning to extend the parking lot. **That** would mean we would have an extra 50 spaces.*
(*that* = extending the parking lot)
*Rémi suggested that we all attend the conference and **that** sounded like a good idea to me.*
(*that* = we all attend the conference)

2 *One* / *ones*

One replaces singular countable nouns and *ones* replaces plural countable nouns.
*I need a pen. Do you have **one**?*
*I prefer the green folders to the red **ones**.*

One or *ones* often follows the demonstrative (*this*, *that*, etc.).
*Here are the folders we ordered. I'll leave **these ones** for you and take **this one** for myself.*

3 *Some* and *any*

We use *some* or *any* with plural countable nouns and uncountable nouns to indicate quantity.

We use *some* in positive statements and in questions indicating a request or an offer.
*I need **some** paper clips.*
*Would you like **some** coffee?*

We use *any* in most other questions and in affirmative statements with a number of options.
*Do we have **any** days off this month?*
*We can meet **any** day next week.*

We use *not* + *any* in negative statements.
*We do**n't** have **any** pencils.*
We can sometimes use *some* and *any* with the same meaning.
*Can I bring you **any** drinks? = Can I bring you **some** drinks?*

Something / anything / nothing; *someone / anyone / no one*; *somebody / anybody / nobody*, *somewhere / anywhere / nowhere* follow the same rules as *some* and *any*.

	People	Things	Places
+	*someone, somebody*	*something*	*somewhere*
-	*not anyone, not anybody / no one, nobody*	*not anything / nothing*	*not anywhere / nowhere*
?	*anyone, anybody*	*anything*	*anywhere*

*Do you have **anything** to add to the agenda?*
*I have **nothing** to add unless you want to say **something** about the coming trade show.*

4 Quantifiers

Quantifiers are words that we use with nouns to indicate quantity.
We use *all, enough, lots of / a lot of, plenty of, more,* and *most* with both plural countable nouns and uncountable nouns.
***All** the warehouses have ventilation systems.* (= every one)
*We budgeted **enough** money to cover the advertisement costs.* (= as much as necessary)
*We have **lots of / a lot of / plenty of** time to prepare for the trade show.* (= a large amount)
*I would like **more** space in my office.* (= a bigger amount)
***Most** people in the area work in agriculture.* (= almost all)

We only use *little, a little,* and *much* with uncountable nouns.
*He needs **little** guidance.* (= almost none)
*He needs **a little** guidance.* (= a small amount)
*He does**n't** need **much** guidance.* (= a small amount)

We only use *few, a few, many, both,* and *several* with plural countable nouns.
*He has **few** requirements.* (= almost none)
*He has **a few** requirements.* (= a small number)
*He does**n't** have **many** requirements.* (= a small number)
*She has **several** pictures in her office.* (= some)
***Both** pictures on her desk are of her family.* (= one as well as the other)

We mainly use *much* and *many* in questions and negative statements.
*Do you have **much** work to finish up?* *No, I don't have **much** work to do.*
*Do you have **many** letters to file?* *No, I don't have **many** letters to file.*

5 *Each* and *every*

We use *each* and *every* with singular countable nouns. They often mean the same thing. However, sometimes they have a different meaning.
We use *each* when individual things or people are considered separately. It can be used with *of*.
*We tested **each** applicant's English speaking skills during the interview.*
(= The applicants were tested one by one.)
*There were parked cars on **each** side of the street.*
(= There were parked cars on both sides of the street.)

We use *every* when all individual things or people are considered as one group.
***Every** member of staff was included in the invitation to attend the opening ceremonies.*
(= All the names of the staff were on the invitation.)

6 *Either*, *neither*, and *either* ... *or* and *neither* ... *nor*

We use *either* and *neither* with singular countable nouns referring to two items.
***Neither** report covers the situation well.* (There are two reports.)
***Either** desk can be moved.* (There are two desks.)

We use *either...or* (= a choice of one, but not both) and *neither* ... *nor* (= not one and not the other) with a set of two countable or uncountable nouns or two groups.
***Neither** the sofa **nor** the chair is comfortable.*
*I think he imports **either** clothes **or** shoes.*

7 *Another*, *the other*, *other*, *the others*, and *others*

We can use *another* alone or with a singular noun to mean *one more*.
***Another** customer came into the store.*
*I just had a cup of coffee but I would like **another**.*

We can use *the other* with a singular countable noun to mean *the last one of the group being discussed* and with an uncountable noun or a plural noun to mean *all the rest*.
*Only the furniture in this room is Victorian. **The other** furniture is modern.*
*This package is damaged, but **the other** packages are in good condition.*

We can use *other* with a plural noun or an uncountable noun to mean *more of the group*.
*There are **other** customers in the shop.*
*You can use an online storage service to save all your files and **other** data.*

Others refers to different members of a group we have already mentioned. *The others* refers to the rest of the members of that group.
*We had lots of customers today. Some were interested in making purchases, but **others*** (= other customers) *were just looking. Only one customer paid cash for his purchase.*
*The **others*** (= the rest of the customers who made purchases) *used a direct debit card.*

C Grammar exercises

1 **Fill in the blanks with this, that, these, or those.**

Margaret: Emma, could you bring me the files from the Jacob's account?
Emma: I've already put **1** *those* ________ files on your desk.
Margaret: Do you mean **2** ________ files here?
Emma: No not **3** ________ ones. The ones by the telephone, beside **4** ________ picture of your family.
Margaret: Oh. **5** ________ files right in front of me. Of course! Thank you. And, Emma, could you also bring the invoice for Mr. Jacob?
Emma: Oh, I put **6** ________ into the file.
Margaret: Is **7** ________ the invoice?
Emma: No, Margaret, **8** ________ is a letter explaining some of the details on the invoice to Mr. Jacob.
Margaret: Oh, yes. You are right. I'm having difficulties because I broke my glasses. **9** ________ pair is old and they're not strong enough.
Emma: Ah, **10** ________ explains everything.

2 **Read Sasha's response to the following TOEIC writing test opinion question. Look at the italicized words and correct the ones that are wrong. Some of the italicized words are correct.**

There are many ways to save money. What is one good way to save money? Why? Give reasons or examples to support your opinion.

Using store coupons is ~~*ones*~~ one great way to save money on *much* of your household purchases. Smart consumers keep their eyes open, since you can find coupons *everywhere*. They can be cut out of *some* magazines, *many* local newspapers, and *another* printed materials. *Other* place you can find coupons nowadays is on the Internet, where they can be printed out from *some* consumer websites. *Many* stores provide them, especially at the checkout counter. *Any* coupons have a real cash value and *another* can be used to get a discount on certain items in the store. *These* will usually state something like "Save two dollars on your next visit," or perhaps "Save 10 percent on *some* purchase over 50 dollars." *Other* types can only be used to get a discount on particular products. It is a good idea to save *this* coupons for *every* time you visit a store. But read the information on *every* of *these* coupons carefully. Sometimes businesses limit the number of coupons you can use on any *one* visit. Also there is usually an expiration date and once the date has passed the coupon doesn't have *some* value.

3 **Use *either* / *or* and *neither* / *nor* to complete the sentences.**

1 The manager says that the number of staff has to be cut, but gave the alternative of cutting the annual salary increase.
Either the number of staff or the annual salary increase has to be cut.

2 I tried to talk to the manager or her assistant but they were in a meeting.
I wanted to talk to ______

3 Becky doesn't drink coffee and she doesn't drink tea.
Becky drinks ______

4 The printers are late and the laptops are stuck in customs.
______ have arrived.

5 Some of my colleagues eat in the staff cafeteria and some bring their own sandwiches.
My colleagues ______

4 **Underline the best choice of the words in italics and circle the correct answer.**

1 Would you prefer the green shoes or the red *ones / others*?
a I've already have one.
b Neither pair.

2 I can't find *any / many* paper.
a Here is some.
b Don't you want any?

3 Is *this / these* coat on sale?
a Yes, either one.
b No, not that one.

4 Do you have *all / enough* money to send this package?
a I've got some small change.
b No, I have something.

5 Has there been *much / many* mail for me while I was gone?
a Yes, anything at all.
b Yes, there is some in the box.

6 Does *every / both* package need to be insured?
a No, neither of them do.
b Yes, each one does.

7 Did you want *any / every* of these documents?
a Yes, that one on top.
b Yes, either of them.

5 **Underline the correct words.**

In 1992 a shipment of toy rubber ducks washed off a cargo ship that was traveling from China to the United States. Since then, **1** *many / much* of these toys have floated all around the world. There are about 30,000, and **2** *every / all* of them were originally a bright yellow color. **3** *Some / Any* of the ducks are being found as far away as the south coast of England and **4** *other / others* are arriving on the coast of Africa. After years of exposure to the sun and salt water, **5** *this / these* ducks have lost their bright yellow color. However, people have started to collect them and **6** *some / both* have sold for hundreds of dollars. There are even children's storybooks about them. **7** *This / These* accident has also proved very useful to scientists. **8** *Every one / All* that people find provides more information about the movement of the ocean currents. So if **9** *another / anyone* finds a discolored rubber duck on a beach **10** *anywhere / nowhere* in the world, it is likely that its journey started in the middle of the Pacific Ocean. It also might be worth quite a **11** *lot / lots* of money.

D Vocabulary

Key Vocabulary

Read the paragraph about exports / imports and check your understanding of the meaning of the words in bold.

Nowadays an increasing amount of **cargo** is being brought from overseas (**imported**) or sent abroad (**exported**) as countries **exchange commodities**, in other words, become involved in **trade**. This **freight** is packed into large **containers** and then **hauled** by road, air, or ship to its destination. If the cargo is **fragile,** then it must be **handled with care** and **cushioned** in **reinforced packaging** to **protect** it from damage. Often, cargo that is going to be **transported** is stored temporarily in a **warehouse** before being loaded onto a vehicle. If the **shipment** is being exported, then each commodity and its quantity or **weight** must be **declared** to the customs officials of the receiving country.

Vocabulary note

Look at the words relating to *ship*:
A *ship* is a boat that is large enough to travel on the sea.
A *shipment* is a group of goods transported together.
To *ship* means to transport something by air, train, boat, or truck.
Shipping is the business of transporting things.

1 Match the verbs in column A with the definitions in column B.

Column A	Column B
contain	1 declare To make a statement about the goods you import or export
~~declare~~	2 ______ To hold inside
exchange	3 ______ To carry from one place to another
package	4 ______ To buy and sell for profit.
protect	5 ______ To give something in return for something received
reinforce	6 ______ To prevent from being damaged, attacked, stolen, or injured
trade	7 ______ To strengthen by adding extra support or material
transport	8 ______ To put into a container for transporting or storing

2 Write the noun form of the words in column A in Exercise 1. There may be more than one possibility.

1 container 3 ______ 5 ______ 7 ______
2 ______ 4 ______ 6 ______ 8 ______

3 Cross out the word that does not belong in each list.

1	cushioned	~~weight~~	reinforced	strengthened
2	breakable	delicate	fragile	strong
3	freight	cargo	warehouse	commodity
4	transport	haul	trade	ship

4 **Fill in the blanks in this article with the words in the box.**

commodity declarations ~~exporting~~ handle import packaging shipments weight

So you think that it is time to expand your business by **1** ___exporting___ your product? Your first task should be researching the market. Is your product a **2** ________________ that buyers in other countries need or want? Have you found someone abroad who wants to **3** ________________ your product? You should consider the name of your product. Too many marketing ventures have failed because the product's name translated into a silly or inappropriate word in the target countries' languages. You also need to think of **4** ________________, since your product should arrive in good condition. Will you have to change the units of **5** ________________ or other measurements? This may require costly changes to your factory floor. Who is going to **6** ________________ the shipping? You will have to take care of shipping documents, verifications, and customs **7** ________________, even though the importer will help your **8** ________________ through customs.

17 Using the phone

Pronouns

Personal and possessive; reflexives; impersonal pronouns; *it / there*

A Context listening

1 **You are going to hear a telephone conversation between Mr. Harrison and Mr. Nesbitt's new Personal Assistant, Rita. Before you listen, look at the pictures and statements below. Underline the answer you think correctly completes the statements.**

1 Mr. Harrison wants to speak to *Rita / Mr. Nesbitt.*

2 Mr. Nesbitt is *busy / out to lunch.*

3 Rita says Mr. Nesbitt will *call him back / take a message.*

4 Mr. Harrison *is an important customer / has the wrong number.*

2 **Listen and check if you were right.**

3 **Listen again and complete these sentences.**

1 Mr. Nesbitt's office. How can ________ help ________ ?

2 I really need to speak to ________ now.

3 Is there any way ________ can put ________ through?

4 I placed an order with ________ company.

5 I'll tell ________ ________ .

6 Please make sure ________ calls ________ .

7 Oh, dear. ________ hung up.

8 Lots of people are calling ________ to complain, but ________ can't help ________ .

9 … could you ask ________ which company ________ are trying to contact?

4 **Add the words you wrote in Exercise 3 to the correct group. One word does not fit in any group.**

1 ____

2 ____

3 ____

5 **Match the word or phrase you heard in the conversation with a sentence.**

1 busy signal — a Answer the phone!

2 disconnect — b Hang up and try again later.

3 put on hold — c The line just went dead.

4 ring — d I'm waiting for someone to return to the phone.

B Grammar

1 Pronouns

We use pronouns to replace nouns to avoid repeating the same word.

We use subject pronouns (*I, you, he, she, it, we, they)* to show who is doing the action.
Rachel only lives two blocks away from the office so ***she*** *walks to work.*
He *hung up.*

We use object pronouns (*me, you, him, her, it, us, them)* to show who is receiving the action.
I saw Sofia and gave ***her*** *the files.*
I'm very anxious to speak to ***him.***

There are two ways to talk about possession or refer to parts of the body. Some possessives (*my, your, his, her, its, our, their*) go before the noun and some (*mine, yours, his, hers, its, ours, theirs*) replace the noun.
I share an office with Samir. This is ***my*** *desk and that is* ***his.***
I called ***your*** *office.*

We use reflexive pronouns (*myself, yourself, himself, herself, itself, ourselves, yourselves, themselves*):

- to refer back to the subject
  She often talks ***to herself*** *when she's concentrating hard.*
- to emphasize who does something.
  Our CEO does his accounts ***himself.***
- in some common expressions
  Make ***yourself*** *at home.*
  Help ***yourselves*** *to some cake.*
  Did they enjoy ***themselves*** *at the party?*

Compare the use of reflexive pronouns and *each other*. We can also use *one another*.
Karen and Michiko talked to ***each other / one another.*** (= Karen spoke to Michiko and Michiko spoke to Karen.)
Karen and Michiko talked to ***themselves.*** (= Karen spoke to Karen and Michiko spoke to Michiko.)

2 Impersonal pronouns

We use *you, we, they,* and *one* when we are not referring to a particular person.

We can use *you* to talk about everyone in general.
You *can travel to all continents.* (= Anyone can travel to all continents.)

We can use *we* to talk about everyone including ourselves.
We *can't go back in time.* (= This limitation is on all people including myself.)

We can use *they* to refer to experts or authorities.
They *advise against traveling because of the weather conditions.* (= someone who knows about the dangers of the current conditions)

We can use *one* to refer to one unspecified person. The impersonal *one* is very formal.
One *should be careful when crossing a busy street.*

3 *It* and *There*

We sometimes use *it* and *there* in the subject position.

It

We use *it* to talk about time, weather, and distance.
***It** is 10:00 am.* ***It** isn't very cold outside.* *How far is **it** to the shop?*

We can use *it* in the subject position to emphasize the normal subject.
Visiting the gold market is interesting. (= **It** is interesting to visit the gold market.)
Tom did most of the work. (= **It** was Tom who did most of the work.)

There

We use *there* + the verb to be to say that something exists or is present. The verb agrees with the noun.
***There is** plenty of **space** here.* ***Are there** only two **hotels** along that coast?*

C Grammar exercises

1 **Underline the correct pronoun in each of the following sentences.**

1 The connection is very bad. Can *you / your / yours* hear me?

2 In the first quarter *we / us / our / ours* met our production goals.

3 I'm sorry, sir. I can't give out *you / your / yours* medical records over the phone.

4 Was there a call for *I / me / my / mine* while I was out?

5 My daughter cancelled *she / her / hers* appointment with the doctor.

6 This was made by skilled craftsmen in *we / us / our / ours* factory.

7 I have misplaced my cell phone. Can I borrow *you / your / yours*?

8 Did *he / him / his* have any comments about today's agenda?

9 This file is for the personnel department. Can you pass it on to *they / them / their / theirs*?

2 **Peter and Paula are discussing medical advice. Fill in the blanks with an impersonal pronoun. In some cases more than one answer is possible.**

we you they one

Paula: Medical authorities have advised everyone to get a flu shot. **1** They say this will reduce the number of flu cases this winter. Aren't **2** ________ told this every year in the fall? **3** ________ would think that everyone knows by now that **4** ________ should get a shot, especially the elderly and people with breathing problems.

Peter: Well, I think **5** ________ should be advising us. Some people might forget that a flu shot is available. **6** ________ never know what viruses are coming in the winter. **7** ________ can't be too careful.

3 **Read the email and choose the correct word.**

File Edit View Insert Format Tools Message Help

Hi Silvia,
You know I told you that Troy bought me a new phone for **1** *my* / ~~*mine*~~ birthday? I never really wanted a cell phone but Troy said it would be easier for us to keep in touch. Well, it's really good. I can take pictures of **2** *me* / *myself* and the family and send them to **3** *you* / *yourself* now. For **4** *me* / *my* though, the best thing is the reminder function. I find it really useful to send **5** *myself* / *me* reminders when I have important things to do–you know how forgetful I can be! Unfortunately, I'm not getting many reminders at the moment because I just let Alex borrow the phone. I think that was a big mistake! He has been running around taking pictures of **6** *him* / *himself* and sending them to **7** *his* / *him* friends. I think he'll want me to buy **8** *him* / *himself* one for his birthday. At least if we do buy **9** *him* / *his* one, I can get **10** *my* / *mine* phone back.
Bye for now,
Helen

4 **Correct any mistakes with *it* and *there*.**

Jenny: Hi, Jane. You look tired. Are you OK?

Jane: Yes, I just didn't get much sleep last night. **1** ~~It~~ There was a party in the apartment below me. It didn't finish until 2:30 A.M.

Jenny: No wonder you are tired. **2** It is some coffee in the pot. Would you like some to wake you up?

Jane: Oh thank you. So, I just got to sleep when the phone rang and woke me up. I picked up the receiver but **3** there was no one on the other end. I tried to get back to sleep and then the phone rang again. That's when I realized that **4** there was my cell phone ringing and not the landline.

Jenny: So who was **5** it?

Jane: **6** There was my husband. He is on a business trip and forgot about the time difference. Of course, after that I couldn't get back to sleep.

Jenny: Well, **7** there is a good thing you didn't have to be at work this morning.

D Vocabulary

Key Vocabulary

Read the text about phoning and check that you understand the meaning of the words in bold.

In most offices everyone has a **landline phone** and people often have their own **extension (number)** so that you can call them directly. Otherwise, you may have to talk to an **operator** who will **transfer your call** to the person you want or **put you on hold** if that person's **line** is busy. To answer a call, you **pick up the receiver** or press the answer key if you're using a wireless phone or **cell phone.** You can find the number of most businesses in the **yellow pages**, which is available online as well as in a book. To make a call on a landline phone, you listen for the **dial tone** and then **dial the number**. The phone at the other end either **rings** or you get a **busy signal**. You may have to **leave a voice message** after the **tone.** Occasionally, you may get **disconnected** and have to make the call again. A cell phone can perform many useful functions not available with a landline phone, such as allowing users to send and receive **text** (or **SMS**) **messages.**

Vocabulary note

Here are some common phoning expressions:
Personal Assistant: *Jane, Anna Gomez is* ***on the line.*** (= Anna has called and would like to speak to Jane.)
Jane: *Could you* ***put her on hold?*** (= ask her to wait)
Personal Assistant: *Anna, Jane has asked if you could* ***hold the line / hold on?*** (= Don't hang up.)
Jane: *Could you* ***put*** *Anna* ***through*** *now?* (= complete the connection)

1 **Match a word from the first box with a word from the second box and correct the errors in the conversation below.**

busy	hold
cell	message
dial	pages
on	phone
voice	signal
yellow	tone

Eileen: I can't make an international call on this ~~voice~~ cell phone.
Jonathan: You can use my phone. Here it is.
Eileen: Thank you. Uh, I can't get a busy tone on your landline. What's wrong with it?
Jonathan: Oh, you know what? It isn't plugged into the wall. Ok. Now try it. Do you know the number of the business?
Eileen: Yes, I got it from the online yellow dial. Oh, now it's just giving me a cell signal.
Jonathan: Oh, you shouldn't hang up. If you wait, you may be able to leave a hold message and ask them to return the call.
Eileen: Either that or they will put me on page to listen to boring music for 10 minutes and pay the international charges.

2 **Find the words to complete the sentences.**

disconnected	transfer	ring	extension
line receiver	dialed	~~text~~	

1 If you're going to arrive late to the meeting, just send me a ____*text*____ message to let me know.

2 I think I ________________ the wrong number. Sorry!

3 Mr. O'Brien is on the ________________ . Should I put him through?

4 I have the number of your company. But could I have your office ________________ ?

5 I'm sorry we got ________________ . I accidentally dropped the ________________ when I answered the phone.

6 Could you hold on while I ________________ your call to customer services?

7 My cell phone shows that I missed a call, but I didn't hear the ________________ because of the traffic noise.

3 **Underline the correct word or phrase.**

1 Thank you for calling. I'll just check if she's in the office. I'll just *put you on hold* / *disconnect you* for a moment.

2 You can call me at home on my *receiver* / *landline* and if there's no reply, try this cell phone number.

3 If you know the extension, dial it now; if you don't know the extension, dial 0 for the *operator* / *SMS*.

4 Please leave a message after you hear the *ring* / *tone*.

5 If you spend a lot of money *transfer* / *text messaging* your friends, you should sign up for our new cell phone package.

18 Office supplies

Nouns

Countable and uncountable nouns; articles

A Context listening

1 **You are going to hear Bill and Mr. Boswell preparing a room for job interviews.**

Look at the picture and decide what changes you think the room needs for holding interviews and what other equipment you think they might need.

2 **Listen and put a check in the box beside the nouns that you hear in the conversation.**

☐ computer	☐ water	☐ scissors
☐ file	☐ music	☐ news
☐ table	☐ furniture	☐ noise
☐ cabinet	☐ advice	
☐ scanner	☐ equipment	

3 **Find words from the list in Exercise 2 that match these descriptions.**

1 Things that you can count *computer* ____________________
2 Things that you cannot count ____________________
3 A noun that can be countable or uncountable ____________________
4 A countable noun that is always plural ____________________
5 An uncountable noun that ends with an *-s*. ____________________

4 **Look at your answers in Exercise 3 and answer the following questions.**

1 Which nouns can we use with the articles *a*, *an*, or *the*? ____________________
2 Which nouns can we use with the article *the* but not with *a* or *an*? ____________________
3 Which nouns can we use without any article? ____________________

5 **Look at the words in Exercise 2. Put them into the following categories. You do not need to use all the words.**

1 Office supplies ____________________
2 Electronic equipment ____________________
3 Furniture ____________________

B Grammar

1 Countable and uncountable nouns

Countable nouns can be singular or plural. They agree with a singular or plural verb and we can replace them with singular or plural pronouns.
__A file is__ on the desk. / The applicants' __files are__ not here.
I put __the file__ down and now __it__ is gone. / I put __the files__ down and now __they__ are gone.

Some countable nouns only have a plural form: *scissors*, *trousers*.

Uncountable nouns are always singular, so they always take a singular verb and we replace them with a singular pronoun.
The __money is__ on the desk.
The __news is__ good.
There is __coffee__ in the staff room. __It__ is fresh.

Some uncountable nouns appear to be plural, but they are not: *economics*, *news*.

Some nouns have countable and uncountable forms with different meanings.
The complete __works__ of Shakespeare are available online. (works = the product of an activity)
She has done a lot of __work__ on this project. (work = effort and activity)
I can hear a loud __noise__ coming from over there. (= a particular sound)
With the construction outside, there is too much __noise__ for me to concentrate. (= sound in general)

2 Articles

We use *a* / *an* before a singular countable noun:

- when you mention a noun for the first time
  I was working on __a__ report. *__A__ stapler would be useful.*
- when you make a general statement about all people or things of a type
  __An accountant__ must have an excellent understanding of numbers. (An accountant = All accountants)
- when you express price and speed
  55 miles __an__ hour

We use *the:*

- when we have already mentioned the noun
  I put a report on your desk. __The__ report concerns the proposed expense account.
- when it is clear which thing or person we are referring to
  We could move __the__ table away from __the__ wall. (= a particular table and wall)
  I went to __the__ bank. (= a particular bank)
- when there is only one of something in a specific group
  __The__ Earth orbits __the__ Sun.
- when you use the superlative form
  This is __the__ best advertisement for our new product.

3 No articles

We do not use *a* / *an* when the noun is uncountable.
Sam gives ***advice*** *to new staff members.* (**not** ~~an advice~~)

We do not use *the* before a singular noun that names a general category.
In this city, ***crime*** *is decreasing.* (= a general category)
We were all shocked by ***the crime****.* (= a particular crime)

We do not use an article before a possessive.
I have to take ***my laptop*** *with me to the trade show.* (**not** ~~the my laptop~~)

4 Amounts

We can use some words to show the amount of something that is uncountable.
I had ***a cup of*** *coffee with my breakfast this morning.*

We use *pair of* for things that that have two parts.
I'm taking ***a pair of*** *sunglasses and two* ***pairs of*** *shoes.*

We use the name of the container for some words.
I carry ***a bottle of*** *water and* ***a tube of*** *toothpaste in my bag.*

We can use the amount without the noun.
Would you like ***a piece of*** *cake?* *Just* ***a*** *small* ***piece****, please.*

C Grammar exercises

1 Put the following words in the correct column.

advice desk equipment fax furniture glass music news noise paper clips printer scanner calendar space stationery tape

Always countable	Can be countable or uncountable	Always uncountable
______	______	advice
______	______	______
______	______	______
______	______	______
______	______	______
______	______	______

2 Read what Max Jones said to a potential customer about his new business. Fill in the blanks with the article *a*, *an*, *the*, or ∅ (if the noun does not take an article).

Hi. My name is Max Jones. I recently opened **1** ___a___ stationery store and am already supplying many of **2** ______ businesses in the area with all their office needs. My store is located in **3** ______ center of town on the corner of 4th and Grand, and is **4** ______ easy walk from **5** ______surrounding offices and stores. I carry **6** ______ paper supplies, computer accessories, and **7** ______ variety of office accessories such as **8** ______ clocks, calendars, and novelty items. Whether you need **9** ______ eraser or **10** ______ box of paper clips, **11** ______ address book or **12** ______ study lamp, we have it.

3 Look at the following phrases. Choose the words in the box to complete the phrases.

scissors marker pens coffee tape water paper

1 A sheet of paper______
2 A cup of ______
3 A glass of ______
4 A pair of ______
5 A set of ______
6 A roll of ______

4 Look at the email that Elena is writing to her friend, Zovig. See how many mistakes you can find.

Delete Reply Reply All Forward Print

Dear Zovig,
In your last ~~an~~ email, you were complaining about a disorganization in your office. I hope it is OK for me to give you advices. I've just redesigned my office because I was spending more time looking for file than getting works done. Well, guess what? I replaced my printer, fax machine, and scanner with one of those printer that does everything. And it makes very little noises. I can hear myself think now! Why didn't I get rid of that old equipments a long time ago? I also got printer stand with shelves that hold my paper and other supply. A change has made a great improvement to my working life. I bet you could easily do a same thing.

D Vocabulary

Key Vocabulary

Read the paragraph about office supplies, equipment, and furniture and check your understanding of the meaning of the words in bold.

Well-equipped offices need a wide variety of **equipment** and **stationery**. Every office needs stationery **supplies** such as pens, **labels**, **paper clips**, **stapler** and **staples**, **tape**, and **scissors**. Many businesses have a large **supply room** that contains **shelves** full of office supplies. Most offices have a **filing cabinet** for important documents and some offices even have a **safe** where they keep money or valuable papers. But that's not enough for the modern office. Each office worker also needs a **PC** or **laptop** on their desk. They also need access to a **printer**, a **scanner**, a **fax machine,** and a **copy machine.**

Vocabulary note

The words *stationary* and *stationery* look and sound similar.
Stationery is a noun.
*I stopped at the office supply store for some **stationery.*** (writing materials: paper, envelopes, pens, pencils, notepads, etc.)
Stationary is an adjective.
*The bus was **stationary.*** (not moving)

Vocabulary note

The word *safe* has more than one meaning.
Safe can be a noun.
*The jewelry was put into the **safe.*** (= a box made of steel used to store valuable objects)
Safe can be an adjective.
*Have a **safe** journey.* (= free from danger or harm)

1 It is Giovanni's first day at a new job. Read this conversation between Giovanni and his new colleague, Andrea. Choose the correct words to complete the conversation.

Andrea: So, this is the **1** *supply / equipment* room. It's got everything you need, I think. Each **2** *laptop / shelf* has a label that tells you what's on it. This one's for pens and pencils.

Giovanni: Oh, you have a lot of supplies here. Can I take some stuff now? I need some **3** *scanners / stationery*. Printing paper and envelopes would be useful, for a start.

Andrea: You'll find that you already have some paper and envelopes in your desk, but I think you should take some **4** *tape / labels* because you might want to stick notices or pictures on your walls.

Giovanni: What else should I take? Are there **5** *scissors / paper clips* in my office desk? I already have quite a few pieces of paper that need organizing.

Andrea: Good idea. You should have a stapler in your desk. But you might want to take a box of **6** *staples / printers* to fill it.

Giovanni: Oh, OK. Those are the kind of things that always run out just when you need them. I think that's all I need for now anyway. Oh, what's that over there? It looks like a **7** *safe / copy machine*.

Andrea: Yes, it is. That's where we keep all the valuables and confidential files. You won't be able to open it though. Only Mr. Henderson knows the combination.

2 Cross out the word that does not belong in each set. Write why the other two words go together.

1 ~~paper clips~~ filing cabinet safe

Filing cabinets and safes are places to keep things.

2 laptop fax machine PC

____

3 stationery labels supply room

____

4 printer stapler copy machine

____

5 scanner tape scissors

____

19 Presentations

Linking words 1

And, but, or; so, such, as, such as; too and *enough; still, yet, already*

A Context listening

1 You are going to hear Leroy and Cheryl talking about Bernard Chertok's product presentation. Before you listen, look at the pictures and write what you think is happening. Use words from the box.

projector	marker	flip chart	whiteboard

1 ______________________

2 ______________________

3 ______________________

4 ______________________

5 ______________________

2 Listen and check if you were right.

3 Underline the correct word and then listen to the conversation again to check your answers.

Leroy: You mean our projector hasn't been fixed **1** *already* / *yet*?
Cheryl: Lucy ran to the supply room to get new ones, **2** *but* / *or* she discovered ...
Cheryl: So, I got out a flip chart **3** *or* / *and* Lucy had already brought a set ...
Leroy: ... better to postpone the presentation **4** *but* / *or* send someone out to buy ...
Cheryl: Well, Bernie was **5** *already* / *yet* here, wasn't he?
Cheryl: These pictures were drawn **6** *so* / *such* quickly ...
Cheryl: The speech was **7** *enough spontaneous* / *spontaneous enough* to keep our interest and not **8** *too* / *enough* conventional.

4 Complete the sentences using the numbers of your answers in Exercise 3.

1 Answers ________ indicate whether a situation has changed or is expected to change.
2 Answer ________ indicates an addition.
3 Answer ________ shows contrast.
4 Answer ________ indicates a sufficient amount and ________ indicates more than a reasonable amount.
5 We use answer ________ with an adverb.
6 Answer ________ shows two options.

5 Look at the following words that could be used when talking about presentations. Underline the ones you heard in the conversation. Listen again and check your answers.

chart	handouts	pointer	summary
diagram	key points	projector	topic
flip chart	markers	screen	visual aids
graph	outline	slides	whiteboard

B Grammar

1 *And*, *or*, and *but*

And, or, and *but* join two or more words, phrases, or parts of the sentence.
Mr. Chertok's key points ***and*** *summary were well presented.*
Wouldn't it have been better to postpone the presentation ***or*** *send someone out to buy some whiteboard markers?*
He arrived with his presentation on his computer ***but*** *our projector wouldn't work.*

And
The most common way to add to a sentence or a phrase is *and*.
I gave the presentation ***and*** *my colleague answered questions.*

We often use *and* with *both*.
We have ***both*** *a schedule* ***and*** *a program.*

Other words we use to add information include *as well as*, *too*, and *also*. (▶ See Unit 23, Linking Words 2 for other phrases we use to add information.)
There are mistakes in the letter ***as well as*** *in the report.*
Susan has a laptop on her desk. She's got a PC ***too****.*
I want to talk to you about your report. I ***also*** *need to ask you a question.*

Or
We use *or* to connect two or more options. We can use *or* with *either*. The negative of *either / or* is *neither / nor*. (▶ See Unit 16.)
We could book a flight ***or*** *take the train. = We could* ***either*** *book a flight* ***or*** *take the train.*

But
We use *but* when the parts of the sentence show a contrast.
Lucy ran to the supply room to get new ones, ***but*** *she discovered that we only had permanent markers.*

But can be used with *not only* and *also*.
I ***not only*** *have experience in research* ***but also*** *in sales.*

2 *So*, *such*, *as*, and *such as*

So* and *such
We use both *so* and *such* for emphasis.
The movie was ***so*** *funny.* *It is* ***such*** *a beautiful day.*

We also use *so* and *such* to show a cause and a result. (▶ See Unit 23 for other cause and result phrases.)
I was tired ***so*** *I left the office party early.* (*I was tired* = cause; *I left* = result)
It was ***such*** *a successful presentation* ***(that)*** *everyone stood up and cheered.* (*It was a successful presentation* = cause; *everyone stood up and cheered* = result)

So

We use *so* before adverbs, adjectives, and some quantifiers (*many, much, little, few*).
*I was **so happy** about the sale **(that)** I brought a cake to the office to celebrate.*
*We walked **so slowly (that)** we missed the bus.*
*We had **so many** customers **(that)** we had to hire an extra salesperson.*

We also use *so* when speaking to introduce a new idea, question, or comment.
***So,** Mr. Chertok didn't have any transparencies.* ***So,** what happened next?*

As

We can use *as* to connect two sentences.
***As** I understood the contract, we have to pay those fees.* (*As* = The way that)
*The alarm went off **as** I was approaching the door.* (*as* = at the same time)
***As** it is my responsibility to protect our security systems, I check the alarms daily.* (*As* = Because, Since)

Such as

We use *such as* to introduce examples.
*We sell home textiles, **such as** linens, curtains, and blankets.*

3 *Too* and *enough*

Too

Too indicates more than one needs or wants. We can use it before an adjective or adverb. We can also use it before *much* + an uncountable noun or *many* + a countable noun.
*There was **too much** noise in the office. It was **too noisy** for me to concentrate.*
*He worked **too quickly** and made **too many** mistakes.*

Enough

Enough means a sufficient amount or number. We can use it before a noun or after an adjective or adverb.
*We saved **enough money** for a new car.*
*The instructions are **clear enough** for everyone to understand.*

We can also use *enough* alone.
Do we need some more milk? *No, we have **enough**.*

4 *Still*, *yet*, and *already*

We use *still* when a situation hasn't changed.
*We are **still** looking into our market possibilities.*
*By the way, we **still** need to replace the light bulb.*

We use *yet* mainly in negative sentences and questions when we are expecting something to happen.
*Has Mr. Jawali hired a new driver **yet**?*
*We haven't **yet** discussed our options.*

We use *already* when something happened in the recent past.
*I've **already** booked a hotel.*

C Grammar exercises

1 Correct the mistake in each sentence.

1 The customer wanted to return the dress or buy a suit.
2 Was the conference postponed but canceled?
3 Mr. Lee wanted to have the meeting today, or several people were out of the office.
4 He but wanted a new mouse for his computer.
5 Sue is going to the trade show but will give a product presentation there.
6 You could go to lunch early and wait until after the meeting for lunch.
7 Our profits are up, or the outlook is still uncertain.
8 Could you bring me some paper clips or as a box of staples?
9 Andrea wanted to invest in the company or.

2 Underline the correct word to complete the sentences.

1 The service in that restaurant was *so / as / such* unpleasant that we can't recommend it.
2 It was hard to hear the talk because the presenter spoke *so / such / such as* quietly.
3 I've never attended *so / such / such as* a motivating conference before.
4 It was *so / as / such* late when I left work that the buses were no longer running.
5 *So / As / Such as* before, you start by opening a new document.
6 Our company has outlets in several cities, *as / such / such as* Paris, Tokyo, and New York.

3 Complete the sentences with *enough* or *too*.

1 A company can never do ________ to attract and retain talented personnel.
2 Sam doesn't have ________ self-motivation to be really successful in his job.
3 Although it paid well, my factory job was ________ repetitive, so I quit.
4 Our profits have increased ________ for us to invest in some new technology.
5 ________ many complaints aren't solved quickly ________. We need to do something to improve the situation.
6 I am ________ shy to give a presentation in front of a large audience.

4 Complete the conversation using *already*, *yet*, or *still*.

Hasmik: Jim is **1** ________ planning to give a demonstration about his new idea for packaging fragile products, but he hasn't got it ready **2** ________.
Birgitta: Really? I thought he **3** ________ gave that demonstration at last week's meeting.
Hasmik: Oh, no. This is different. He's demonstrating a new product.
Birgitta: That's exciting. Has he told you what it is **4** ________?
Hasmik: Not exactly, although I know he's **5** ________ prepared a slide show of the development process and that he's **6** ________ interested in packaging innovations.
Birgitta: Well, there's **7** ________ a week to go before the demonstration. He can **8** ________ get it ready by then.

5 **Choose two of the words from each set to complete the answers to the questions.**

and / or / but   as / such as   so / such   ~~still / already / yet~~   too / enough

1 Did you agree with Mr. Adams's key points?
   a I'm ____still____ thinking about them. He had a lot to say and I can't decide at the moment.
   b I ____already____ discussed them with him earlier and I really think he's got a point.
2 How do you think the presentation went?
   a ________ a visitor knowing nothing about that topic, I can say that I learned quite a lot.
   b I'd never thought about some of those points before, ________ the way you can restructure departments. It gave me a lot of think about.
3 Lydia gave a great talk and she even brought several new products to show.
   a Yes, she presents her products in a way that is entertaining ________ to keep her audience interested.
   b I've heard that, but I was ________ busy to attend because I had to meet the visitors from Amsterdam.
4 Will the hotel provide things such as a projector, a screen, and laser pointers in their conference rooms?
   a Yes, we just have to let them know, ________ they can move the equipment into the conference rooms we've booked.
   b Yes, they have ________ a lot of conferences there that I'm sure they'll have everything we need.
5 The presentation was so successful that we've been asked to repeat it at the trade show.
   a Have you already agreed to do that ________ are you waiting to see if you can take the time off?
   b Oh, you could repeat it there ________ give it at the conference as well.

6 **Use the words in parentheses in any order to write sentences.**

1 (and / ask / office) I went to the main office and asked for a raise.
2 (apply / or / promotion) ________
3 (business trips / but / tiring) ________
4 (handouts / presentation / so) ________
5 (such / interesting / movie) ________
6 (produce / such as / frozen foods) ________
7 (visit / Tokyo / too) ________
8 (not enough / gigabytes / computer) ________
9 (met / new boss / yet) ________
10 (finish / report / already) ________

D Vocabulary

Key Vocabulary

Read this paragraph about presentations and check your understanding of the words in bold.

Giving a successful presentation takes practice and preparation. You must decide what kind of **visual aids** will effectively support your **topic**. These could be simple materials such as a **flip chart** or a **whiteboard** with a **marker**. But nowadays many presenters use a laptop and **projector** to show PowerPoint® **slides** on a screen. In addition, a stick or **laser pointer** is useful for indicating a particular area of the **screen**. It is important to know your **audience** and their expectations.

You should also prepare a clear **outline** with **key points** that will enable you to speak confidently. You can clarify information in the form of **diagrams**, such as **charts** and **graphs**. It is also a good idea to finish the presentation with a **summary** of the main ideas. A presenter may also prepare **handouts** of the key points, although some people give them out after the presentation so that they do not create a distraction.

1 Match the words in the first column with their meanings in the second column.

1 Charts and graphs are — e
2 Flip charts and whiteboards are
3 Laser pointers are
4 The audience are
5 Key points are

a the essential ideas in a presentation.
b the people who attend the presentation.
c equipment to write information on.
d hand-held objects used to point at a screen.
e pictures of data.

2 Cindy's colleague gave her the following feedback after she practiced giving her presentation to her coworkers. Complete the feedback using the words in the box.

audience	graphs	handouts	key points	screen
outline	visual aids	summary	projector	~~slides~~

Your information was well-organized. You gave a nice overview and showed the important features of our services. However, you wrote too much information on each of your **1** ___slides___ . Your audience read that information instead of listening to your talk. For the same reason, I suggest that you distribute your **2** ________ after the talk. You read through your presentation instead of talking to your **3** ________ . I suggest that you just make an **4** ________ on note cards and be sure to make eye contact with the audience.

Your **5** ________ were attractive, and showed up nicely on the **6** ________ , but in one case you had too many **7** ________ on one slide. They were too small to be seen properly. Decide which ones show the **8** ________ most effectively, make them bigger, and show them one at a time. Delete the ones that are secondary. You made a nice **9** ________ of all the points at the end.

One last thing. Don't forget to call the conference center and make sure that they've got a **10** ________ in the room you're going to be using.

3 **Look at these sets of words. Cross out the one that doesn't belong in each set.**

1 ~~marker~~ computer projector microphone

2 slides expectations transparencies visual aids

3 pointer chart graph diagrams

4 audience viewers listeners presenters

5 whiteboard flip chart outline screen

6 summary key points topic handouts

20 Investments

Passives

Passive voice; *have something done*

A Context listening

1 **You are going to hear Jackie and Isaac discussing with Maruka what they think she should do with her money. Can you guess what they will advise Maruka to do?**

1 Put the money into a bank account? ________

2 Play the lottery? ________

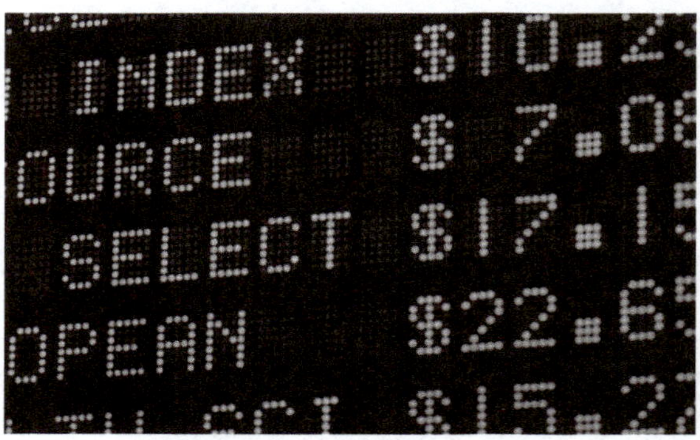

3 Invest in the stock market? ________

4 Invest in property? ________

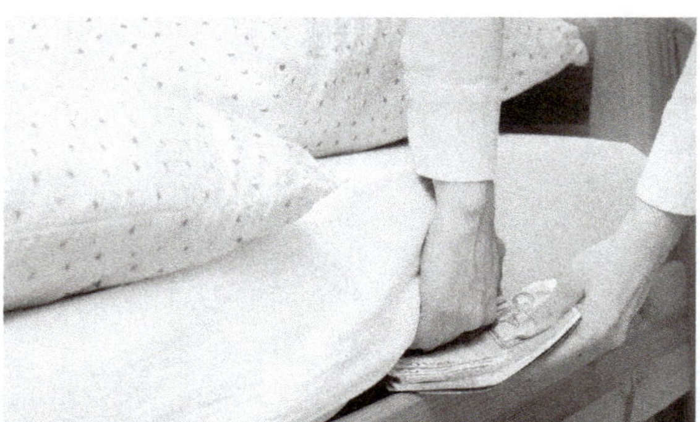

5 Hide the money under a mattress? ________

Vocabulary note

When talking about finances, the word *stock* means a share of ownership in a company.
*We own 100 shares of J.C. Penny **stock**.*
When talking about merchandise, the word *stock* means the supply of items that a storekeeper or manufacturer has available for sale.
*The trade show will give us the opportunity to exhibit our new line of **stock**.*

2 **Listen and write *yes* or *no* by the options that Jackie and Isaac mention. What does Maruka say she plans to do?**

____

3 **Complete the second sentence so that it has a similar meaning to the first sentence. Then listen to the recording again and check your answers.**

1 Someone has left Maruka a large sum of money.
Maruka, we heard that you _have been left_ a large sum of money.
2 You should pay back any money you owe first.
Any money you owe ____________ first.
3 You should invest your money in a bank fund that has a higher interest rate.
Your money ____________ in a bank fund that has a higher interest rate.
4 You can withdraw the money in case of an emergency.
The money ____________ in case of an emergency.

4 **Write the form(s) of the words you heard in the conversation. You may need to listen again.**

1 invest _invested_
2 capitalist ____________
3 liquidity ____________
4 diversification ____________

B Grammar

1 Passive voice use

We use the active voice when we focus on the person or thing doing the action. We use the passive voice when we focus on the person or thing affected by the action.

Active voice

Daniel Murphy ***opened*** *his first shop in 1986.* (active voice – the focus is on Daniel Murphy)

Passive voice

The first shop ***was opened*** *in 1986.* (passive voice – the focus is on the shop)

We use the passive voice when:

- the action is more important than who or what is responsible for the action
  Your debts ***should be paid*** *off first.*
- we do not know who or what is responsible for the action
  Two hundred XF70 cell phones ***were stolen*** *from the warehouse last night.*
- the person or thing that is responsible for the action is known
  The thief ***was arrested.*** (We know the police arrested him.)
- we talk about impersonal situations
  It ***is rumored*** *that we are going to get a raise.*
- we do not want to say who is responsible
  The computer files ***were*** *accidentally* ***deleted.***

2 Passive voice form

When an active verb becomes a passive verb, the person or thing that has been affected by the action becomes the subject of the verb.

Active

*Investors **are following** the stock market movement quite closely.*

Passive

*The stock market movement **is being followed** quite closely.*

The verb *be* is followed by the main verb in its past participle form.

Tense / Part of speech	Active	Passive
present simple	*follow(s)*	*am / is / are followed*
present continuous	*am / is / are following*	*am / is / are being followed*
past simple	*followed*	*was / were followed*
past continuous	*was / were following*	*was / were being followed*
present perfect	*has / have followed*	*has / have been followed*
past perfect	*had followed*	*had been followed*
will future	*will follow*	*will be followed*
going to future	*am / is / are going to follow*	*am / is / are going to be followed*
would	*would follow*	*would be followed*
would have	*would have followed*	*would have been followed*
infinitive	*to follow*	*to be followed*
gerund	*following*	*being followed*

We can also put the modal form into the passive.

*We **can put** an ad in the newspaper. An ad **can be put** in the newspaper.*

*I **should have sent** those forms last week. Those forms **should have been sent** last week.*

When we mention the person or thing doing the action, we use the word *by*.

Of Mice and Men *was written* ***by John Steinbeck.***

*Our user guides are translated **by a technical writer.***

*He was attacked **by a dog.***

When we are changing an active sentence with two objects into the passive voice, we can use either object as the subject.

Active *Simon **sent** the documents to the client.*

Passive *The documents **were sent** to the client.*

*The client **was sent** the documents.*

3 *have something done*

Sometimes we ask or pay someone else to do something for us. We say we are *having something done* and do not usually need to say who is doing the job for us.

*Gerald **is having** the offices **repainted.***

*I **had** my hair **done** for the inerview.*

***Is** Audrey **going to have** the accounts **checked** over?*

C Grammar exercises

1 **Change the active sentences to passive sentences and the passive sentences to active sentences using the verb from the first sentence.**

1 Are you offering the weekend training course to staff members this year?
Are staff members being offered the weekend training course this year?

2 I have been offered a job as a sales representative for the Tidy Lawn Company.
The Tidy Lawn Company __________ me a job as a sales representative.

3 The courier brought the package this morning.
The package __________ by the courier this morning.

4 The R & D people won't present their new software tomorrow.
The new software __________ by the R & D people tomorrow.

5 All Yamaguchi San's clients are sent greeting cards every year.
Yamaguchi San __________ all his clients greeting cards every year.

6 Can customers assemble our desks quickly?
__________ our desks __________ quickly?

7 We haven't replaced the old equipment yet.
The old equipment __________ yet.

8 Have you been introduced to all the staff members?
__________ anyone __________ you to all the staff members?

2 **Complete the text with the passive form of the verbs in parentheses.**

To connect to a wireless internet network, you need a router and a wireless adapter. The information **1** is received (*receive*) by the router through a normal internet cable and then it **2** __________ (*send*) to the wireless adapters. Radio waves **3** __________ (*use*) to transmit the information to the adapters. In the right conditions, the signal transmission travels up to a mile in all directions. The signal **4** __________ (*pick up*) by the wireless adapter and the computer reads the information. When the wireless system **5** __________ (*set up*), several computers can **6** __________ (*connect*) at the same time, without the need for cables. Problems with the signal **7** __________ sometimes __________ (*cause*) by microwaves and mobile phones.

3 **Match the two halves of the conversations and fill in the blanks with the correct form of the verbs in parentheses.**

1 Can I send out the price list today? ___c___

2 Where are the old documents? ______

3 This office looks different. ______

4 Are we going to the trade show this year? ______

5 When will we know about the raises? ______

6 This letter has a lot of mistakes in it. ______

7 We need more skilled workers. ______

8 I need to make a new chart. ______

a Intensive training ______ (*could / offer*) to our new employees.

b I agree. It ______ (*should / rewrite*).

c No, it ___is___ still ___being updated___ (*update*).

d Oh, try this program. A new one ______ (*can / make*) in minutes.

e That ______ not ______ (*have / decide*) yet because it conflicts with our move to the new office building.

f They ______ (*shred*) yesterday for security reasons.

g We ______ not ______ (*tell*) until next month.

h Yes, the old curtains ______ (*have / replace*).

4 **Correct the underlined passives in the following article.**

Mushrooms make a tasty addition to a variety of meals. But mushrooms **1** may soon being used in a completely new way. A technique **2** has be found to produce the beautiful sound quality of the famous Stradivarius violins – and it uses mushrooms! Real Stradivarius violins **3** are desiring by musicians all over the world because of their unique sound quality, but they are too expensive for most people. However, when the wood of a normal violin **4** is treat with a certain mushroom, the sound quality is so good it **5** could be mistake for a real Stradivarius. The researchers found that the wood of the violin **6** was breaked up by the mushroom so that the density of the wood **7** was reducing. The sound quality of the violin **8** are much improved through the "mushroom" method.

5 **Read the situation and answer the question using the correct form of *have something done*.**

1 Ron's car engine is making strange noises. It is time for a tune up, so he's going to take his car to a mechanic. What is he going to do there?

He is going to have his car tuned up.

2 Maggie is going to present the Award for Business Excellence this evening. She has gone to the beauty parlor where a hairdresser is styling her hair. What is Maggie doing?

____

3 Bill and Natasha want to paint their house, but they don't have time to paint it themselves. They have hired a professional painter. What are they doing?

____

4 Jackie tore her favorite dress. She took it to a tailor. What did she do?

____

5 Dmitri needed some passport pictures. He has gone to see a professional photographer. What is he doing?

____

D Vocabulary

Key Vocabulary

Read this paragraph about investments and check your understanding of the words in bold.

Saving and investing your money in a profitable way takes both skill and luck. You should keep some money **liquid,** which means that you can **access** it immediately. This money should be used to pay regular **expenses** and **debts.** The **capital** that is left could be invested in a long-term deposit or a **bond,** where you will get a better **interest rate.** The next level of investing is either to purchase **stocks** in companies or to buy property. Both **investment strategies** carry **risks,** so it is important to **diversify** your investments. This means that your money should not be put in just one company or just one kind of company. If you can't study the stock market regularly, you can go to a **financial advisor** for help. These experts will design a **portfolio** that fits your specific needs depending on your total **assets,** and they will make the **financial transactions** for you. For this service, they **take a commission.**

1 Match the words with the definitions.

1	assets	a	ability to get to
2	capital	b	a collection of investments
3	access	c	money
4	debt	d	money owed
5	portfolio	e	possessions, including money

2 Fill in the blanks with the words in the box.

financial advisor | bonds | commission | transactions | interest rates | stocks | ~~expenses~~

1 I don't have any cash left after I pay my monthly ___expenses___.

2 Jim suggested that I balance my portfolio by buying ________ in several sectors.

3 Marta is a real estate agent and she gets a good ________ on all house sales she makes.

4 I don't have time to study the stock market. I need a ________ to help me invest.

5 I suggest putting some investments in ________ instead of putting it all in stocks.

6 I'm not sure whether to invest in stocks or bonds. What ________ are you offering on your bonds?

7 Financial ________ range from buying a house all the way to buying a candy bar.

3 Read the extract from an article and underline the correct form of the words in italics.

Today the PID pension fund has announced plans to **1** *diversification / diversify / diverse* and invest in a wider portfolio of stocks. This **2** *diversification / diversity / diverse* is part of the change in **3** *strategic / strategy / strategically* developed by the new management of PID. Previously, a large proportion of the pension fund's assets had been in the form of **4** liquidity / liquid / liquidation accounts.

The fund is planning to increase its **5** *investment / investor / invest* in biotechnology stocks although it will be careful to evaluate the **6** *risky / risk / riskier* level before making any new investments.

Practice test 4

TOEIC® TIP
In question 8 of the Writing test, make sure you answer the question and give good reasons and examples to support your opinion.

Listening

Part 1: Photographs

Directions: In this section, you will hear four statements about a photograph. The statements will not be printed on the test. As you listen, select the statement that best describes the photograph. You will hear the statements only once.

1 (A) (B) (C) (D)

Part 2: Question-Response

Directions: In this section, you will hear a question or statement followed by three responses. They will not be printed on the test. As you listen, select the best response. You will hear the question and statements only once.

2 (A) (B) (C)
3 (A) (B) (C)
4 (A) (B) (C)
5 (A) (B) (C)
6 (A) (B) (C)
7 (A) (B) (C)

Part 3: Conversations

Directions: In this section, you will hear two people having a conversation and will answer questions about what you heard. The conversations will not be printed on the test. Select the response that best answers the question. You will hear the conversations only once.

Questions **8–10** refer to the following conversation.

8 Why is the couple unsure about whether to make an offer?
(A) They don't know if the bank will give them a loan.
(B) They think the price is too high.
(C) They are not sure about the neighborhood.
(D) They don't know if their children will like it.

9 What does the man say he will do tomorrow?
(A) Visit the agent
(B) Check the supermarket
(C) Talk to the seller
(D) Call the bank

10 What facilities are NOT mentioned as being near the house?
(A) A supermarket
(B) A post office
(C) A school
(D) A park

Part 4: Talks

Directions: In this section, you will hear a speaker giving a talk and will answer questions about the talk. The talks will not be printed on the test. Select the response that best answers the question. You will hear the talks only once.

Questions **11–13** refer to the following talk.

11 Where was this announcement heard?
(A) At the bank
(B) On the radio
(C) At the library
(D) On the Internet

12 What does the speaker suggest to the listener?
(A) Buy a flat screen TV
(B) Go to Disney World
(C) Take charge of his / her finances
(D) Get items at summer sales

13 What problem does the speaker NOT mention?
(A) Credit card debt
(B) A negative bank balance
(C) Out of control spending habits
(D) Lost investments in the stock market

Reading

Part 5: Incomplete Sentences

Directions: In each sentence below, a word or phrase is missing. Select the best answer from the four choices to complete the sentence. Mark (A), (B), (C), or (D).

1 We are renting office space in the building that is _________ the parking lot from our plant.
(A) across
(B) among
(C) into
(D) from

2 Improve your company's _________ through effective advertising.
(A) appearance
(B) image
(C) icon
(D) logo

3 You need to present your identification _________ you enter the factory.
(A) how
(B) why
(C) what
(D) when

4 I was _________ by the chairperson's presentation this morning.
(A) impressed
(B) impression
(C) impress
(D) impressive

5 Security cameras were installed on city buses for the _________ of everyone.
(A) protected
(B) protection
(C) protecting
(D) protective

6 You should try to make a good impression at _________ interview.
(A) his
(B) my
(C) your
(D) their

7 Can we have a show of hands to _________ on this point?
(A) decision
(B) decided
(C) decide
(D) decisive

8 _________ careful you don't get Mr. Carr and Mr. Marr mixed up.
(A) Be
(B) Are
(C) To
(D) At

9 What is the difference _________ this point and the last one?
(A) in
(B) for
(C) between
(D) with

10 Imelda signed the _________ for the McNulty account.
(A) venue
(B) trademark
(C) contract
(D) innovation

Part 6: Text Completion

Directions: Read the text below. Select the best word or phrase to complete the sentences. Mark (A), (B), (C), or (D).

Questions **11–13** refer to the following memo.

Trusoft Concrete, Inc.
Dublin
Ireland

Dear Peter:

I would like to express my thanks to you for the truly excellent display for our Trusoft concrete products. At our first trade show in Munich, many visitors to our booth remarked on the attractiveness of our exhibit space. It ________ confirms our

11 (A) yet
(B) soon
(C) already
(D) just

belief that we were right to depend on your company to design our display.

In my opinion, one never gets a second chance to make a good impression. Your display impressed many people and ________ this, I am sure it

12 (A) because of
(B) of course
(C) as of
(D) obviously

will encourage them to purchase our products. I would like to mention also that for the quality and service we received, your ________ was very reasonable.

13 (A) promotion
(B) product
(C) pricing
(D) convenience

I look forward to doing more business with you in the near future. We have appreciated working with you. Thank you.

Sincerely,
Jake Blake
President
Trusoft Concrete, Inc.

Part 7: Reading Comprehension

Directions: In this section, you will read documents such as advertisements, email correspondence, newspaper articles, and letters. Select the best answer. Mark (A), (B), (C), or (D).

Questions **14–17** refer to the following page from a tourist guide.

If you are at a public telephone and do not have any way of paying for a call yourself, or if you are at someone else's home or office, you can make what is known as a collect call. With a collect call, the person on the other end agrees to accept the charges for the call. First, call the operator of the service provider and say, "Collect call, please." You must give your name and the operator will connect you. If the person at the other end accepts the call, you can speak to them wherever they are in the world without worrying about how much money you have with you. The person receiving the call is the one who must be careful. If you receive a collect phone call, you should only agree to accept the charges if you know the person calling. If you are not sure who it is, you should tell the operator that you will not accept the charges and then you should hang up immediately.

14 When should you make a collect call?
(A) When you do not have a way of paying for the call
(B) When you only have cash with you
(C) When you think someone else will pay for the call
(D) When the operator does not accept your money

15 Who pays for a collect call?
(A) The caller
(B) The service provider
(C) The person who receives the call
(D) The person whose house you are visiting

16 What should you do when you receive a collect call?
(A) Ask the operator how much it will cost.
(B) Check if the service provider is genuine.
(C) Give the operator your name.
(D) Make sure you know who is calling you.

17 What should you do if you receive a collect call from someone you do not know?
(A) Ask the operator to put the person on hold.
(B) Tell the person to call back later.
(C) Tell the operator that you will not accept the call.
(D) Introduce yourself to the caller.

Questions **18–22** refer to the following advertisement and flyer.

Advertisement

ATB Bank 24 Hour Call Center

A free service for ATB Bank customers: phone banking with a difference!
Welcome to ATB Bank personalized 24 Hour Call Center. Serving you year-round, including weekends and holidays. Access your account details and pay telephone, electricity, credit card, and internet bills without leaving your home. The automatic call center is open 24 hours a day, and multilingual phone bankers are at your service from 8:00 A.M. to 8:00 P.M. from Monday to Friday and 8:00 A.M. to noon on Saturdays. Phone bankers provide extra services, including setting up direct deposits.

Flyer

ATB Bank 24 Hour Call Center

Automatic Call Banking Services
- Account Details
- Statement of Account
- Information on Loans
- Pay Telephone, Electricity, Water and Internet Bills

Multilingual Phone Banker Services
- Pay Credit Card Bills
- Issue Standing Orders
- Set Up Direct Deposits
- Make Credit Card Related Enquiries
- Resolve Problems

Call us at 1-000-555-9722 or drop into your local branch to apply for this fast, totally secure, and very convenient service.

18 Which of the following services requires a phone banker?
(A) paying a telephone bill
(B) getting account details
(C) issuing a standing order
(D) making an automatic call

19 What is the latest time to use this service to set up direct deposits on Friday?
(A) 8 A.M.
(B) Midnight
(C) 8 P.M.
(D) Noon

20 What is the purpose of the advertisement?
(A) To promote a service
(B) To offer free accounts
(C) To improve bank security
(D) To issue new details

21 Why is the call center convenient?
(A) Customers can use it at the branch.
(B) Customers can pay a phone banker.
(C) Customers can do their banking at any time.
(D) Customers can write checks without going to the bank.

22 Which of the following statements is NOT true?
(A) Customers do not have to pay for this service.
(B) Customers can get a bank statement automatically.
(C) Customers can apply for this phone banking in any branch.
(D) Customers have to speak to a phone banker to pay electricity bills.

Speaking

Questions 1–2 Read a text aloud

Directions: In this section, you will read a text aloud. You will have 45 seconds of preparation time and then 45 seconds to read aloud.

Question 1:
The first store coupons were handwritten tickets issued by an Atlanta drugstore owner in 1894. These entitled customers to one free glass of a new drink called Coca Cola. Less than a year later, another store owner, C.W. Post, started distributing coupons worth one penny off his new health cereal, Grape Nuts. During the Great Depression of the 1930s, coupons became a regular way to reduce grocery bills and save money. Supermarket owners soon realized the promotional benefits of issuing discount coupons on their produce and nowadays 89% of consumers use coupons while shopping at supermarkets.

Question 2:
The first mobile phones were launched in Sweden in 1956. However, since they weighed about forty kilograms, few people were interested. The first prototype of the modern mobile phone was demonstrated in 1973 in New York when its inventor made a call in front of a group of amazed journalists. Despite the prototype's success, another ten years passed before it went on sale as a phone installed in a car. The light hand-held version soon followed, but needed to be recharged within 15 minutes of use. Improvements in battery technology and electronics led to the much smaller and more efficient phones of today.

Question 3: Describe a picture

Directions: In this section, you will see a photograph and describe it in as much detail as possible. You will have 30 seconds of preparation time and 45 seconds to talk about the photograph.

Questions 4–6: Respond to questions

In this section, you will hear and answer three questions. Begin speaking immediately after you hear a beep. You will not have any preparation time. You will have 15 seconds to answer Questions 4 and 5, and 30 seconds to answer Question 6.

Imagine that a European market research company is doing research in your country about the kinds of home and office furnishings you prefer and why.

You agree to answer some questions about your preferences.

4 Describe your favorite piece of furniture and why you like it.
5 How would you improve the look of your home if you had the time and money?
6 Describe your workplace or study area and say what you like about it and how it could be improved.

Questions 7-9: Respond to questions using information provided

Directions: In this section, you will read information and then answer three questions based on what you have read. You will have 30 seconds to read the information. You will not have any additional preparation time. You will have 15 seconds to answer Questions 7 and 8, and 30 seconds to answer Question 9.

Movefast Shipping Company (Singapore)
ASSISTANT MANAGER SEA FREIGHT FORWARDING

An excellent opportunity to join the Freight Division of the region's major shipping and transportation organization in their Far East operations.

Ideal candidates for the position would be graduates with 10 years or more experience in the freight transportation industry with proven communication and leadership skills.

The candidate should also be familiar with Pacific Rim customs procedures and have a thorough understanding of correct shipping practices.

An excellent salary and benefits package will be offered to the right candidate.

Qualified candidates should fax their résumé before Friday, July 15th to:

The Personnel Manager, Movefast Shipping Company, Singapore. Fax 1-000-555-2094

Question 10: Propose a solution

Directions: In this section, you will be told a problem. After 30 seconds preperation time, you should respond, showing you understand the problem and suggesting a solution. You will have 60 seconds to give your answer.

Quesiton 11: Express an opinion

Directions: In this section, you will be asked your opinion on a particular subject. You then have 15 seconds to prepare and 30 seconds to give your answer.

What is more important for success: hard work or good luck?

Writing

Questions 1–5: Write a sentence based on a picture

Directions: In this section, you will be given two words or phrases and a photograph. You will be asked to write one sentence about the photograph, using the two given words or phrases. You can change the forms of the words and use them in any order. Your sentence will be scored on grammar and how relevant the sentence is to the photograph. You will have 8 minutes for this part.

Question 1:

but / graph

Question 2:

demonstration / enough

Questions 6–7: Respond to a written request

Directions: In this section, you will write a response to an e-mail. Your response will be scored on vocabulary, organization, and the quality and variety of your sentences. You will have 10 minutes to read and respond to each e-mail.

Directions: Read the email. In your email, describe ONE problem and ask TWO questions.

Delete Reply Reply All Forward Print

From: Jim Prager
To: Dr. Sean Baldwin
Subject: Upcoming presentation
Sent: April 22nd

Dear Dr. Baldwin:

Thank you for agreeing to give a presentation titled "New Materials for the New Generation" at our upcoming biannual Construction Engineers Conference. We are delighted to be able to have you as our main speaker and look forward to your visit.

Could you please confirm your arrival time so that we can meet you at the airport? Also, would you like us to reserve accommodations for the three days of the conference? We have private guest accommodations at our main facility. Please let me know as soon as possible.

Best regards,
Jim Prager

Question 8: Write an opinion essay

Directions: In this section, you will write an essay about a given issue. You will be asked to state your opinion and explain and support the opinion. A successful essay will usually contain a minimum of 300 words. Your essay will be scored on grammar, vocabulary, organization, and whether your opinion is supported with reasons and examples. You will have 30 minutes to complete your essay.

Essay question:
Describe a presentation that you have watched. Did you enjoy the presentation? Explain why / why not. Use specific reasons and examples to explain your answer.

Grammar Focus Task

Underline the word that was used in the test.

1. Improve your company's image through effective *advertising / advertised*.
2. They do not know if the bank will give *they / them* a loan.
3. I was *impressed / impressing* by the chairperson's presentation this morning.
4. We are delighted to be able to have you *as / such* our main speaker.
5. What is the difference between this point *or / and* the last one?

Vocabulary Focus Task

Complete these sentences with words from the box.

access	exchange	financial	chart	fax

1. Have you spoken to your ________________ advisor?
2. Has the ________________ rate changed?
3. ________________ your account details and pay telephone, electricity, credit card, and internet bills without leaving your home.
4. They are pointing to a ________________ .
5. Qualified candidates should ________________ their résumé before Friday, July 15th.

21 Innovations

Relative clauses

Relative clauses; relative pronouns; relative pronouns with prepositions

A Context listening

1 **You are going to hear Linda Evans interview an inventor on her radio show. Before you listen, look at the pictures and describe what you think is new and different about Terry's inventions.**

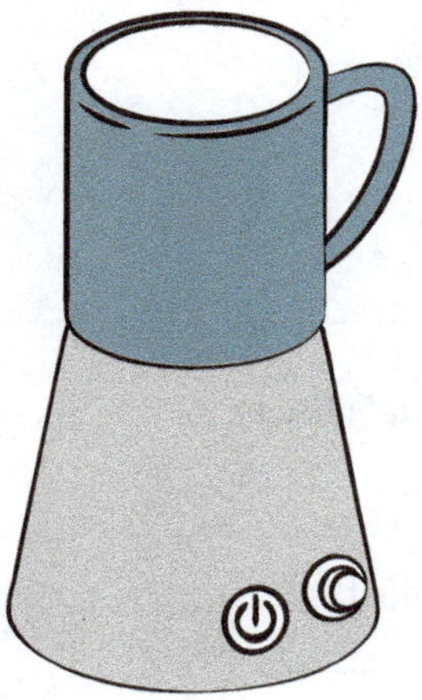

1 ____________________

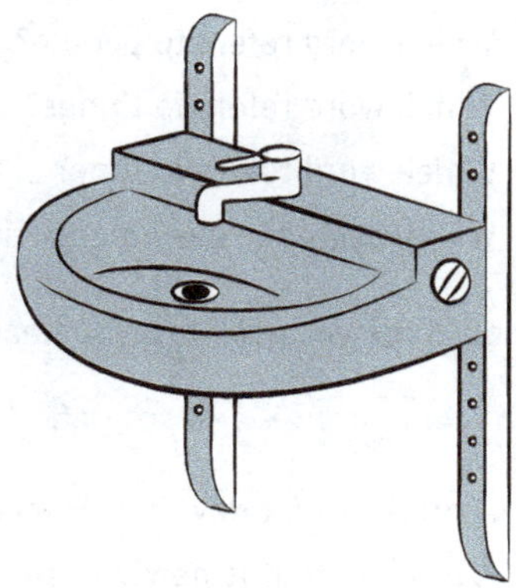

2 ____________________

3 ____________________

2 **Listen and check if you were right.**

3 Listen again and complete the sentences.

1 We have a guest who is going to tell us ______ about his inventions.
2 The days ______ cold coffee are over.
3 Different people in the same house can change the height of the sink to the position ______ most comfortable.
4 Your sink is one invention ______ really ______.
5 In fact, my SqueakyClean dishes are dishes ______ themselves.

4 Underline the first word in each of your answers to Exercise 3. Answer the following questions about the word you underlined.

1 Which word refers to a place? ______
2 Which word refers to people? ______
3 Which word refers to things? ______
4 Which word refers to time? ______
5 Which sentence has an underlined word that you can delete? ______

5 Choose the correct word you heard in the listening for these definitions.

a breakthrough | a spin-off | an invention

1 A product that develops from another more important product is ______ .
2 A product that is newly designed or created is ______ .
3 An important discovery or event that helps solve a problem is ______ .

B Grammar

1 Relative clauses

The relative clause describes, identifies, or gives more information about a noun or indefinite pronoun (*anyone, someone, everyone, anywhere,* etc.). When we join two sentences that are related through a noun or pronoun that are the same, one of the sentences becomes a relative clause.

The two sentences below are related because *the man* and *he* refer to the same person.
*I saw **a man. He** was running for the bus.*

We can join these two related sentences by making a relative clause.
*I saw a man **who** was running for the bus.*

2 Relative pronouns

The relative clause begins with a relative pronoun (*who*, *which*, *that*, *whose*, etc).

Who, which* and *that
We use *who* or *that* when the relative clause is talking about a person.
*We have a guest **who** is going to tell us about his inventions.*
*For someone **that** really likes a hot cup of coffee, your invention sounds like a great idea.*

We use *which* or *that* when the relative clause is talking about a thing.
*This is the copy machine **which** we just had serviced.*
*I have a pad of paper **that** I always keep by the telephone.*

Leaving out the relative pronoun
We can leave out the relative pronoun when it is the object of the relative clause.
I am training a woman. She is our new salesperson. (*woman* = object)
*The woman (**who**) I am training is our new salesperson.*
I had to move the boxes. They were heavy. (*boxes* = object)
*The boxes (**that**) I had to move were heavy.*

It is not possible to leave out the relative pronoun when it is the subject of the relative clause.
*The woman **who** is standing next to the door is our new salesperson.* (**not** ~~*The woman is standing next to the door is*~~)

Whose
We use *whose* to show possession.
*I helped the customer **whose** complaint was about a coffee pot.*

Where, when,* and *why
We use *where* to refer to a place, *when* to refer to a time, and *why* to refer to a reason.
*The office **where** I work is near the freeway.*
*You can reduce your bills by using electricity at times **when** demand is low.*
*There are many reasons **why** the workload is heavy this month.*

3 Relative pronouns with prepositions

The relative pronoun sometimes replaces the noun in a prepositional phrase.
*The records **to which** I was referring are in the filing cabinet.* (**not** ~~*The records to that*~~)
*The records **that** I was referring **to** are in the filing cabinet.*
*The records I was referring **to** are in the filing cabinet.*

*That is a problem **for which** I don't have an answer.* (**not** ~~*That is a problem for that*~~)
*That is a problem **that** I don't have an answer **for**.*
*That is a problem I don't have an answer **for**.*

*The man **with whom** I was speaking is one of our managers.*
*The man **who(m)** I was speaking **with** is one of our managers.*
*The man I was speaking **with** is one of our managers.*

C Grammar Exercises

1 Complete these sentences with *who, whose, that, which, where,* or *when*.

1 The delivery ___that___ came today was incomplete.

2 The woman ______ office is next to mine does the accounts.

3 I booked a hotel room ______ faces the ocean.

4 This is the assembly line ______ we package the eggs.

5 The man ______ is talking to the director is a very important client.

6 I remember the day ______ Evelyn took over the director's job.

2 Underline the relative pronouns in this article. Decide which relative pronouns are optional and put them in parentheses.

The History of the Smartphone

The first smartphone was designed by IBM in 1992. It was a mobile phone that had a variety of extra functions, including email and fax. It was a phone that we would think is quite normal today, but at the time was very advanced. The use of smartphones increased in the 1990s when Nokia introduced the 9000 series. These were phones that people could buy relatively cheaply. Consumers who bought them were impressed with the greater range of functions combined with their light weight. In the first decade of the new century, several companies introduced smartphones that were easier to use and more powerful. Some models that contain millions of downloadable music tracks for no extra cost have been introduced. This is a technology that experts claim will continue to improve in terms of performance and range of functions.

3 Match the beginnings (1–6) and endings (a–f) of these sentences, and join them by adding a relative pronoun. Sometimes more than one pronoun is possible.

1 A bar code is a set of black and white lines ___that___ ___f___

2 Millions of people communicate using social networks ______ ______

3 Ruben Rausing was the man ______ ______

4 Those sales predictions were published at a time ______ ______

5 There are several locations ______ ______

6 SCUBA refers to a device ______ ______

a you can return our recyclable bottles.

b the market was shrinking.

c link them to computer users around the world.

d invented the milk carton.

e allows divers to stay underwater for long periods of time.

f ~~a laser reads for product information~~

4 **Join these pairs of sentences with *who, which,* or *that.* Sometimes more than one relative pronoun is possible.**

1 The items were not ordered. They were removed from the bill.
The items that were not ordered were removed from the bill.

2 We employ craftsmen. They build traditional wooden furniture.
______

3 An accountant works in the building next door. Why don't you contact the accountant?
______

4 The phone had no dial tone. I took it over to the maintenance department.
______

5 My brother got a new job. The job requires some training in marketing.
______

6 Our R & D department has proposed a new design. The design has many advantages.
______

7 The customer brought back her microwave. She gave in the receipt.
______

8 We have to contact those board members. The board members were unable to attend the meeting.
______

5 **Complete the sentences using a relative pronoun and preposition.**

1 I'd like to introduce you to the people who I work with / the people with whom I work.
(I work with the people)

2 Gianna wants to show us ______.
(she's been working on the project)

3 Jane tried to book a hotel room, but ______ was booked up.
(she wanted to stay in the hotel)

4 Lee is looking for a job, but ______ are very competitive.
(he's applying for the positions)

5 We went to ______.
(we told you about the movie)

D Vocabulary

Key Vocabulary

Read this paragraph about the process of developing a new product and check your understanding of the words in bold.

Many companies have a department called the **Research and Development** department, or "R & D" for short. The people in this department are **creative** thinkers who look for ways to improve existing products or come up with **innovative** ideas that may lead to a totally new **invention.** The **creative process** to develop one may take months or even years. During this **trial and error** period, the researchers may make important **breakthroughs** while **experimenting with materials** and **designs**. Their **discoveries** can lead to **revolutionary** new products. The company has to get a **patent** that gives it **exclusive rights** to manufacture the product. Alternatively, it may grant a **license** that allows another company the right to produce the product. Frequently, there are important **spin-offs**, or unexpected products in an unrelated area, that make good profits for the company and are valuable for the end user.

1 Underline the correct words.

1 We need to think *creative* / *creativity* / *creatively* about the development of this product.

2 Our plans include the *developmental* / *development* / *develop* of a robotic device for use in medical operations.

3 This idea will *revolutionize* / *revolution* / *revolutionary* the way we work.

4 Mike Lewis *inventors* / *invents* / *inventions* gadgets that help people with disabilities.

5 Many important *discoveries* / *discovery* / *discover,* such as penicillin, Teflon, and even potato chips, have been accidental.

6 Our research team's *innovation* / *innovator* / *innovative* products include a range of solar powered insulated containers.

7 Our company is *license* / *licensing* / *licensed* to manufacture a new kind of lightbulb.

8 If we are to travel further into space we must *designer* / *design* / *designing* a new generation of spaceships.

2 **Match the words that are frequently used together and complete the description of the process of developing a product.**

1	creative	development
2	exclusive	error
3	research and	~~off~~
4	~~spin~~	process
5	trial and	rights

I was reading an article about research that was being done on space suits and realized that there was a lot of potential for a **1** ___spin-off___ of the fire-resistant textiles for the emergency services. It wasn't easy to get **2** ________ for developing the textiles, but eventually we convinced the space agency to let us go ahead and do our own **3** ________ in this field. The **4** ________ for developing such new material is challenging and time consuming. Sometimes we make a breakthrough, but we have made many mistakes and have had to redesign the textiles on several occasions. It is really a process of **5** ________ .

3 **Complete the following sentences with the correct word from the box.**

breakthroughs	exclusive rights	~~experiments~~	
patent	research	spin-offs	trial and error

1. We are performing a series of ___experiments___ to see if the treatment has any negative side effects.
2. One of our most important ________ last year was finding a way to manufacture a new kind of plastic.
3. We should ________ this new lightweight folding ladder as soon as possible so that we have the rights to it.
4. High-tech athletic shoes, freeze-dried food, and water purification systems have all been ________ from research in unrelated areas.
5. The cartoon character Mickey Mouse was developed over several years by ________ until the version we recognize now was created.
6. Our company has the ________ to the profits from this energy-efficient hair dryer.
7. Before we develop a new product we have to do a lot of technological ________ .

22 Insurance

Conditional sentences

Zero, first, and second conditionals

A Context listening

1 **You are going to hear three conversations. Look at the pictures below. Before you listen, match the kind of insurance to the situation you see in the illustrations.**

1 liability ________ 2 accident ________ 3 fire ________

a

b

c

2 **Listen and check if you were right.**

3 **Match the first and second halves of these sentences from the recording.**

1 As long as it was the other driver's fault,
2 Your claim should be approved quite quickly provided that
3 There shouldn't be a problem with compensation unless
4 If you suspect it was done intentionally,
5 If you give me some details,
6 Your liability insurance premiums will increase if

a you'll need to file a police report.
b I'll be able to put you through to a claims advisor.
c you send us all the paperwork.
d she wins her claim.
e there are unusual circumstances.
f his insurance company should pay for the damage.

Listen again and check your answers.

4 **Look at the sentences in Exercise 3 above. Which three words or phrases other than *if* are used to show condition?** ____________________

5 **Listen again and underline the words you heard in the conversations.**

Conversation 1:
a dedication / deductible
b approved / proved

Conversation 2:
a policy / privacy
b compensation / conversation

Conversation 3:
a negligent / negotiate
b legality / liability

B Grammar

Conditional sentences contain two parts or clauses: the conditional clause is the part of the sentence that begins with *if*, and the main clause contains the result. The condition can come before or after the result.

1 Zero conditionals (general truth)

We use the present simple or the present continuous in both parts of the sentence to talk about conditions and results that are generally true.
*If it **isn't** raining, I **walk** to work, but if it **is raining**, I **drive**.*
*I **leave** home half an hour later if I **drive** to work.*

We can use *when* instead of *if* in a sentence showing a general truth.
***When** it isn't raining, I walk to work.*

We use the past simple for a situation that was generally true in the past.
*In my old job if a customer **phoned** with a problem, we **transferred** the call to the sales advisors.*

2 First conditionals (probability)

We use a present tense or a present perfect tense in the conditional clause and the future tense in the main clause when the result will probably be true.
***I'll be** late to the meeting if my flight **is** delayed.*
*How much **will** they **have to pay** her if she **wins** her claim?*
*If you **are planning** to stay late, you**'ll need** to let the security guard know.*

We can also use a modal or an imperative in the main clause in a first conditional.
*If you **haven't reported** the accident yet, we **can't file** the claim.*
*If an accident **is** your fault, then your rates **may / might / could rise**.*
***Have** our visitors wear hard hats if you **take** them into the shop.*

We don't usually use *when* to replace *if* in the conditions of probability.

3 Second conditionals (imaginary)

We use a past tense in the conditional clause and *would / could / should / might / must* + verb in the main clause to talk about a condition and result in the present or future that we think is very unlikely or improbable.
*If I **finished** this report, I **could leave** work early today.* (= I am working on the report now. I haven't finished it yet and I probably won't finish it, so I am unlikely to leave early.)

4 Other ways to introduce conditions

If is the most common way to introduce a condition, but we can use other words or phrases to make conditional sentences.

Unless
We use *unless* with a positive verb to mean *if ... not.*
*You can't get a job in our factory **unless** you have training.* (= . . . **if** you do**n't** have computer skills.)

In case

We use *in case* to introduce the reason why you take a precaution.

I put the file on your desk ***in case*** *you need it.*
We will bring a laptop ***in case*** *we have to check our accounts.*
We should aim to get there early ***in case*** *there are a lot of people.*

In case has a different meaning from *if*.
I'll come to our exhibition table early ***in case*** *you want my help.*
(= I'll be there because you might want my help.)
I'll come to our exhibition table early ***if*** *you want my help.*
(= I'll only come if you say you want me to be there.)

Provided / providing that, as long as, only if, and *on condition that*

Provided / providing (that), as long as, only if, and *on condition that* can be used instead of *if* when there is a restriction.

We can give refunds ***provided (that)*** *you have the receipt.*
People will realize that we haven't really been negligent ***as long as*** *they know all the facts.*
The product will ***only*** *be withdrawn from the market* ***if*** *a fault is found.*
I accepted the job ***on condition that*** *I could have a company car.*

C Grammar exercises

1 **Complete each sentence with the correct form of the word in the box.**

tell	~~be~~	walk	forget	get	meet	try	put

1 If my flight is delayed, I ___'ll be___ late to the meeting.
2 These documents ________________ lost if you don't file them.
3 When I ________________ to work, I leave the house 20 minutes earlier.
4 If you are free at that time, we ________________ in the staff room.
5 More people come into the store when we ________________ coupons in the paper.
6 I'll open the safe if you ________________ me the combination number.
7 If we ________________ the brochures again, we'll really get in trouble.
8 If Jake gives a presentation, we always ________________ to attend.

2 **Complete this conversation between Hyo and Kelly, using the correct form of the verbs. You may have to use a modal verb.**

Hyo: If **1** ___it's___ (it / be) sunny this afternoon, would you like to go for a walk on the beach?
Kelly: Maybe, but I can't go unless **2** ________________ (I / get) this work done first.
Hyo: OK. But I don't think you can finish all that before this afternoon.
Kelly: I can, provided that **3** ________________ (I / be / not) interrupted.
Hyo: Oh, I'm sorry. I'll let you get back to work. Let me know if **4** ________________ (you / need) anything.
Kelly: OK. Well, I'd like a cup of coffee, if **5** ________________ (there / be) any left.
Hyo: There isn't, but if you just wait a minute, **6** ________________ (I / make) a fresh pot. I'll also bring you some sandwiches in case **7** ________________ (you / get) hungry later.
Kelly: Oh, thanks.
Hyo: OK. But what **8** ________________ (I / say) if your boss calls?
Kelly: Tell her that if **9** ________________ (she / want) me to do more work over this weekend, I quit.
Hyo: No, I won't do that. If you want to quit your job, **10** ________________ (you / have) to tell her yourself.

3 **Complete the sentences using *if* or *unless* so that they have the same meaning.**

1 We'll have the shipment tomorrow unless there is a delay.
We'll have the shipment tomorrow ___if there isn't___ a delay.
2 We will approve your claim unless you haven't paid your premiums.
We will approve your claim ________________ your premiums.
3 If the traffic is not heavy, we can get there in 10 minutes.
________________ heavy, we can get there in 10 minutes.
4 Unless I can't avoid it, I never arrive late for work.
________________ it, I never arrive late for work.

5 We will only approve the design if you make the changes we discussed.

We won't approve the design ______________________ the changes we discussed.

6 If the door isn't locked, just go in.

______________________ locked, just go in.

4 Underline the correct words.

1 I won't go to the trade show <u>unless</u> / *if* I can get a company car for that weekend.

2 Let's go for an early lunch *in case* / *if* you are finished with that report.

3 Should I put the file in my briefcase *in case* / *provided that* we need to refer to it?

4 *When* / *If* my train is late, I will miss the connecting train.

5 I will go *on condition that* / *in case* we come home early.

6 *As long as* / *Unless* you have paid the premium, you are covered.

5 Mandy is telling Christine about insurance. Match the beginnings of the sentences (1–8) with the endings (a-h).

1 If I didn't have insurance

2 If you want to save money on insurance

3 These websites can be useful

4 You can get a reduced premium

5 Special rates are also given

6 You may be turned down for insurance

7 I wouldn't take out a policy

8 I recommend NTZ insurance company

a as long as you check the details carefully.

b if you have a bad driving record.

c if you want excellent service.

d to people in certain categories.

e if I didn't trust the company.

f provided you are a nonsmoker.

g you could look on a comparison website.

h I could lose everything I own.

6 Complete each sentence with your own ideas.

1 I walk to work if the weather is fine ______________________.

2 I can leave the office early on Fridays provided that ______________________.

3 If I go on vacation, ______________________.

4 When I talk to my boss, ______________________.

5 You should always back up your computer files in case ______________________.

6 I enjoy my job as long as ______________________.

7 I'll do some training at work if ______________________.

8 Insurance companies don't approve claims unless ______________________.

9 If we made the packaging biodegradable, ______________________.

10 You would get a good commission, ______________________.

D Vocabulary

Key vocabulary

Read this paragraph about insurance and check your understanding of the words in bold.

People and companies buy **insurance policies** in case there is an **accident** or **damage** to their property. If something happens, they will **receive compensation** from the insurance company. This means that they are protected against **risks** to their health, home, car, or even financial loss. With most kinds of insurance, the **insured party** pays the insurance company annual or monthly **premiums** to pay for the **coverage**. When loss or damage occurs, the **policy holder files a claim** to the insurance company. The insurance company will **assess** the amount of loss or damage to the policy holder and then will either **approve** or **deny** compensation. If they approve the claim, they **pay out** to the **claimant**, although there is often a **deductible** that the policy holder must pay. These days, many property owners and businesses carry **liability insurance** that **covers** them **against** claims that they were **negligent**.

Vocabulary note

In business a **party** is a person or group involved in a legal agreement, such as signing a contract.
*There are two **parties** to this contract: you and the insurance company.*

Vocabulary note

The word *cover* can be a noun or a verb. *Cover* gives protection.
*We stood under the tree to get **cover** from the rain.*
Coverage or *cover* is the amount of protection provided by the insurance policy.
*We have **coverage** on the house itself, but not on the furniture.*
In the insurance business, *to cover* means to protect from loss through insurance.
*All employees driving our company cars are **covered** for accidents.*

1 Match each word with an appropriate definition.

1 accident	a a document showing an agreement with an insurance company
2 pay out	b a request for payment of money that you believe is owed you
3 claim	c a type of insurance for protection from claims against you
4 damage	d give money as compensation for a loss, damage, or injury
5 liability	e an amount of money paid at regular times to insure something
6 policy	f an unintended event that causes damage or injury
7 premium	g harm or break

2 **Use the words in the box to complete the sentences. Use each word twice, once as a verb and once as a noun. You may have to change the form.**

claim	cover	damage	file	risk

1 You are taking a _risk_ if you don't get _coverage_ for earthquake _damage_ in this area.

2 I bought insurance to ________ my house in case of fire, but I hope I never have to ________ a ________ .

3 You don't want to ________ not having insurance in the case of an accident where you need to ________ a lot of expenses.

4 After the fire ________ Maria's home, the insurance company said that its ________ showed that her premiums were not up-to-date.

3 **Read this article about insurance claims and underline the correct word.**

Take a look at our list of unusual claims for vacation insurance. If you're going on vacation this year, don't forget to take out an insurance policy. You never know what might happen!

A tourist was seriously injured by a coconut that fell on her head while she was reading under a coconut tree. The insurance company decided to **3** *compensation / compensate* her for the medical costs, although she had to pay the **4** *deductible / deduct.*

A woman went on a skiing vacation but there was not enough snow for skiing. She tried to ski anyway and destroyed her skis. Then she claimed the price of a new pair of skis. The company **1** *denial / denied* her compensation because she was **2** *negligent / negligence* in trying to use the skis.

Two children buried their parents' video camera on a beach to hide it while they went swimming. Later they couldn't find the camera, so the parents filed an insurance claim. Fortunately for them, after the insurers made an **5** *assessment / assess*, they gave **6** *approval / approved* for the payment.

A truck carrying sheep turned over on a bridge and the sheep escaped. One of them jumped over the bridge and landed on a car traveling underneath it. The owner had **7** *coverage / covers* on the car and the insurance company paid out to the **8** *claimant / claim.* No one knows what happened to the sheep.

23 Trade shows

Linking words 2

Giving reasons; giving results; making contrasts; adding information; showing sequences; showing attitude

A Context listening

1 You are going to hear two employees of Kaiser's Kitchen Appliances talking about their company's participation in a trade show. In what way are the two pictures different?

2 Listen to the conversation and circle the picture that shows last year's stand.

3 **Listen again and fill in the blanks. Stop the recording if you need to.**

1 Last year we didn't do a very good job of representing the company, so ________________ we started planning early this year.

2 We waited until the last minute to book a space in the exhibition hall. ________________ , the space they gave us was very small...

3 ________________ our rebuilt stand was so much smaller than we had planned, we didn't have space to showcase our products properly.

4 And ________________ , we noticed that our promotional leaflets had lots of spelling mistakes in them.

5 And ________________ , we are sponsoring a couple of social events and will be handing out cups and bags with our logo.

4 **Look at your answers to Exercise 3 and answer the following questions.**

1 Which word or phrase introduces a reason? ________________

2 Which words or phrases introduce a result? ________________

3 Which word or phrase introduces a sequence? ________________

4 Which word or phrase introduces more information? ________________

5 **Match the word you heard in the conversation with its meaning.**

1 stand	a a fashion or style
2 competitor	b a promotion of a new product
3 trend	c a company selling similar products or services
4 launch	d a place set up for a company to exhibit its products

B Grammar

We use linking words and expressions to connect ideas within a sentence, ideas between two sentences, and ideas within a paragraph.

1 Giving reasons

We can use *because, as,* and *since* to introduce the reason for doing something.
*We will be closed tomorrow **because** it is a national holiday.*
*Our meeting was longer than usual **since** we had to discuss the preparation for the trade show.*
*We have lowered the prices **as** the production costs have dropped.*

We can use *because of, due to,* and *on account of* with a noun.
*We will be closed **because of / due to** a national holiday.* (**not** ~~*because of it is a national holiday*~~)
*The launch didn't go well **because of** our lack of organization.*

2 Giving results

We can use *therefore, consequently, so,* and *as a result* to introduce the result of a situation or action.
*We have to take inventory. **Therefore / Consequently**, we will be closed on Saturday.*
*At first the stand was too large, **so** we had to rebuild it once we got to the show.*
*Conference sales were down by 60 percent, and **as a result** the event was canceled.*

3 Making contrasts

We can use *although, even though, though, whereas,* and *while* to join two contrasting sentences. The linking expression can be at the beginning or in the middle of the sentence. *Though* can also go at the end of the sentence.
***Although** we have discussed opening a new branch, we haven't made a decision.*
*We specialize in soft furnishings for the home, **whereas** our partner company specializes in hard furnishings.*

> *Even though* means *despite the fact that*. The condition is true.
> *Even if* means *whether or not*. The condition may or may not be true.
> *I'll try to be there **even though** I'm busy.* (= I am busy, but I will still try to be there.)
> *I'll try to be there **even if** I'm busy.* (= I may or may not be busy. Either way, I will try to be there.)

We can use *however, in contrast, on the other hand*, and *nevertheless* to contrast two sentences.
*The Hotel Lyon is the cheapest. **However**, it is much further from the conference center than the Ferris Hotel.*
*We could carpool. **On the other hand**, there is a good bus service.*

We can use *unlike, in contrast to,* and *instead of* + noun to contrast two ideas in the same sentence.
***Unlike** our competitors, we offer a 24-hour service.*
***In contrast to** last year's poor performance, this year we have done very well.*

We can use *despite* and *in spite of* + noun / *-ing* to contrast two ideas in the same sentence. The linking expression can be at the beginning or in the middle of the sentence.
In spite of* / *Despite *the heavy snow, the shipment arrived on time.*
The shipment arrived on time ***in spite of* / *despite*** *the heavy snow.*
Rafael hasn't been promoted for five years, ***in spite of* / *despite*** *being one of our most successful salespeople.*

4 Adding information

We can use the words *additionally, in addition, furthermore, moreover,* and *also* to add more sentences with more information.
We have decided to adopt this new strategy because we think it will increase our sales. ***Furthermore,*** *it will give us tax advantages.* ***Moreover,*** *the costs of implementing the strategy won't be very high.*

5 Showing order

We can use the words *first, second, third,* (etc.) *then, after that,* and *finally* to show the order of a series of points or events.
First, *I would like Dan to welcome everyone to the presentation.* ***Then,*** *Sally is going to give a short talk about the company.* ***After that,*** *Sally can introduce our guest speaker.* ***Finally,*** *we will present our top salespeople with the gift certificates.*

6 Showing attitude

We can emphasize an idea or point with the words *indeed, above all,* and *most importantly.*
Indeed, *we have made a major effort to make our company more energy efficient.*
And ***above all* / *most importantly,*** *the Moscow trade show is an opportunity to look at what our competitors are doing.*

We can indicate our point of view with the words and phrases *clearly, fortunately / unfortunately, in my opinion, personally, interestingly,* and *surprisingly.*
Fortunately, *the flood only damaged the parking lot and main entrance.*
Personally, *I think that the current prices are too high.*
Not surprisingly, *there were a lot of applicants for this job.*

We can indicate that information or opinions have come from someone else with the words and phrases *according to* (*someone* or *something*), *apparently,* and *evidently.*
According to *the market report, we should expect a drop in profits.*
Apparently, *South Korea would be a good market to investigate.*

C Grammar exercises

1 For each pair of sentences, decide whether they have exactly the same meaning. Write S (same) or D (different).

1 a There may be delays on public transportation because of the bad weather.
b There may be delays on public transportation due to the bad weather. S

2 a We ordered these cabinets for the office because they are made of steel.
b We ordered these cabinets for the office even though they are made of steel. ______

3 a As the new parking lot isn't ready yet, please use the temporary area behind the main building.
b Since the new parking lot isn't ready yet, please use the temporary area behind the main building. ______

4 a We decided to attend the reception in spite of the terrible weather.
b We decided to attend the reception despite the terrible weather. ______

5 a We were promised a raise even though the profits were low.
b We were promised a raise even if the profits were low. ______

6 a After we have drafted a proposal, we will call a meeting.
b We have drafted a proposal, so we will call a meeting. ______

7 a Tunes Music Shop carries musical instruments. Furthermore, they have technicians for repairing them.
b Tunes Music Shop carries musical instruments. Moreover, they have technicians for repairing them. ______

8 a I would not have given a refund to that customer. Not surprisingly, she did not follow the washing instructions on the label.
b I would not have given a refund to that customer. Apparently, she did not follow the washing instructions on the label. ______

2 Match the beginnings and endings of these sentences.

1 As a result of the ongoing price war, b
2 Although all our products are of high quality, ______
3 On account of the Internet being down, ______
4 Despite the candidate's lack of experience, ______
5 In spite of the large discount we offered, ______
6 Unlike our competitors' products, ______

a we really think he's the right person for the job.
b our profits are down.
c the customer continued to complain.
d they are reasonably priced.
e ours are biodegradable.
f we didn't finish the report.

3 **Underline the correct word to complete the letter.**

Dear Mr. Tyson,

I regret to inform you that our production has been interrupted **1** *due to / despite* a large earthquake that has temporarily closed down our factory. **2** *Consequently / Whereas*, we cannot promise to fill your order by June 2nd , the date we had previously agreed to. **3** *Not surprisingly / Fortunately*, no one was injured. **4** *However / Finally*, there was considerable damage done to the building **5** *because / despite* the roof collapsed. But, **6** *unlike / since* the roof was made of a light material, it did not damage our equipment. We have already moved to a temporary building. **7** *After / However,* we cannot yet work to full capacity. **8** *Therefore / Furthermore*, some major rail lines were damaged, affecting the transportation of goods. We will be able to fulfill part of your order by the requested date, **9** *so / although* not all of it. We will let you know when the factory reopens and, **10** *most importantly / personally,* when your final order will be ready.

We appreciate your understanding of our situation.

Best regards,

Alfred Horowitz

4 **Fill in the blanks with the linking expressions in the box.**

because	consequently	due to	first	on the other hand	~~unlike~~

1 FlyFast Air has increased the number of advantages it offers, ___unlike___ its rival airlines.

2 There has been a drop in the housing market. ______ , there has also been a reduction in property taxes.

3 We haven't met today's targets ______ a faulty machine slowed down production.

4 Our products are selling better than last year ______ the successful ad campaign that we launched in July.

5 We could replace this old machine. ______ , we could repair it again.

6 To operate this machine, ______ push down on this button until you hear the control lever click into place.

5 **Complete these sentences using your own ideas.**

1 I was late for the meeting because of ___a flat tire.___

2 The employees at the suppliers' factory are on strike. Therefore, ______

3 It will be necessary to postpone the meeting, as ______

4 Customer satisfaction is extremely important, so ______

5 James Walsh has excellent references from his previous employer. In my opinion, ______

6 We are going to renovate the offices on the ground floor. Furthermore, ______

D Vocabulary

Key Vocabulary

Read this paragraph about the organization of trade shows and check your understanding of the words in bold.

A trade show is an event that often takes place once a year and gives companies from a particular industry the opportunity to **showcase** their products. Access to the **venue** can be restricted to only those companies involved in that particular trade or can be open to the public. Participants use this opportunity to **demonstrate** and sometimes **launch** their products, find out what their **competitors** are doing, and observe new **trends**. They can also **network** during the fair and this is useful for meeting new **contacts**. Before attending a trade show, companies should **liaise** with the trade show organizers to organize the **stand** where they will **exhibit** their products. Some companies **sponsor** events for extra publicity. They may also decide to print **leaflets** to promote their brand as well as produce items with their **logo** to **distribute** to fair participants.

1 Match the phrases in the two columns to describe the italicized word.

1 A *stand* is where __d__
2 A *competitor* is a company that sells ______
3 A *logo* is a symbol used to ______
4 A product *demonstration* is a way to get potential ______
5 A *venue* is where ______
6 *Networking* is making contacts with ______
7 A *trend* is the general direction ______

a identify the company.
b buyers interested in an item.
c a fashion or movement is going.
d the company exhibits its product.
e people who may be useful to know.
f a similar product to those of its rival companies.
g a planned event takes place

2 Underline the correct form.

1 The telecommunications market is very *competitive* / *competition*.
2 Jerry helped me prepare our stand at the *exhibit* / *exhibition* hall.
3 Are you going to *distribute* / *distribution* those leaflets at the trade show?
4 We're thinking of *sponsoring* / *sponsorship* the annual city marathon run.
5 I like to see the different *demonstrations* / *demonstrates* at trade shows.

3 Look at the following sets of words. Cross out the word that does not belong in each set.

1	network	~~promote~~	liaise	interact
2	contacts	display	showcase	exhibit
3	logo	brand	slogan	launch
4	flier	competitor	leaflet	poster

24 Marketing

Verb + verb patterns

Verb + *to* infinitive; verb + *-ing*; infinitive without *to*

A Context listening

1 **Scott, a marketing manager, and Jan, an executive director, are discussing the research done for marketing a new product. Look at the picture. What do you think the new product is and who would be most interested in buying it?**

2 Listen and check if you were right.

3 **Complete the sentences you heard using the verbs in parentheses.**

1 People who enjoy _going out_ (*go out*) all year round are looking for a hiking boot that is long lasting.

2 These people also tend ________________ (*develop*) a loyalty for a particular brand.

3 They also like ________________ (*wear*) comfortable shoes.

4 I'd suggest ________________ (*target*) most of our advertising at these consumers.

5 Well, at least we should think ________________ (*about concentrate*) on the occasional hikers.

4 **Look at your answers to Exercise 3. Underline the word before the blank in Exercise 3 and answer the following questions.**

1 What type of words did you underline? ________________

2 What are the three forms you can see in the blanks? ________________

5 **Match the words in the first column with the words in the second column to make common marketing phrases.**

1 special	a research
2 potential	b markets
3 market	c offers
4 target	d customers

B Grammar

When one verb follows another verb, the second verb can take one of three different forms: *to* infinitive (*to go*), the infinitive without *to* (*go*), or *-ing* (*going*).

1 Verb + *to* infinitive

We use these verbs with verbs in the *to* infinitive form.

agree appear arrange attempt claim
decide demand deserve fail hesitate
hope learn manage offer plan
promise refuse seem wait wish

*We **agreed to work** on the project together.*
*We didn't **attempt to expand** at that point in time.*

Compare these negative forms
*He **didn't promise to** buy anything.* (He didn't make a promise.)
*He **promised not to** buy anything.* (He made a promise. The promise was that he would not buy anything.)

We **always** use these verbs with an object and the verb in the *to* infinitive form.

advise allow cause challenge convince encourage
force hire instruct invite order permit
persuade remind require teach tell warn

*We **require our employees to take** safety training courses.*
*TV and internet ads will **persuade people to buy** our new footwear.*

We **sometimes** use these verbs with an object and the verb in the *to* infinitive form. The meaning is different if we do not use an object.

ask beg choose expect help
intend prepare dare need want

*I **chose to give** the presentation.* (= I gave the presentation.)
*I **chose him to give** the presentation.* (= He gave the presentation.)

We can also use *would like* and *would prefer* with an object and the *to* infinitive form.
*I **would like you to give** the presentation.* (= You will gave the presentation.)
*I **would like to give** the presentation.* (=I will give the presentation.)

2 Verb + infinitive without *to*

We use the modal verbs *can*, *could*, *may*, *might*, *must*, *shall*, *should*, *will*, *would*, *had better*, and *would rather* with the infinitive without *to*.
*You **should bring** that problem to your boss's attention.*

We use *make* and *let* with an object and the infinitive without *to*.
*We **made the company replace** the faulty item.*
*We **let everyone take** the afternoon off.*

We can use *help* with the infinitive with or without *to* without a change in meaning.
*The search button **helps** our customers **(to) find** what they want on the website quickly.*

3 Verb + *-ing*

We use these verbs with verbs in the *-ing* form.

admit anticipate appreciate avoid consider delay discuss enjoy
finish keep mention mind miss postpone practice quit recall
recommend resist resume risk suggest

*Has he **finished writing** the yearly report?*
*We **recommend spending** another week on this project.*

We use the *–ing* form with most verb + preposition patterns, including phrasal verbs.

approve of be better off call for confess to count on depend on
give up insist on keep on object to look forward to put off
rely on succeed in think about think of worry about

*I'm **looking forward to** seeing the launch.*
*He **hasn't succeeded in** convincing all of the team yet.*

4 Verb + *to* infinitive or + *-ing*

We can use these verbs with verbs in either *to* infinitive or *–ing* form without much difference in meaning.

begin can't stand continue hate like love prefer propose start

*We **continue to improve / continue improving** our production techniques.*
*Our customers don't like **having / to have** to buy a new pair of shoes every year.*

We can use some verbs with verbs in either *to* infinitive or *–ing*. *However there is a difference in meaning*.

forget remember regret stop try

*I **remembered to lock** the door and I **remember locking** it.* (= I didn't forget to lock the door and I can think back to when I locked it.)
*I **stopped to chat** with the waiter, but the café got busy so I **stopped chatting** with him.* (= I stopped my journey and talked to the waiter. However, I couldn't continue talking to him because he had to take care of customers.)

5 Verb + *that* clause

We can use some verbs with a *that* clause.

admit agree appreciate arrange confess consider
decide demand deny forget hope imagine
mention pretend promise propose regret remember
suggest threaten expect intend

*I **propose going** to the convention.*
*We **decided not to sign** the contract.*

*I **propose that we go** to the convention.*
*We **decided that we wouldn't sign** the contract.*

C Grammar exercises

1 **Complete this conversation using the verbs in parentheses.**

Lee: I've been asked **1** ___to join___ (*join*) the advertising team. They are attempting **2** ________________ (*break*) into the dog food market and they've asked me **3** ________________ (*produce*) an animated cartoon to promote the product.

Kim: Really? I didn't know that you knew how to do animation.

Lee: Yeah, I've always enjoyed **4** ________________ (*do*) animation. In my own time, I've managed **5** ________________ (*complete*) several advanced courses in computer animation, so I always planned **6** ________________ (*use*) my new skills at work if possible. This opportunity was really perfect for me.

Kim: That's great. So when do you begin **7** ________________ (*work*) on this project?

Lee: Well, I hope **8** ________________ (*start*) as soon as possible. I'm really excited about it.

Kim: I can imagine. Is the advertising team intending **9** ________________ (*use*) your animation for TV or internet ads?

Lee: Internet ads, I think. I hope they are successful because I'd love **10** ________________ (*make*) more ads.

2 **Underline the correct word.**

1 I forgot *lock* / *to lock* / *locking* the door when I left home this morning.

2 I'd recommend *use* / *to use* / *using* the same design company again.

3 We let the staff *decide* / *to decide* / *deciding* where to hold the office party.

4 My brother encouraged me *visit* / *to visit* / *visiting* the new museum.

5 We'll make them *understand* / *to understand* / *understanding* how important this project is.

6 We waited two hours *catch* / *to catch* / *catching* the next train.

7 I quit *smoke* / *to smoke* / *smoking* last year.

8 She offered *buy* / *to buy* / *buying* me lunch.

9 Would you mind *close* / *to close* / *closing* the window; it is cold in here.

10 We are trying to avoid *spend* / *to spend* / *spending* as much money as we did last year.

11 I invited Dr. Yamaguchi *give* / *to give* / *giving* a presentation at the conference.

12 I finished *eat* / *to eat* / *eating* lunch and left the restaurant.

3 **Read the first sentence and ✓ the correct response. Sometimes both answer choices are possible.**

1 Can you remind me to phone Carolina?
  a I won't remember to do that if I'm really busy. ✓
  b I won't remember doing that if I'm really busy.
2 What do you think of my work so far?
  a I regret to say that you'll have to do better.
  b I regret saying that you'll have to do better.
3 Suzy sometimes stays at the office until 8 P.M.
  a I know she likes to work overtime.
  b I know she likes working overtime.
4 You're late getting in today.
  a That's because we stopped picking up the orders.
  b That's because we stopped to pick up the orders.
5 What should we do when we arrive?
  a Let's begin organizing the conference stand first.
  b Let's begin to organize the conference stand first.

4 **Rewrite the sentences using either the *-ing* form or the *to* infinitive.**

1 We decided that we would file the documents.
  We decided to file the documents.
2 I propose that we wait until after next week.
  I propose ______________________.
3 He agreed that he would come at five o'clock.
  He agreed ______________________.
4 I hope that I meet you soon.
  I hope ______________________.
5 She mentioned that she finished the market analysis.
  She mentioned ______________________.

5 **You are giving some advice to a coworker who wants to impress his or her boss. Use your own ideas to complete the sentences.**

1 Avoid arriving late to work.
2 You should quit ______________________ at work.
3 I recommend ______________________ with difficult projects.
4 Why don't you stop ______________________ the tasks you have to do?
5 You should learn ______________________ better.
6 Don't forget ______________________ every day.
7 You can try ______________________ before the deadlines.
8 You could offer ______________________ when they are having problems.

D Vocabulary

Key Vocabulary

Read the paragraph about marketing and check your understanding of the meaning of the words in bold.

Many businesses face **tough competition,** so if a company wants to become the **market leader**, it needs to **analyze consumption habits** by doing some effective **market research**. Some companies do their research **in-house** while others pay an **agency** to do it. Their findings help companies choose the best way to **promote** their **product range** to **potential customers** and can also help identify a **target market** for new products. Promotion is usually done through an advertising campaign, and companies might decide to make **special offers**, give out **free samples,** and even hold **competitions**. The company may also produce an online or paper **catalog** with details of its products. Through marketing, a company **builds customer loyalty** within their **market segment** and creates an **image** that helps the consumer to distinguish its **trademark** from those of competitors.

1 Match the following words with their definitions.

1 consumer ___b___
2 potential ______
3 range ______
4 market leader ______
5 loyalty ______
6 segment ______
7 trademark ______
8 target market ______
9 image ______
10 catalog ______

a a part or section
b ~~a person who buys goods or services~~
c a series of products of a certain kind manufactured by a company
d the segment of the population who are expected to buy the company's products
e a listing, sometimes with pictures or explanations, of items for sale
f an opinion or an idea or mental picture of what something is like
g a symbol that identifies a product or company
h a company that is first or most important in its field
i the support given to a brand or company
j possible, not yet achieved

2 **Underline the correct form.**

1 The *consume* / *consumer* / *consumption* of dental hygiene products has risen sharply in recent years.

2 This is *potential* / *potentially* / *potentiality* the most important breakthrough in the car industry in 30 years.

3 This segment of the population has remained *loyal* / *loyalty* / *loyalties* to our products.

4 I'm applying for a job as a market *analyze* / *analysis* / *analyst* with Hendersons.

5 We are trying to break into a very competitive *market* / *marketing* / *marketer*.

6 What's the best way to keep the *image* / *imagine* / *imagery* of our product in the minds of our target customers?

7 Tinpots Cookware claimed during its *promotion* / *promote* / *promoting* that their pots and pans were the easiest to clean.

8 In the meeting, we discussed whether we had the finances to expand our *production* / *product* / *producer* range.

3 **Match a word from the first box with a word from the second box and add them to the sentences below.**

~~market~~	in	special	free	consumption	tough

competition	samples	habits	~~research~~	house	offers

1 If we want to know what the public thinks of our new candy bar, we really have to do some market research.

2 I don't think we have the funds available for paying an agency so we'll need to do our research ________________ .

3 Rochester's has ________________ with great low prices on all its kitchenware for this week only.

4 The aim of our research is to discover the ________________ of different age groups so that we can target our products more precisely.

5 I like the job of giving away ________________ at Spencer Foods. People are always happy to take them.

6 There is very ________________ in the car insurance market so we have to provide excellent service.

25 Employee perks and benefits

More verb patterns and phrasal verbs

Adjectives + *to* infinitive or *-ing*; nouns + preposition and *-ing*; phrasal verbs

A Context listening

1 **You are going to hear Iris and Doug talking about some of the advantages of a job at SmartThink. What do you think some of those benefits might be? Can you think of some other perks they might talk about?**

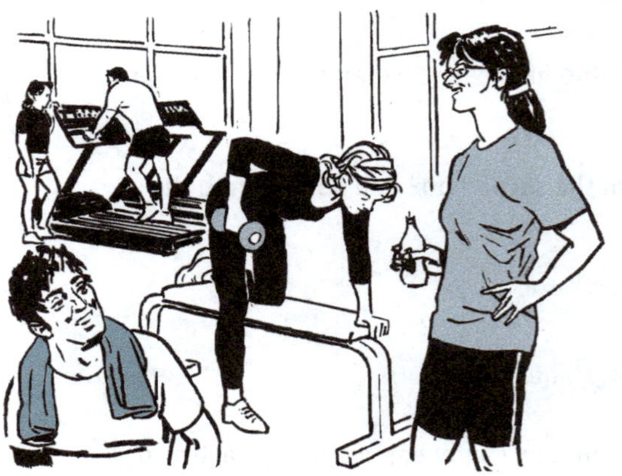

1 ______________________

2 ______________________

3 ______________________

4 ______________________

5 Other benefits or perks ______________________

2 **Listen and check if you were right.**

3 **Read the definitions 1–5. They all refer to phrasal verbs that Iris and Doug use in their conversation. Listen again and complete the phrasal verbs. Stop the recording when you need to.**

1 *request* = ____ask____ for

2 *complete* = ________ in

3 *get information* = ________ out

4 *introduced* = ________ in

5 *keep* = ________ on to

4 **You heard the following benefits mentioned in the conversation. Match the person's need with a benefit or perk.**

1 Mahmood has to drive a lot doing company business.

2 Kaisu wants some recognition for her inventive ideas.

3 Sam has been in the same job for over 10 years.

4 Johannes wants to work on the computer from his home.

5 Tomo needs to arrive and leave at unusual times.

a incentives

b company car

c flexible working hours

d promotion

e telecommuting

B Grammar

1 Adjectives + *to* infinitive or *-ing*

When a verb follows an adjective, we use the *to* infinitive or the *-ing* form. We usually use the *to* infinitive after these adjectives:

boring	common	dangerous	difficult	easy	good
hard	pleased	prepared	ready	strange	usual

*I'm not **prepared to make** a final decision at this stage.*
*Are you **pleased to hear** about the new perks the company is offering?*

We usually use a preposition and the *-ing* form after these adjectives:

afraid of	capable of	intent on	interested in
successful in	tired of		

*Sara has shown that she is **capable of leading** a successful team.*
*They aren't **interested in expanding** into that area.*

2 Nouns + preposition and *-ing*

We use the *-ing* form after most nouns + prepositions. Some common nouns + prepositions are:

choice of	excuse for	intention of
method of / for	possibility of	reason for

*We have the **choice of driving** to the convention or **taking** a company bus.*
*The **possibility of working** from home two days a week is a great advantage.*

3 Phrasal verbs

Phrasal verbs consist of two parts: the verb and the particle(s). Some phrasal verbs have one particle and some have two. Particles can either be adverbs (*out*, *up*, etc.) or prepositions (*on, off,* etc.).

verb + adverb	get up, look out, back down
verb + preposition	get at, go on, turn over
verb + adverb + preposition	go up against, get away with, run out of

We can sometimes understand the meaning of the phrasal verb from the meaning of its individual parts.
*If you are in favor of the plan, please **put up** your hands.* (= Raise your hand into the air.)
*He **pulled down** his hat to protect his eyes from the bright sun.* (= lowered his hat)

However, usually the meaning of a phrasal verb is different from the meaning of its individual parts.
*You don't have to **knock** yourself **out** trying to get here on time.* (= try exceptionally hard)
*That design **stands out** as the best in my opinion.* (= is noticeably the best)

Sometimes one phrasal verb has several meanings.
*I'll **pick** you **up** outside of the office building.* (collect or go and get someone)
*I had to **pick up** the pieces of the cup that I broke.* (lift something with your hands)
*Business has really **picked up** this quarter.* (increase)
*I **picked up** a bit of Spanish while I was living in Mexico.* (learn)
*Can you **pick up** some office supplies during your lunch break?* (go and buy)

Phrasal verbs without an object
We can use some phrasal verbs that consist of verb + adverb without an object.
*I will **set out** early tomorrow morning.*

Phrasal verbs with an object
We use an object with some phrasal verbs that consist of a verb + adverb, and all verbs that consist of a verb + preposition or have two particles.
*I just **gave in** my notice.* (*my notice* = object)
*Can you **go over** these documents with me?* (*these documents* = object)
*We have **run out** of printer cartridges.* (*printer cartridges* = object)

Some verbs have different meanings with and without an object.
*I **ran off** some extra photocopies of the report.* (= I made copies.)
*He **ran off** immediately after the meeting.* (= He left quickly.)

Separable phrasal verbs
When we use phrasal verbs that consist of verb + adverb, we can put the object between the two parts of the verb.
*I just **gave** my notice **in**.* (or *I just **gave in** my notice.*)
*Is he going to **turn** the job **down**?* (or *Is he going to **turn down** the job?*)

When the object is a pronoun (*it*, *him*, *her*, etc.), we must put the pronoun between the two parts of the phrasal verb.
*I just **gave** it **in**.* (**not** ~~*I just gave in it.*~~)
*Is he going to **turn** it **down**?* (**not** ~~*Is he going to turn down it?*~~)

Inseparable phrasal verbs
When we use phrasal verbs that consist of verb + preposition or that have two particles, we can not put the object between the two parts of the verb.
*I started **looking for** a new employer.* (**not** ~~*I started looking a new employer for.*~~)
*Can we **back out of** that deal?* (**not** ~~*Can we back out that deal of?*~~)

We can use many particles as adverbs or prepositions, so you might need to look them up in a dictionary to check how you can use them.
*The taxi arrived and they **got in** it.* (*in* = preposition)
*She gave me a form and asked me to **fill** it **in**.* (*in* = adverb)

Common phrasal verbs
► See Appendix 1 for common phrasal verbs that are used in the TOEIC test.

C Grammar exercises

1 Fill in the blank with a verb in the infinitive or preposition + -*ing* form.

1 I am anxious ___to meet___ (*meet*) with you and discuss your ideas.
2 The new CEO is intent __________ (*make*) more money from our online business.
3 It is hard __________ (*find*) the right tires for this classic car.
4 It's common __________ (*see*) office workers taking a break in this park on sunny days.
5 We are interested __________ (*test*) this new design of air bags.
6 Chelsea is pleased __________ (*be*) one of the team members.
7 It would be good __________ (*get*) out of the city this weekend.
8 We are not afraid __________ (*lose*) business in the recession.

2 Replace each of the underlined nouns with a pronoun and rewrite the sentences with the pronoun in the correct place.

1 I brought up <u>the topic</u> at the meeting. I brought ___it up at the meeting.___
2 You can't back out of <u>the contract</u>. You can't __________
3 We'll have to cut <u>the salaries</u> back. We'll have to __________
4 I would have backed up <u>Elizabeth</u>. I would have __________
5 We have to put up with <u>noisy machines</u>. We have to __________
6 I want to get out of <u>the field of information technology</u>. I want to __________
7 Can we throw out <u>this agenda item</u>? Can we __________
8 He really doesn't get along with <u>many of his colleagues</u>. He really doesn't __________
9 They've called off <u>the meeting</u>. They've __________
10 She turned down <u>the offer</u>. She __________

3 Find and correct the mistakes in the underlined phrasal verbs.

Home

FAQs

Contact Us

When your company is **1** cutting back on spending on, it can be difficult to **2** ask a raise for. But have you considered negotiating for some extra perks? The best way to start is **3** to drawing up a list of the things that you want, which might include some extra time off, flexible working hours, or perhaps some education to help your career. Perhaps you really don't want to **4** deal working with so many hours in a week because you need to **5** catch up things with in your home life. If this is the case, you might try **6** for asking unpaid leave either for a few hours a week or perhaps for an extended period. Also remember that many companies are interested in encouraging "green" ideas at work. So you could perhaps negotiate for a bonus by **7** give up your parking space. Think carefully about what is important to you before you **8** up bring this with your supervisor. Of course, you may be **9** down turned, but it is certainly worth a try.

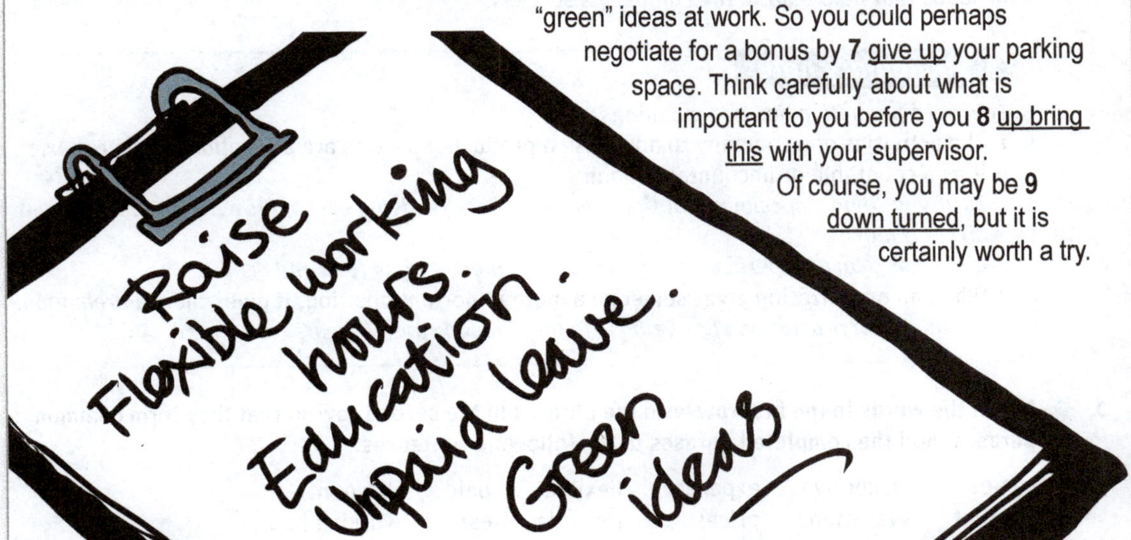

4 Respond to these questions and statements with your own ideas. Use complete sentences.

1 Do you get along with your supervisor? *Yes, I get along with her. She's very nice.*

2 I bet you are looking forward to your next vacation. ______

3 Do you have to put up with any annoying noises at work? ______

4 Will you let me pay for your lunch? ______

5 Have you ever run out of motivation? ______

6 When can you bring back my books? ______

7 I hope you didn't turn down that job. ______

8 Don't back out of that agreement you made. ______

9 Would you like to go through that explanation again? ______

10 How long will it take you to catch up with your work? ______

D Vocabulary

Key Vocabulary

Read this paragraph about the advantages a company can offer employees and check your understanding of the words in bold.

When **recruiting**, most companies offer prospective employees a package of benefits that may include **paid vacations, retirement plans, bonuses, leaves of absence,** and regular **promotions** as well as a basic salary and **health insurance**. In order to **attract**, **retain,** and **motivate** good workers, many companies also offer a variety of extra **benefits**, known as **perks**. Common examples include **discount prices** for certain products, a **company car**, or an **expense account** for business trips. In addition to these benefits, companies may offer the employees the opportunity to take advantage of **flexible working hours**, **subsidized gym facilities**, **telecommuting,** and **training programs**. An increasingly popular way some companies motivate their employees is with **incentive rewards** for creativity or good performance. These are earned for ideas that help lead to the company's success.

Vocabulary note

The word *promotion* has two meanings.

1 The activities of a company to advertise a product or service are *promotion(s)*. We can use it as a countable or uncountable noun.
Thrifty is doing a special ***promotion*** *this week. They're giving customers a 20 percent discount on car rentals.*
Chloe has a lot of experience in ***promotion*** *and marketing of food and drink.*

2 When an organization gives someone a more important position, it gives them a *promotion*.
I finally got a ***promotion*** *after being with the company for five years.*

1 Match the words in the first row with the phrases in the second row so that they form common phrases. Add the completed phrases to the following sentences.

~~company~~	incentive	expense	flexible	paid	discount
account	vacations	prices	rewards	~~car~~	working hours

1 We should provide our sales personnel with a ___company car___ because they have to do a lot of traveling.

2 Is it OK to put the meal costs of visitors to the company on my ________________ ?

3 One of the best things about working for this chocolate company is that you get great ________________ on the products!

4 Our company is thinking of introducing a system of ________________ for employees who come up with new ideas.

5 I prefer to choose my times for being in the office so I like the new ________________ .

6 In my job I get two weeks of ________________ but I haven't taken any yet this year.

2 **Complete the table with the correct form of the word. Add the correct form to the blanks in the following conversation.**

Noun	Verb	Adjective
attraction	________	________
________	________	beneficial
________	motivate	________
________	train	________
recruitment	________	________

1 Jim: So, Helen, how do you suggest we ___recruit___ highly competent candidates?

2 Helen: Well, Jim, salary is important of course, but I think our positions would be more ________ if we offered better perks.

3 Jim: I totally agree. And if we offer good perks, then people will also be ________ enough to stay with us.

4 Helen: Exactly. So we need to think about offering more ________ than our competitors. Have you got any suggestions?

5 Jim: How about introducing some practical ________ programs?

3 **Match the beginnings of the sentences (1–8) with their endings (a–h).**

1 There was no chance of a promotion in my job so
2 I also asked for a personal leave of absence and
3 I don't think a company can retain good employees
4 Anyway, I decided to move to a company that
5 In my new job I telecommute and so
6 I also have been given a special bonus
7 My new job is really challenging so now
8 I like to exercise regularly so I'm really happy about

a has better perks than my old one.
b I didn't feel very motivated.
c for coming up with a creative idea.
d I am really motivated to work.
e unless it offers some perks.
f my request was turned down.
g the new subsidized gym facilities
h most days I don't have to go to the office.

4 **Match the words in the first box with a word in the second box and put them into the correct column.**

~~discount~~ subsidized paid
retirement health training

insurance plans ~~prices~~ programs
vacations gym facilities

Benefits package	Perks
________	discount prices
________	________
________	________
________	________

Practice test 5

Reading

Part 5: Incomplete Sentences

Directions: In each sentence below, a word or phrase is missing. Select the best answer from the four choices to complete the sentence. Mark (A), (B), (C), or (D).

1 I was planning to go to the conference but I ________ my trip because of the air traffic controllers' strike.
(A) cancel
(B) canceled
(C) was canceling
(D) were canceling

2 Do you have ________ knowledge of new software developments?
(A) many
(B) either
(C) same
(D) any

3 We require someone who is ________ the challenge.
(A) up to
(B) over
(C above
(D) higher than

4 We need to be prepared ________ the safety inspectors will arrive without warning.
(A) although
(B) so that
(C) because
(D) then

5 You need to find the best marketing strategies to keep your product ________ .
(A) attract
(B) attraction
(C) attractive
(D) attractively

6 Have you ________ over the new insurance policy?
(A) looked
(B) watched
(C) seen
(D) observed

7 Mr. James ________ his company credit card to pay for all his business expenses.
(A) uses
(B) useful
(C) were using
(D) usefulness

8 Let's move on to the next ________ on the agenda.
(A) motion
(B) summarize
(C) item
(D) ballot

9 I apologize for being ________ from yesterday's meeting.
(A) absence
(B) absent
(C) to absent
(D) absenting

10 Mr. Jennings has a clear strategy and a deep ________ of what his customers want.
(A) avoidance
(B) sympathy
(C) relationship
(D) understanding

Part 6: Text Completion

Directions: Read the text below. Select the best word or phrase to complete the sentences. Mark (A), (B), (C), or (D).

Question **11–13** refer to the following memo.

To: All personnel
From: Jade Perkins (Human Resources)
Subject: New company initiative

I am pleased to bring to your notice a new company initiative that gives loyal employees the possibility **11** ________ earning paid winter vacations.
(A) of (B) for (C) to (D) in

This company perk will give employees who have been with us for at least five years the
12 ________
(A) risk (B) odds (C) luck (D) chance

to be rewarded with a company-paid three-day vacation at a variety of specified locations. I'm sure you will be interested in this initiative. If you would like to find out more details of the plan, please see the attached notice. We will also **13** ________ off some

(A) to run (B) running (C) ran (D) run

brochures giving full details. They will be distributed around the offices during next week.

Part 7: Reading Comprehension

Directions: In this section, you will read documents such as advertisements, email correspondence, newspaper articles, and letters. Select the best answer. Mark (A), (B), (C), or (D).

Questions **14–15** refer to the following newspaper article.

London —Copper prices jumped on the London Metal Exchange (LME) yesterday, after major copper producer Valumetal said it was cutting back production by 75,000 tons per year at their mines, because of slow demand.

The latest production cut follows an initial 150,000 tons per year cut made by Valumetal in December of last year. "This is good news for the market. It is timed to get maximum market attention," said analyst Richard Fuller of brokers A Z Securities. On the LME, the world's largest metals market, the response led to an immediate leap in price to $1,705 a ton, the highest since March. "We are forecasting that the copper market will move into a metal deficit of 200,000 tons next year as demand recovers due to improvements in the global economy. We remain optimistic about the copper market outlook over the next few years," added Fuller.

14 Which company mines copper?

(A) LME
(B) Valumetal
(C) Fuller
(D) AZ Securities

15 What is the current dollar value of copper per ton?

(A) 75,000
(B) 150,000
(C) 1,705
(D) 200,000

Questions **16–18** refer to the following promotional material.

Online Product Solutions

We are a web-based company that focuses on bringing new products to market using internet-based resources to finance the development and marketing of your great ideas. Getting a new idea from development to the point of sale is very expensive because of the cost of making prototypes, tooling, and marketing and distribution. Because of this, many inventors whose ideas have great potential never see these ideas get to the market. Quite simply, manufacturers do not want to spend money on development.

At Online Product Solutions we use the huge potential of the Internet, which allows us to distribute costs over a large number of people. We do this by pre-selling the production costs. If the product is never manufactured, you, the consumer, get your money back. If the product is made and sells, you get a percentage share of the profits along with the original inventor. For a more detailed account of how this arrangement works and for FAQs, click on the links at the right of the web page.

16 Why do many good ideas NOT get turned into products?

(A) Not enough people think they are good ideas.
(B) It is too expensive to distribute them.
(C) The development process costs too much.
(D) Prototypes do not have enough potential.

17 How does Online Product Solutions function?

(A) People want what they manufacture.
(B) Many users share the development costs.
(C) Inventors risk their own money.
(D) Inventors share the profits.

18 How can ordinary consumers benefit from this scheme?
(A) They can sell their inventions to the largest company.
(B) They get products for a reduced cost.
(C) They share in the profits of marketed products.
(D) They do not need to pay for the products.

Questions **19–20** refer to the following memo.

From: Bill Dickens (Organizing Committee of Innovations Week)
To: All employees of Gerald Greenway Science Park
Subject: Presentations during Innovations Week
Date: April 6th

This is to remind all employees of the following presentations scheduled as part of our Innovations Week at Gerald Greenway Science Park (April 10th –14th).

We hope you will be able to attend these presentations, which will be given by recognized researchers.

Monday, April 11th, 4:00 P.M.–6:00 P.M. Presentation on "Latest research into flexible screen technology" by Dr. Paulette Kumar (*ScreenTech Industries of Greenway Science Park*) at the ground floor Lecture Hall.

Tuesday, April 12th, 4:00 P.M.–6:00 P.M. Presentation on "Plastic electronics: research that will revolutionize our lives" by Prof. Paul McLachlan and Dr. Brian Han (*Both of Plastic Solutions, Inc.*) at the Nelson Auditorium.

19 What is the purpose of the memo?
(A) to introduce employees to Dr. Brian Han
(B) to send employees a reminder of the upcoming presentation
(C) to organize a schedule for the Innovation week
(D) to present the innovations to employees of Gerald Greenway

20 Which of the following people is NOT mentioned as a well-known researcher?
(A) Gerald Greenway
(B) Paulette Kumar
(C) Brian Han
(D) Paul McLachlan

Questions **21–23** refer to the following newspaper story.

With stocks recovering and company profitability rising, Zsmart has designed a new employee retirement benefits package, according to the company's Human Resources office. A Zsmart spokesperson refused to discuss details with the newspaper since employee benefit details are confidential information. But the company issued a statement saying that it is working hard "to draw up a competitive benefits package, including a company savings plan that will help attract and retain the best talent." Company employees are looking forward to the new contract, which will be issued in the coming months.

21 Why won't Zsmart allow the newspaper to have details of the benefit package?
(A) The package is not ready yet.
(B) The company has no savings plan.
(C) The information is confidential.
(D) They cannot keep good employees.

22 Why is Zsmart able to draw up a new benefits package?
(A) They are a large company.
(B) The company is doing well financially.
(C) Fewer employees are retiring.
(D) Employees are working very hard.

23 What is the stated purpose of the new benefits package?
(A) To keep good workers with the company
(B) To issue new guidelines for workers
(C) To prevent workers from retiring early
(D) To make sure information is kept secret

Questions **24–26** refer to the following notice.

HOLIDAY BEACH HOTEL

announces

MALAYSIAN FOOD AND CULTURAL WEEK

May 12–22, at the **Holiday Beach Hotel**

We promise to give you a spectacular day out. Taste our authentic Malaysian cuisine and enjoy our magnificent live cultural show at the **Tropical Sunset** restaurant on the second floor. We look forward to serving you.

Lunch: from 12 noon to 3:00 P.M.
Dinner: from 7:30 P.M. to 11:00 P.M.
Show Time: Twice daily at 2:00 P.M. and 9:00 P.M.

Tickets: adult 4.5 Dinars, children below 6 free. Children between 6 and 12 years old get 50 percent discount.

In addition, visit our consumer fair at **Salalah Ballroom** on Sunday, May 12th, from 10:00 A.M. to 2:00 P.M. (open to the general public). From 5:00 P.M. to 8:00 P.M. open to **Travel Agents**, **Media** personnel, and **Airline** representatives only.

For further information, don't delay calling Said al Alawi, at (555) 513–1922.

24 What is the main purpose of the notice?
(A) To advertise a cultural event
(B) To sell airline tickets
(C) To display Malaysian food
(D) To familiarize representatives with prices

25 Who is invited to the Holiday Beach Hotel?
(A) Employees of airlines
(B) The general public
(C) Families with children only
(D) Hotel guests only

26 Where is this notice probably posted?
(A) In government offices
(B) In college dormitories
(C) In a newspaper ad section
(D) In city restaurants

Questions **27–31** refer to the following agenda and report.

Everywhere Express, Inc
Meeting of Supervisors
Saturday, May 14th 10:00 A.M.
Venue: Boardroom

AGENDA

Presentation of new company logo
James Daniels of Logosmart, Ltd.

New packaging regulations
Teresa Sidcup

Preparation for Hong Kong Trade Show
Emile Grass

The redecoration of the boardroom
Brainstorming session

To: Dieter Hansberger
From : Celia Chan
Subject: Report of supervisors' meeting

In general, the meeting went well and progress was made in two areas. The presentation by James Daniels was well received. We agreed to submit a separate report giving our recommendations before a final choice is made. Next, Teresa invited us to become acquainted with packaging regulations, especially in relation to airline security. She also showed us samples of packaging innovations that may contribute to package strength. She plans to repeat this "show-and-tell" for other interested staff at next week's lunch-hour discussion.

Unfortunately, due to the length of the discussions involving the first two agenda items, we did not finish discussing the trade show nor get to the final item. This has been moved to the first agenda item at next month's meeting (on the 16th), which will be held in the Conference Annex.

27 In which room was the meeting held?
(A) The Boardroom
(B) The Annex
(C) The Supervisor's Office
(D) The Packaging Room

28 Which agenda item was NOT discussed at the meeting?
(A) Packaging regulations
(B) Boardroom redecoration
(C) The Hong Kong Trade Show
(D) The new company logo

29 Who was absent from the meeting?
(A) James Daniels
(B) Celia Chan
(C) Dieter Hansberger
(D) Emile Grass

30 What samples will Teresa Sidcup show next week?
(A) Airline regulations
(B) Security systems
(C) Packaging innovations
(D) Reports of recommendations

31 What is true about the new company logo?
(A) It has been recommended to the committee.
(B) It has not been decided on yet.
(C) It will be ready for the trade show.
(D) It will be presented at the meeting.

Writing

Questions 1–5: Write a sentence based on a picture

Directions: In this section, you will be given two words or phrases and a photograph. You will be asked to write one sentence about the photograph, using the two given words or phrases. You can change the forms of the words and use them in any order. Your sentence will be scored on grammar and how relevant the sentence is to the photograph. You will have 8 minutes for this part.

Question 1:

accident / damage

Question 2:

office / but

Question 3:

banana / unless

Question 4:

auction / buy

Questions 6–7: Respond to a wrtitten request

Directions: In this section, you will write a response to an email. Your response will be scored on vocabulary, organization, and the quality and variety of your sentences. You will have 10 minutes to read and respond to each email.

Directions: Read the email. In your email, ask TWO questions and make ONE request.

Delete Reply Reply All Forward Print

From: Jones and Associates
To: Judy McAnsh
Subject: Sunderland National Insurance
Sent: October 11, 8:09 A.M.

Dear Ms. McAnsh:
In past correspondence you indicated that you wanted to have your life insurance policy run its course without any extra payments. In June of this year your policy will cease to exist. If that is still your intention, nothing needs to be done. However, if your situation has changed and you now wish to continue your policy, the monthly payments will need to be increased. You should contact our office so that we can calculate these new payments.

Please respond to this email and confirm that you wish to keep the policy longer or that you wish to discontinue it.

Thank you.

Douglas K. Jonson
555-343-9876

Question 8: Write an opinion essay

Directions: In this question, you will write an essay about a given issue. You will be asked to state your opinion and explain and support the opinion. A successful essay will usually contain a minimum of 300 words. Your essay will be scored on grammar, vocabulary, organization, and whether your opinion is supported with reasons and examples. You will have 30 minutes to complete your essay.

Essay question:
Do you think it is important to buy insurance? Use specific reasons and examples to explain your answer.

Grammar Focus Task

Match the two parts to complete the sentences from the test.

1 If the product is made and sells, ________
2 Company employees are looking forward to the new contract, ________
3 We need to be prepared because ________
4 I was planning ________
5 Mr. James uses his company credit card to pay ________

a for all his business expenses.
b the safety inspectors will arrive without warning.
c to go to the conference.
d which will be issued in the coming months.
e you get a percentage of the profits.

Vocabulary Focus Task

Underline the word that was used in the test.

1 Have you looked over the new *insurance / insure / insured / insuring* policy?
2 Many *inventions / inventors / invent / invented* whose ideas have great potential never see these ideas get to the market.
3 Visit our *consumer / consume / consumption / consuming* fair at Salalah Ballroom.
4 Some brochures giving full details will be *distribution / distribute / distributing / distributed* around the offices.
5 A company savings plan will help *attraction / attract / attractive / attractively* and retain the best talent.

Answer Key

Unit 1

A Context listening

1/2

1 the man, Kevin Bates
2 the woman, Laila Joseph
3 secretary

3

2 impressive 3 impressed 4 enthusiastic
5 applied 6 qualifications 7 Qualified
8 enthusiasm

4

a The main part of the word is the same for each pair, but the ending is different.
b 2 adjective 3 verb 4 adjective
6 noun 7 adjective 8 noun

5

2 d 3 b 4 a

C Grammar exercises

1

nouns: application, employment, interview
verbs: interview, experienced, qualify, require
adjectives: beneficial, experienced, manageable, successful
adverbs: suitably, enthusiastically, impressively

2

noun	verb	adjective	adverb
benefit	benefit	beneficial	
employment employee employer	employ	employed employing	
enthusiasm		enthusiastic	enthusiastically
experience	experience	experienced	
impression	impress	impressive impressed	impressively
interview interviewee interviewer	interview	interviewed interviewing	
manager management	manage	manageable managerial	manageably
qualification	qualify	qualified qualifying	
requirement	require	required	
success	succeed	successful	successfully
	suit	suitable	suitably

3

2 economically 3 suitable 4 officially
5 polite 6 successfully

4

2 excited 3 challenging 4 encouraging
5 amazed 6 interesting 7 annoyed

5

2 What motivated you to apply for this position?
3 When did you qualify to become an accountant?
4 What challenges you?
5 What have you accomplished in your career so far?

6 Tell a friend or teacher your answers.

2 I was successful at ... I succeeded in ...
3 I am planning ...
4 As an employee, I would be ... Employment here would ...
5 My motivation in a job ... . I find ... very motivating. I am motivated by ...

D Vocabulary

1

2 hire 3 candidates 4 vacancies
5 employment 6 temporary 7 reject

2

2 qualifications 3 résumé 4 references
5 interview 6 impress 7 offering 8 candidate

3

2 a 3 b 4 e 5 c

Unit 2

A Context listening

2

1 Emma is in her office / at work.
2 John is in his hotel room / at a conference.
3 John wants Emma to send him a copy of a report and give him figures from an account.

3

1 report 2 fax, attachment 3 file, folder

4

2 John wants a copy of the Newhaven report.
3 The fax machine guarantee covers the repair costs.
4 Emma is sending her copy as an attachment to an email.
5 John needs a printer.
6 Emma is looking in the folder for the file.

5

1 1
2 3
3 4 and 6
4 Present simple
5 Present continuous
6 No. They are in the present simple tense, but they are not regular actions or general truths. (See B4, State verbs.)

C Grammar exercises

1

2 is taking off 3 isn't working
4 Do you finish 5 are currently taking

2

1 a (*uses* = regular event, *travels* = regular event)
2 b (*is preparing* = at the time of speaking, *wants* = state verb)
3 a (*Does ... input* = regular event, *is* = permanent situation)
4 b (*am locking* = at the time of speaking, *have* = state verb)
5 a (*clears* = regular event, *goes* = regular event)

3

1 looks 2 am not having; have 3 enjoys; is enjoying
4 am thinking; don't think 5 see; am seeing

4 Sample answers

2 Don't smoke in this area.
3 Ride on the bike route. Don't ride on the highway.
4 Don't trespass. Don't climb over the fence.
5 Watch for animals crossing the road.
6 Be careful on the slippery stairs.
7 Don't go the wrong way down this street. Follow the arrow.

5 Sample answers

2 I always have a cup of hot chocolate before bedtime.
3 At this moment I am shopping online.
4 For most holidays I drive home to my parents' house.
5 Every morning I see what the weather is like.
6 I am currently thinking about applying for an office job.
7 This week I am working overtime because of a promotional sale at work.

D Vocabulary

1

2 photocopy 3 file 4 report 5 folder 6 memo
7 attachment 8 correspondence 9 fax

2

2 copy 3 folder 4 in-box 5 report 6 inventory

3

2 copies 3 confidential 4 hard copy 5 files

Unit 3

A Context listening

1/2

1 at the airport/ in front of airport arrivals
2 Bill 3 Jenny

3

2 pulled, set off 3 am used to setting off
4 was causing 5 misplaced 6 was working
7 did, turn up 8 were waiting

4

1 2, 5, and 7 2 4, 6, and 8 3 1 4 3
5 2, 5, and 7 6 4, 6, and 8

5

1 cabin crew
2 boarding gate, baggage pick-up, check-in, lost luggage counter
3 boarding pass, carousel

C Grammar exercises

1 a Sample answers

2 met clients and did the accounts
3 didn't have lunch at noon
4 I finished the PPM report
5 What did you do in the evening?
6 I met Paula and Diane and we went out to eat at the Chez Jean Paul restaurant.

b

2 was talking with clients
3 was finishing the PPM reports
4 wasn't driving home
5 was talking with Paula and Diane while we were waiting for a taxi

2

2 noticed 3 was running 4 tripped 5 dropped
6 fell 7 was picking up 8 saw 9 was reaching
10 heard 11 went 12 was talking 13 left
14 arranged 15 were going 16 met 17 married

3 Sample answers

2 I was walking along the river bank when I fell and hurt my foot.
3 I was talking on my cell phone and didn't see the red light.
4 While I was reading the newspaper, I heard a strange noise behind me.

4

2 used to find 3 used to enjoy
4 am used to staying 5 didn't use to pay

5 Sample answers

2 I used to swim every day at 6 a.m..
3 I used to play football before I got my job.
4 I used to work in a car rental office.
6 I am used to going to sleep around midnight.
7 I am used to commuting daily.
8 I am used to working long hours.

D Vocabulary

1

2 delayed 3 time zones 4 check-in 5 carousel
6 aisle 7 cabin crew 8 baggage

2 a

2 e 3 a 4 c 5 d

b

terminal, flights, delays, passengers

3

2 luggage 3 boarding 4 flight 5 terminal

Unit 4

A Context listening

1/2

1 Mary has been to / in New York City
Mary has been at the New York City book fair.
2 She has been .... traveling / driving / putting signs in the window / working on the accounts.
3 Mary has forgotten to change her watch.

3

1 T 2 F 3 F 4 T

4

1 3 2 1 3 2, 4

5

2 sale 3 display 4 cash register
5 counter 6 order

C Grammar exercises

1

2 has just called 3 has received
4 have invited 5 have reserved
6 have been attending 7 has been expanding

2 Sample answers

2 She has unpacked a shipment. She has been cleaning up the delivery room.
3 She has made a sale. She has been replacing old stock.
4 She has just finished a call. She has been talking to her supplier.
5 People have been coming into the store. They have come because of the sale.
6 A customer has just made a large purchase. She has been making a lot of sales all day.

3

2 has become (an action that happened at a time that is not specified)
3 has been relying (an action that began in the past and continues to the present)
4 have just placed (the focus is on a completed activity)
5 have finished (the focus is on a completed activity)
6 has brought (the focus is on a completed activity)
7 has always been (an action that happened at a time that is not specified)
8 has been waiting (an action that began in the past and continues to the present)
9 has been sitting (the focus is on an ongoing activity)
10 have been (an action that began in the past and continues to the present)
11 has been working (an action that began in the past and continues to the present)

4

2 for 3 since 4 for 5 since

D Vocabulary

1

2 Purchases 3 A cash register 4 A gift certificate
5 A chain 6 A coupon 7 A retail store
8 A sales clerk

2

2 store, order 3 stocks, display
4 store, purchase 5 purchase, order

3

2 counter 3 labels 4 order
5 coupon 6 merchandise 7 price tag

Unit 5

A Context listening

1/2

Inez will fly to her destination and take a taxi from the airport. She will not take a bus. She will not stay at a guesthouse, but she may not have a room in a hotel. The weather will not be warm. It will snow.

3

2 is going to be closed 3 will, take 4 are sending

4

1 3 future *will* 2 1 present simple
3 2 future *going to* 4 4 present continuous

5

1 guesthouse, hotel **2** book, reserve
3 amenities, complimentary breakfast

C Grammar exercises

1

2 I'm attending a birthday lunch for our assistant manager.
3 I'm visiting our local retail outlets.
4 I'm making arrangements for the trade fair.
5 I'm having lunch with Wing Chou, the manager of King Kitchen Utensils.
6 I'm flying to Helsinki for the trade fair.

2

2 Will you make **3** 'll be
4 will I do/should I do/do I do **5** finish
6 'll let **7** 'll give/give **8** do
9 'll come **10** starts **11** leaves/will leave
12 stay/will stay

3

2 I'll get **3** Are you going to attend
4 I'm going to go **5** We're going to get
6 will come **7** are you going to go/will you go
8 are going to / will pick **9** they'll have
10 Will you call

D Vocabulary

1

2 accommodations, guesthouse
3 transportation, destination **4** itinerary, conferences
5 registered, facilities **6** booked/vacancy

2

2 receptionist **3** cancel **4** exhibition
5 registration

3

2 d **3** b **4** a

Practice test 1

Listening

1 C	**6** C	**11** D	**16** C
2 D	**7** A	**12** A	**17** A
3 B	**8** B	**13** D	**18** B
4 B	**9** C	**14** B	**19** D
5 B	**10** C	**15** A	**20** A

Reading

Part 5

1 D	**4** C	**7** B	**9** C
2 B	**5** B	**8** A	**10** A
3 A	**6** B		

Part 6

11 C **12** B **13** D

Part 7

14 A	**17** C	**20** A	**23** B
15 B	**18** C	**21** C	
16 D	**19** B	**22** A	

Grammar Focus Task

1 participated
2 working
3 bought
4 has depended
5 will be opening

Vocabulary Focus Task

1 interview
2 file
3 flight
4 chain
5 complimentary

Unit 6

A Context listening

1/2

1 Her cell phone was broken. **2** No, it wasn't.

3

1 At the customer service desk in a store
2 No, she didn't.
3 To get her cell phone fixed or replaced
4 Yes, she did.
5 No, she isn't.
6 Yes, she can.

4

1 2, 4, 5, and 6
2 1 and 3
3 In 2 and 6 the auxiliary verb (e.g., *did*) or modal *can* is before the subject. In 4 and 5 the question is a tag question (*didn't she*, *is she*) at the end of a statement.

5

complaint, guarantee, expectations, quality, reliability

C Grammar exercises

1

2 Have we had any complaints about our opening hours? / Have you had any complaints about your opening hours?
3 Should we postpone the meeting?
4 Is the sales representative coming today?
5 Did the committee decide on the new sales campaign?

2

2 I didn't 3 it could (be) 4 you did
5 I can't 6 there isn't 7 I will 8 I did

3

2 When was Carlos hired? f
3 Where can I return this suit? a
4 How long has Ms. Wong been working in the sports department? e
5 Why did Anita retire so early? b
6 What do you plan to do in Paris? d

4

2 did you 3 didn't you 4 haven't we
5 weren't they 6 can it 7 don't you
8 wasn't he 9 do they

D Vocabulary

1

2 guarantee, quality 3 committed, feedback
4 satisfaction, expectations 5 service, reliable

2

2 guarantee 3 courteous 4 complaint
5 deal with 6 trust 7 expectations 8 satisfaction
9 unreliable 10 relationships

Unit 7

A Context listening

1 Sample answers

1 Lydia wants to rent or buy an apartment.
2 Robert wants to sell his house.
3 Alex wants to lease a commercial site.

2

1 Lydia is more interested in buying an apartment but doesn't know if she can.
2 Robert will be moving in three months and wants to sell his house.
3 Alex wants to lease a commercial site with an option to buy.

3

Frank's and Lydia's questions

2 I need to know whether you are looking for a place to buy or rent.

Frank's and Robert's questions

3 Could you tell me where your residence is?
4 Can you give me an idea of how quickly you need to sell it?

Frank's and Alex's questions

5 I need to know how much renovation the owner will allow me to do.
6 Could you find out if the owner would consider a lease that gives me the option to buy the building later?

4

1 first 2 different from 3 infinitive

5

2 d 3 a 4 b

C Grammar exercises

1

2 what time/when 3 how much/what 4 if
5 who 6 what 7 how many 8 whose

2

2 when it will be available
3 if you want to accept
4 how much the electricity costs
5 how much the last tenants paid / were paying
6 if there is a good school / if a good school is
7 if the school year has started
8 if my children can start late
9 when I can sign the contract

3

2 Should I bring a coat or not?
3 Where can I get a lunch voucher?
4 Who should I include on the guest list?
5 When should I bring the files over to the main office?
6 Which color do you want me to paint the garage doors?

4 Sample answers

2 if there are stores nearby / when I can move in
3 what the monthly rent is / why the owner wants to sell
4 how much the rent is / which apartment in the building is for rent
5 where the local schools are / whose car is parked in the driveway
6 who the realtor is / how much the bills are

D Vocabulary

1

2 tenant 7 mortgage
3 landlord 8 offer
4 realtor 9 owner
5 suburb 10 commission
6 down payment

2

2 furnishings 3 rentals 4 renovation
5 owns 6 residences

3

2 tenants, landlords 3 down payment, mortgage
4 commercial spaces, residences 5 suburbs, apartment
6 lease, offer

Unit 8

A Context listening

1/2

1 Mike is talking to a bank teller about his bank account.
2 Mike is talking to the loan officer about a loan.
3 Mike is telling his wife what happened in the bank.

3

2 business loans 3 loan officer
4 borrowing 5 credit rating 6 balance

4

2 want 3 have 4 are / 're 5 are thinking 6 was
7 wanted 8 had 9 were 10 were thinking

5

1 a 2 and 4; b 3 and 5; c 1
2 a 7 and 9; b 8 and 10; c 6

6

The verbs in column A are in present tenses and the verbs in column B are in past tenses.

C Grammar exercises

1

2 had 3 was 4 covered 5 didn't cover
6 was 7 would

2

2 a 3 a 4 b 5 b 6 a 7 b

3

2 suggested 3 congratulated 4 offered
5 advised 6 thanked 7 insisted

4

2 Mimi reminded Ajay and Hae-Won not to forget to send the schedule for the trade fair to the Paris branch.
3 Mimi congratulated Linda on the previous week's/last week's promotion.
4 Mimi apologized for sending the agenda to everyone so late.
5 Mimi suggested that we / they ask Nathan what he thought of the proposal.
6 Mimi offered everyone some chocolate brownies.

5 Sample answers

2 James advised me to switch off the computer before I left.
3 I suggested that they come early to work the following day.
4 She advised me to talk quietly in the open offices.
5 I advised Mimi not to drive so fast.

D Vocabulary

1

2 deposit, loan 3 credit, balance 4 loan, cash
5 check, balance 6 cash, credit

2

2 checking 3 interest 4 borrow 5 loan
6 financial advisor 7 ATM machine 8 transfer

3

2 savings 3 debit 4 withdrawing 5 funds
6 checking 7 financial 8 accounts

Unit 9

A Context listening

1

2 Francisco 3 Cindy 4 Jack

2

2 unpleasantly 3 impatiently
4 often 5 extremely 6 conveniently

3

2 expensive 3 long 4 quiet 5 fast 6 bored

4

1 The words in 2 are adverbs. The words in 3 are adjectives.
2 actions / what the person is doing, adjectives and other adverbs
3 people, places, and things

5

2 d 3 a 4 e 5 b

C Grammar exercises

1

2 new (adj), electric (adj), soon (adv)
3 normally (adv), open (adj), late (adv)
4 early (adv), long (adj), quiet (adj)
5 expensive (adj), sometimes (adv) conveniently (adv)

2

2 quickly 3 daily 4 fast 5 accurately
6 patiently 7 late

3

2 late 3 nearly 4 barely 5 immediately
6 high 7 deeply 8 warm

4

2 a rapidly b rapid 3 a sharply b sharp
4 a gradual b gradually 5 a steep b steeply
6 a suddenly b sudden

5 Sample answer

The place I like best is the beautiful yard behind my house. I go there as often as I can, but especially when the sun is shining. After a hard day at work I really enjoy sitting in a comfortable chair in such a relaxing place, reading a good book or just looking at the colorful birds and flowers. When I feel energetic, I walk around my yard and pick up the fallen leaves and twigs. Sometimes I cut the grass if it is too long because I like to keep the yard looking nice. It's a wonderful place to be.

D Vocabulary

1

2 c **3** f **4** g **5** d **6** h **7** a **8** b

2

2 rush hour **3** road rage **4** private vehicles
5 parking spaces **6** public transportation
7 commuter passes **8** bike lanes

3

2 public transportation **3** subway
4 bike lanes **5** highways **6** traffic jams
7 carpool **8** route **9** tank **10** road rage

4

Teacher's analysis: Riitta, you have started your paragraph with a weak introductory sentence. Try to avoid "There are." You could replace this sentence with "People get to work and back home using different methods." You have immediately jumped into your preferred method of commuting and you have provided several good reasons to support this. I think it would be better to start by naming and describing the most common ways of getting to work. You could make a summary of the ways and then use a transition like the word "Personally," to change from talking about people and methods in general to your commuting specifically. Then you can continue by stating whether you enjoy commuting and then giving your supporting reasons.

Unit 10

A Context listening

1/2

A	B	C
1	2	3
2	1	2
3	3	1

3

2 True
3 False, Brochures and flyers will be handed out in shopping malls.
4 False, A jingle will be written for the radio.
5 True

4

1 a promotional campaign
2 advertisements, target audiences
3 Brochures, flyers, a promotion
4 A jingle, a TV ad **5** A slogan, publicity

5

2 a traveler's steamer **3** the industrial steamer
4 No, an iron is not as effective as a steamer.
5 Yes, they are. / Yes, steamers are better.

6

1 3
2 2 (In question 2, two costs are being compared: paying for services and buying a steamer. In question 5, two groups are being compared: a group of "steamers" and a group of "irons".)
3 *(not) as . . . as*

C Grammar exercises

1

2 the cheaper **3** the least convenient
4 the most productive **5** the more flexible
6 a shorter **7** fewer **8** The fastest

2

2 the most effectively **3** less frequently
4 more noisily **5** the hardest

3

Before I announce the award for the most innovative ad of this year, I'd just like to say that this is <u>the most difficult</u> decision the judges have ever had to make. We had to look at these ads <u>more carefully</u> than ever. The entries this year were of <u>much higher quality</u> than last year and we were all extremely impressed. But in the end, we decided that one entry was <u>more innovative</u>, not to mention <u>funnier</u> than all the others. It is the <u>most humorous</u> ad we have seen for a long time. It is also the one that <u>most clearly</u> showed the use of new technology. The ads that we awarded second and third place to were also excellent and the judges gave them only slightly <u>fewer</u> points than the winner. They were both as good as the winning ad in the quality of the acting, but in the end we thought the winning ad made <u>the greatest</u> impact because it was <u>the most original</u>, and we think the public will like it <u>the best</u>.

4

2 not as big as **3** as serious as
4 not as comfortable as **5** as up-to-date as
6 not as enthusiastic as

5 Sample answers

2 The small car uses less fuel than the big car.
3 This pair of shoes feels the most comfortable.
4 My favorite pair of shoes has the highest heels.

5 Your favorite pair of shoes is as expensive as my favorite pair.
6 The small car is not as roomy as the large car.

D Vocabulary

1

2 classified ads 3 target audience
4 air time 5 brand recognition

2

2 ad 3 commercial 4 slogan
5 target audience 6 jingle 7 promote
8 promotional campaign

3

2 budget 3 media 4 publicity 5 posters
6 flyers 7 air time 8 commercial
9 advertising agency 10 slogan

Practice test 2

Listening

1 C	11 A	21 D	31 D	41 D
2 C	12 B	22 B	32 A	42 C
3 C	13 A	23 A	33 C	43 A
4 B	14 A	24 C	34 D	44 C
5 B	15 C	25 A	35 A	45 A
6 C	16 A	26 D	36 A	46 D
7 C	17 A	27 D	37 D	47 D
8 B	18 C	28 A	38 D	
9 A	19 A	29 C	39 B	
10 C	20 D	30 A	40 C	

Writing

Sample answers

Question 1:
Although the woman has an apple on her desk, she can't eat it until she is off of the phone.
Although she is working, she is talking on the phone.
She is taking phone calls although it is her lunch break.

Question 2:
The cyclist is going to the building because he works there.
The cyclist is riding in the bicycle lane because it is dangerous to ride in the street.
Because of the weather, the cyclist is enjoying a ride to the museum.

Question 3:
She is getting money out of the bank machine.
Unfortunately, the machine is out of money.
The woman ran out of money so she stopped at the ATM.

Question 4:
City streets are always busy and have lots of advertisements.
Busy people in taxis only notice bright advertisements.
The busy streets beneath the advertisements are full of taxis.

Question 6:
Dear Mr. Kumar:
Thank you for the email. I would be interested in coming to your dealership to test drive one of your vehicles. Could you send me your opening hours? It would be ideal if you were open on Sundays, as that is the only day that I'm off work.
If you aren't, I would suggest that you consider opening on Sundays. I am most interested in a 4-wheel drive vehicle.
Would we be able to go out of town so I can see how well it handles on country roads?
I look forward to hearing from you.
James Kaiser

Question 7:
Dear Sally:
Thank you so much for the email about the 50th Anniversary reception. I'm looking forward to attending, and I plan to bring a guest. Will you be providing camping facilities for members who plan to stay overnight? Such facilities would be very much welcomed.
I would like to make a couple of requests. First, could you ask the catering company to offer a vegetarian menu as one of their meal choices? Second, I know the area surrounding the Grove Institute is large and has beautiful gardens. My guest is elderly and I was wondering if you have a wheelchair so that he can enjoy your gardens.
Charles Lake

Question 8:
Everywhere we go these days, there are lots of advertisements for all kinds of products we don't need. For example, when we turn on the television, it seems that we have to watch commercials for longer than we watch the actual programs. The same is true of the radio and the Internet. I like to listen to music on the radio, but in between my favorite songs more often than not I have to listen to annoying jingles and people who are trying to persuade me to buy bigger and better products. On the Internet I often have to close ads that pop up and prevent me from seeing or reading what I am most interested in. So I agree that it often seems like there is too much advertising. However, on the other hand, I admit that some advertising is very useful and informative. We are often made aware of new products through advertising. For example, last year my family chose their vacation destination by looking at ads in magazines. The vacation was very successful and we plan to return to that place next year. I also bought a new digital camera based on a TV ad that I watched. I have to say that I am very happy with the purchase. Also, there are a lot of informative ads that give useful information about, for example, health issues or where to go to get help with all kinds of problems. Other useful ads give us ideas on what to do with our leisure time, such as the times of movies or concerts. These kinds of ads make life easier and more enjoyable. On balance, we can't really do without advertisements. They can be an annoyance but they are an essential part of our lives. The worst that can be said about them is that they are a necessary annoyance.

Grammar Focus Task 1

1 d **2** c **3** b **4** a **5** e

Grammar Focus Task 2

1 carefully **2** successful **3** as readable as
4 worse than **5** more quickly

Vocabulary Focus Task

2 tenant **3** funds **4** advertising **5** route

Unit 11

A Context listening

1/2

1 A store that sells toys for young children
2 Their profits are falling.
3 They could include toys for older children.

3

2 might **3** couldn't **4** can't **5** can **6** mustn't

4

The meaning of the phrase in the question is the same as the meaning of the modal in the answer.

5

partner, stockholders, expand, profits

C Grammar exercises

1

2 could **3** couldn't **4** can't **5** can **6** could

2

2 may **3** can **4** might **5** must **6** could
7 could **8** may **9** may **10** can't

3

2 b **3** a **4** a **5** b

4 Sample answers

2 I might have an accident on my snowboard, but I must take that risk.
3 I must give a presentation to business executives, but I may not do a good job.
4 I may build my own house, but I might not be able to start for a few years.
5 I can't fix a computer, but I might learn how to do that someday.
6 I can climb mountains, but I must be very careful.

D Vocabulary

1

2 partnership **3** directors **4** corporation
5 Stockholders **6** expansion **7** produce

2

2 merger, merge **3** management, manage
4 expand, expansion **5** corporate, corporation
6 restructuring, restructured

3

It has been a very busy year. As you know, a few years ago we merged with a soft drinks company and the whole business has been restructured. When that happened, all employees were given the opportunity to buy shares in the company, so I became a stockholder. Some employees sold their shares, but I kept mine. The directors have made good decisions and the company has been making good profits despite very high overhead. So, I have received some nice dividends. Now it seems that management is planning to make a takeover bid for another company.

Unit 12

A Context listening

1/2

1 Alex wants to know if he gets vacation time and how much time he gets.
2 He wants to know about sick leave.
3 He asks about what happens if he gets fired.
4 He asks how much time he must give before he quits.

3

2 must give **3** should let **4** don't need to tell
5 have to tell **6** don't have to give
7 mustn't assume **8** had / 'd better go

4

strong obligation or necessity: must, have to, mustn't
advice or suggestions: should, had better
no obligation or necessity: don't need to, don't have to

5

2 f **3** e **4** a **5** c **6** b

C Grammar exercises

1

2 b must **3** g won't **4** a should **5** h shouldn't
6 c should **7** d must **8** f mustn't

2

2 don't have to **3** mustn't **4** mustn't
5 don't have to **6** don't have to **7** mustn't

3

2 should calm **3** should have listened
4 should have kept **5** must have overheard
6 should apologize **7** must have worked
8 had better not

4 Sample answers

2 You should sign the contract. You had better read the terms and conditions.
3 He had better see the doctor. He needs to get a doctor's note.
4 You must obey the police officer. You mustn't run a red light.

D Vocabulary

1

2 terminate **3** conditions **4** misconduct
5 sick leave **6** per annum **7** sign

2

2 absent **3** acceptance **4** sign
5 terminate **6** entitlement

3

2 signature **3** notice **4** fired **5** vacation time
6 quit **7** sick leave **8** lay off

Unit 13

A Context listening

1/2

1 in a restaurant
2 salmon salad and water
3 today's special / the asparagus and salmon entrée with a tossed salad

3

2 may **3** can **4** would **5** May

4

1 5 **2** 1, 4 **3** 3 **4** 2

5

drink–beverage, entrée–main dish, menu–meal choices

C Grammar exercises

1

2 b **3** a **4** b **5** d **6** a **7** c

2

2 Could you speak **3** Would you like
4 Can I book **5** Would you mind
6 Let me look **7** Could I suggest

3

2 How about ~~to~~ going to ...
3 Yes, let's ~~can~~ go there.
4 Should we ~~be~~ look at the website
5 Couldn't we just ~~to~~ pass the movie theater
6 What about inviting the new ...

4

2 Will, d **3** May, a **4** What / How, e
5 can't/don't, f **6** Would, c

5 Sample answers

2 Would you mind forwarding that email please?
3 Could we sit by the window, please? Do you mind if I make a quick call?
4 Let me check the figures for you. Could I fill your glass for you?
5 Why don't you try the apple pie and ice cream? It would be better if you pay with a credit card.

D Vocabulary

1

Places to eat	Food and drinks	People	Payment
cafeteria restaurant	dinner dessert entrée	waiter hostess	bill / check tip

2

2 recommend **3** dishes **4** dessert **5** starter

3

2 menu 3 waiter 4 course 5 starter
6 dishes 7 dessert 8 cafeteria 9 buffet

Unit 14

A Context listening

1/2

1 fire escape, fire-proof doors, fire extinguisher, posters, hard hats, safety goggles
2 protection from noise

3

2 at **3** into **4** beside **5** from **6** at **7** in

4

1 1 and 6 **2** 2, 4, and 7 **3** 3 and 5

5

2 safety 3 fire 4 slippery 5 hard
6 warning 7 fire

C Grammar exercises

1

2 at **3** at **4** beside **5** at **6** on **7** in
8 by **9** from **10** out of **11** into **12** over

2

2 correct **3** on **4** correct **5** across **6** correct
7 in **8** between / around **9** at / in front of

3

2 during **3** in / at **4** on **5** onto
6 against / over / onto **7** from / out of **8** to
9 in / at **10** on **11** on 12 at **13** on

4 Sample answers

3 We put up safety notices in every room.
4 It's a good idea to have a smoke detector in your house.
5 Mary hurt her hand when she was doing some repairs at her house.
6 I attached the sign by the door warning people to step carefully.

D Vocabulary

1

2 g 3 a 4 c 5 f 6 e 7 d

2

2 emergency exit 3 hazardous material
4 ventilation system 5 hard hat 6 first aid
7 safety goggles

3

2 safety 3 extinguisher 4 ventilation
5 flammable 6 comply 7 slip

4

2 fire escape; The other words indicate the possibility of a life-threatening situation.
3 blue jeans; The other words are clothing used for protection against work hazards.
4 ventilators; The other words are possible dangers.

5

2 risks 3 ear plugs 4 hard hat
5 first aid kit 6 fatalities 7 guidelines

Unit 15

A Context listening

1/2

They are discussing the possibility of holding an auction.

3

2 understanding of 3 agreed on 4 thinking about
5 responsibility for 6 interested in

4

1 thinking about 2 interested in
3 anything about; understanding of; responsibility for

5

2 d 3 b 4 a

C Grammar exercises

1

2 anything ~~with~~ about 3 correct
4 impact ~~of~~ on 5 contact ~~on~~ with
6 change ~~for~~ in 7 correct 8 opinion ~~over~~ of

2

2 interested 3 enthusiastic 4 aware
5 annoyed 6 pleased 7 anxious

3

2 He apologized for the damaged order.
3 I have searched everywhere for the missing file.
4 I finally succeeded in opening the door.

4

2 meet with 3 impact on 4 excited about
5 agreement with 6 satisfied with
7 increase in 8 prepare for

5

2 for 3 for 4 of 5 with 6 about
7 about 8 of

D Vocabulary

1

2 a 3 f 4 b 5 c 6 e

2

2 propose a solution 3 brainstorm ideas
4 agenda items 5 motion passed

3

2 h 3 e 4 a 5 b 6 g 7 d 8 f

Practice test 3

Listening

1 B	6 C	11 D	16 A
2 A	7 B	12 B	17 C
3 C	8 B	13 A	18 D
4 A	9 B	14 B	19 B
5 A	10 C	15 C	20 B

Reading

1 C	6 D	11 D	16 B	21 C
2 B	7 D	12 C	17 D	22 C
3 C	8 C	13 A	18 D	23 C
4 D	9 C	14 A	19 C	
5 B	10 D	15 D	20 D	

Speaking

Sample answers

3

This picture shows a man working in a factory storage room. He is holding a device that he is using to tape a box closed. Three papers are on the table beside the box that the man is closing. In the middle of the picture, there is a conveyor belt, but it doesn't have anything on it. The conveyor belt stretches from where the man is working to the far side of the room. Shelves that appear to be made of metal are on both sides of the conveyor belt and also stretch to the far wall. Boxes and other materials are on the shelves.

4

I have always enjoyed eating out. Later I became interested in cooking. My friends told me how great my food was and that I should think about setting up a business. I decided I would like doing that, so I took the risk and started a restaurant.

5

I am sure my restaurant is a success because I am so enthusiastic about the work and I know there is a great demand for good food. So far I have done well because I am very careful about choosing fresh produce and offering interesting choices.

6

When I started the restaurant, I discovered that frequently customers were pleased with the freshness of our salads. In my restaurant, we do not use prepackaged or frozen vegetables. The presentation of food is very important, so we serve colorful combinations. We provide healthy meals that children like. If the kids are happy, parents bring them back frequently. We also serve senior meals for older people who often like smaller portions and enjoy a discount.

7

The convention will take place in the Main Hall of the Hurshel's Business Institute.

8

Registration costs $100 for nonmembers and $55 for Association members.

9

There are three talks in the afternoon. The first one at 1:30 is about chairs of the future and it is being given by Simone Maxwell of Maxwell Associates. At 3:00 Don Esterhazi of Esterhazi Enterprises will give a talk about current research in ergonomics and then at 4:30 Ben Fossett will give a talk about the virtual office.

10

Good afternoon, Ms. Blomqvist. Please accept our sincere apologies. I am very sorry to hear that you received some of the wrong items. I am not sure why there were mistakes in your order and I will look into it immediately. I think you received notepaper that was designed for a different company with a name that is very similar to your company's name. In fact, that same company also ordered desk lamps, so it is possible that you received their complete order, including the number and color of lamps. Please rest assured that we will deliver the correct order and pick up the mistaken order by tomorrow at the latest.

11

First of all, I would like a job that is interesting. Although a good salary would be nice, it is not as important as being able to enjoy what I do. If I enjoy my job, then it's like a hobby instead of work. I would also like a job in which I am learning a lot of new things so that I don't get bored doing the same thing over and over again. I would also find it satisfying to be valued by my employer and colleagues for the work I do. Having a job that gives me the opportunity to travel and meet new people from time to time would also be nice. A position that has all these features is my idea of an ideal job.

Grammar Focus Task

1 Suzuki San is an authority *on* marketing strategies.
2 We called for it to come *at* 7 o'clock, didn't we?
3 *Could you fax* Mr. Chang the corrected contract?
4 You *can increase* the number of customers.
5 The elevators must not *be* used during the drill.

Vocabulary Focus Task

1 first aid kit 2 expand 3 adjourn 4 sign 5 lunch

Unit 16

A Context listening

2

Harry's business involves making containers for shipping and his problems are caused by the types of products that people ship.

3

2 some 3 some 4 these 5 this
6 Both 7 neither 8 nor 9 This
10 every 11 One 12 that 13 Those

4

1 any, some 2 this, these 3 every, one, that

5

2 f 3 e 4 c 5 b 6 a

C Grammar exercises

1

2 these 3 those 4 that 5 these 6 that
7 this 8 that 9 this 10 that

2

Using store coupons is ***one*** great way to save money on ***many*** of your household purchases. Smart consumers keep their eyes open since coupons can be found *everywhere*. They can be cut out of *some* magazines, *many* local newspapers and ***other*** printed materials. ***Another*** place you can find coupons nowadays is on the internet where they can be printed out from *some* consumer websites. *Many* stores provide them, especially at the checkout counter. ***Some*** coupons have a real cash value and ***others*** can be used to get a discount on certain items in the store. *These* will usually state something like "Save two dollars on your next visit," or perhaps "Save 10 percent on ***any*** purchase over 50 Dollars." *Other* types can only be used to get a discount on particular products. It is a good idea to save ***these*** coupons for *every* time you visit a store. But read the information on ***each*** of *these* coupons carefully. Sometimes businesses limit the number of coupons you can use on any *one* visit. Also there is usually an expiration date and once the date has passed the coupon doesn't have ***any*** value.

3

2 I wanted to talk to either the manager or her assistant.
3 Becky drinks neither coffee nor tea.
4 Neither the printers nor the laptops have arrived.
5 My colleagues either eat in the staff cafeteria or bring their own sandwiches.

4

2 any, a 3 this, b 4 enough, a 5 much, b
6 every, b 7 any, a

5

2 all 3 Some 4 others 5 these
6 some 7 This 8 Every one
9 anyone 10 anywhere 11 lot

D Vocabulary

1

2 contain 3 transport 4 trade 5 exchange
6 protect 7 reinforce 8 package

2

2 declaration 3 exchange 4 package / packaging
5 protection 6 reinforcement 7 trade
8 transport / transportation

3

2 strong 3 warehouse 4 trade

4

2 commodity 3 import 4 packaging 5 weight
6 handle 7 declarations 8 shipments

Unit 17

A Context listening

1/2

1 Mr. Nesbitt 2 busy
3 call him back 4 has the wrong number

3

2 him 3 you, me 4 your 5 him, myself
6 he, me 7 He 8 us, we, them 9 them, they

4

1 you, he, we, they 2 you, him, us, them 3 your

5

2 c 3 d 4 a

C Grammar exercises

1

2 we 3 your 4 me 5 her 6 our
7 yours 8 he 9 them

2

2 we 3 You / One 4 they 5 they
6 You/We 7 You / One

3

2 myself 3 you 4 me 5 myself
6 himself 7 his 8 him 9 him 10 my

4

2 ~~It~~ There 3 correct 4 ~~there~~ it
5 correct 6 ~~There~~ It 7 ~~there~~ it

D Vocabulary

1

Eileen: Thank you. Uh, I can't get a ~~*busy*~~ (dial) *tone*
Eileen: Yes, I got it from the online *yellow* ~~*dial*~~ (pages). Oh, now it's just giving me a ~~*cell*~~ (busy) *signal*.
Jonathan: . . . If you wait, you may be able to leave a ~~*hold*~~ (voice) *message* and ...
Eileen: Either that or they would put me *on* ~~*page*~~ (hold) ...

2

2 dialed 3 line 4 extension
5 disconnected, receiver 6 transfer 7 ring

3

2 landline 3 operator 4 tone 5 text messaging

Unit 18

A Context listening

2

file, table music, furniture, advice
scissors, noise

3

1 computer, file, table, cabinet, scanner
2 water, music, furniture, advice, equipment
3 noise 4 scissors 5 news

4

1 The words in answer 3 #1
2 The words in answer 3 #2, #4, and #5
3 The words in answer 3 #2, #3, #4, and #5

5

1 file, scissors 2 computer, scanner 3 table, cabinet

C Grammar exercises

1

Always countable: calendar, desk, fax, paper clips, printer, scanner
Can be countable or uncountable: glass, noise, space, tape
Always uncountable: advice, equipment, furniture, music, news, stationery

2

2 the **3** the **4** an **5** the **6** ∅ **7** a
8 ∅ **9** an **10** a **11** an **12** a

3

2 coffee **3** water **4** scissors
5 marker pens **6** tape

4

In your last ~~an~~ email, you were complaining about *the* disorganization in your office. I hope it is OK for me to give you *advice*. I've just redesigned my office because I was spending more time looking for *files* than getting *work* done. Well, guess what? I replaced my printer, fax machine, and scanner with one of those *printers* that does everything. And it makes very little *noise*. I can hear myself think now. Why didn't I get rid of that old *equipment* a long time ago? I also got *a* printer stand with shelves that hold my paper and other *supplies*. *The* change has made a great improvement to my working life. I bet you could easily do *the* same thing.

D Vocabulary

1

2 shelf **3** stationery **4** tape **5** paper clips
6 staples **7** safe

2

2 ~~fax machine~~ Laptops and PCs are computers.
3 ~~supply room~~ Stationery and labels are supplies.
4 ~~stapler~~ Printers and copy machines are large, electronic pieces of equipment.
5 ~~scanner~~ Tape and scissors are stationery supplies.

Unit 19

A Context listening

1/2

1. There is a problem getting the computer or projector to work.
2. The markers have dried up and cannot be used.
3. They can't find any markers.
4. A woman is setting up a flip chart.
5. The presentation is a success and the man is using a marker and flip chart.

3

2 but **3** and **4** or **5** already **6** so
7 spontaneous enough **8** too

4

1 1 and 5 **2** 3 **3** 2 **4** 7, 8 **5** 6 **6** 4

5

flip chart, graph, handouts, key points, markers, projector, summary, whiteboard

C Grammar exercises

1

2 or **3** but **4** also **5** and **6** or
7 but **8** as well **9** too, also

2

2 so **3** such **4** so **5** As **6** such as

3

2 enough **3** too **4** enough **5** Too, enough **6** too

4

2 yet **3** already **4** yet **5** already
6 still **7** still **8** still

5

2 a as b such as **3** a enough b too
4 a so b such **5** a or b and

6 Sample answers

2. I'll either get a promotion or apply for another job.
3. I enjoy going on business trips, but they can be tiring.
4. I'm giving a presentation so I need to make some handouts.
5. That was such an interesting movie that I think I'll go see it again.
6. They produce various food items, such as frozen foods and instant mashed potatoes.
7. I'm going to Kyoto for the conference, but I will stop off in Singapore on the way.
8. There are not enough gigabytes on this computer to download this software.
9. Have you met the new boss yet?
10. I just gave her the information yesterday, and she's already finished the report.

D Vocabulary

1

2 c **3** d **4** b **5** a

2

2 handouts **3** audience **4** outline
5 visual aids **6** screen **7** graphs
8 key points **9** summary **10** projector

3

2 expectations **3** pointer **4** presenters
5 outline **6** handouts

Unit 20

A Context listening

1/2

1 yes **2** no **3** yes **4** yes **5** no

2

Put some money under her mattress and buy lottery tickets with the rest.

3

2 should be paid back 3 should be invested
4 can be withdrawn

4

1 invested, investments 2 capital
3 liquid 4 diversify

C Grammar exercises

1

2 has offered 3 was brought 4 won't be presented
5 sends 6 Can, be assembled
7 hasn't been replaced 8 Has, introduced

2

2 is sent 3 are used 4 is picked up
5 is set up 6 be connected 7 are, caused

3

2 f were shredded
3 h were replaced, have been replaced
4 e hasn't been decided
5 g will not (won't) be told
6 b should be rewritten
7 a could be offered
8 d can be made

4

2 has been found 3 are desired 4 is treated
5 could be mistaken 6 was broken up
7 was reduced 8 is much improved

5

2 She is having her hair styled (done).
3 They are having their house painted.
4 She had her dress mended (sewn, fixed).
5 He is having his picture taken.

D Vocabulary

1

2 c 3 a 4 d 5 b

2

2 stocks 3 commission 4 financial advisor
5 bonds 6 interest rates 7 transactions

3

2 diversification 3 strategy 4 liquid
5 investment 6 risk

Practice test 4

Listening

1	C	8	A
2	C	9	D
3	B	10	B
4	A	11	B
5	A	12	C
6	B	13	D
7	A		

Reading

1	A	7	C	13	C	19	C
2	B	8	A	14	A	20	A
3	D	9	C	15	C	21	C
4	A	10	C	16	D	22	D
5	B	11	D	17	C		
6	C	12	A	18	C		

Speaking

Sample answers

3

I can see four women in an office. They all seem to be busy. There are computers on desks. A large desk is in the center with piles of papers stacked in trays and on the desk itself. On top of one pile there is a CD. There are two office workers in the front sitting on opposite sides of the desk. One worker is using a mouse. The other worker is looking at a paper document that she is holding. Two other office workers are sitting at desks in the back. Behind the woman at the far end is a bookcase with books on its shelves. There are also pictures in the office.

4

My favorite piece of furniture is the chair in the living room. The back of the chair can be adjusted so that I can sit back and put up my feet. It is very comfortable.

5

I would have beautiful carpets in every room and interesting paintings on the walls. I would also have comfortable chairs to sit in and lots of nice lamps that give a soft light to read by.

6

I work in a big office building with hundreds of offices. Each office is well equipped, but is quite small. There are nice big windows with a good view. I like being able to look out at the city. My biggest complaint is that the walls between the offices are too thin so it is possible to hear the people in the next room. The walls should be thicker and the gray color of the office rooms could be brighter.

7

The Movefast Shipping Company operates in the Far East, around the Pacific Rim.

8

You should fax your résumé to the Personnel Manager at this number: 1-000-555-2094. You must do this by Friday, July 15.

9
The best candidate should be a graduate and have at least 10 years of experience in the shipping business. He or she should have knowledge of the Pacific Rim import and export procedures and correct shipping practices. I also think that the right candidate must be able to prove that he or she is a disciplined worker who can work well with a large team of workers and professionals.

10
Thanks for the warning. I'll call the maintenance people to see if they can get the barrier fixed before people arrive on Monday morning. I'll also send a text message to all the employees and warn them so they won't try to get in before the barrier is working. As for the tree, Maintenance is probably equipped to remove that.

11
I think both hard work and good luck are important for success for most things in life. Of course, luck is important and sometimes it is all that is necessary. For example, you might meet someone just by chance and that person turns out to be someone who helps you on the road to success. Maybe he has the right connections or knows about a job vacancy that has just come up. Or someone might leave you some money in their will and you invest that money in a business that becomes a great success. However, most of the time you need to combine that luck with a lot of hard work in order to achieve something useful. Without careful attention and hard work you will not get far.

Writing
Sample answers

1
The man is showing a graph, but he really wants finish the presentation.
The man is pointing to a drop in the figures, but the graph shows a subsequent rise.

2
The man's demonstration shows that the teapot holds enough water for two cups.
The man has enough water in the teapot for his demonstration.

6
Thank you for your email. I would like to stay in your private guest accommodation. My flight has been rescheduled, but I still haven't heard if the new flight has been confirmed yet. I will let you know my arrival time as soon as I hear back from the travel agent.
I intend to bring a PowerPoint® presentation on my laptop. Do you have a projector that is suitable for this type of presentation? If not, I could print my slides onto transparencies to use on a projector. I am also bringing several products to present to the audience. Could you set up a large table so that I can easily exhibit these items to the audience? These will be used to demonstrate some of our materials.

8
Several years ago, a teacher in my economics course required us to give a presentation. The teacher made a video of all of our presentations. We then got to watch the video so that we could improve on our presentations. I did not enjoy this experience as it was one of the most embarrassing experiences in my life, but I think I learned some very important lessons.
I made mistakes in every part of the presentation. First of all, my body language was awful. I didn't realize before looking at the video how much I wave my hands around while I talk. I also had this annoying habit of pushing up my glasses every few seconds, even though they were not sliding down. Whenever I picked up the laser to point at my slides, my hand was shaking so much that the red point went all over the screen. Second, I not only didn't talk loud enough, but I also spoke too quickly. If I didn't already know what the presentation was about, I would have had difficulty understanding. Third, I read my note cards instead of looking at the audience. And then I dropped the cards on the floor. They got all mixed up and I had to stop and try to reorganize them quickly, but I got them in the wrong order, so some of my points didn't make sense. Finally, I managed my time badly and ran out of time before I was able to summarize the points. The teacher made me go on to answer questions before I was completely out of time.
It was a terrible experience and watching the video was painful. The teacher was very encouraging though. She pointed out the things that I did well and talked to me about ways to improve. That video has made me very aware of things that I should be careful about, not only in giving a presentation, but also in daily life. For example, I no longer push up my glasses every few seconds.

Grammar Focus Task
1 advertising **2** them **3** impressed **4** as **5** and

Vocabulary Focus Task
1 financial **2** exchange **3** Access **4** chart **5** fax

Unit 21
A Context listening
1/2
1 a mug that can keep a drink warm
2 a sink that can be adjusted
3 dishes that are self-cleaning

3
2 when I have to drink
3 where they feel
4 that people with back trouble will / appreciate
5 that clean

4
1 where **2** who **3** that
4 when **5** 4 (that)

5

1 a spin-off 2 an invention 3 a breakthrough

C Grammar exercises

1

2 whose 3 that / which 4 where
5 who, that 6 when, that

2

The first smartphone was designed by IBM in 1992. It was a mobile phone that had a variety of extra functions, including email and fax. It was a phone (that) we would think is quite normal today, but at the time was very advanced. The use of smartphones increased in the 1990s when Nokia introduced the 9000 series. These were phones (that) people could buy relatively cheaply. Consumers who bought them were impressed with the greater range of functions combined with their light weight. In the first decade of the new century, several companies introduced smartphones that were easier to use and more powerful. Some models that contain millions of downloadable music tracks for no extra cost have been introduced. This is a technology (that) experts claim will continue to improve in terms of performance and range of functions.

3

2 which / that, c 3 who / that, d 4 when, b
5 where, a 6 that / which, e

4

2 We employ craftsmen who/that build traditional wooden furniture.
3 Why don't you contact the accountant who/that works in the building next door?
4 I took the phone that/which had no dial tone over to the maintenance department.
The phone that/which I took over to the maintenance department had no dial tone.
5 My brother got a new job that/which requires some training in marketing.
6 Our R & D department has proposed a new design that / which has many advantages.
7 The customer who/that brought back her microwave gave in the receipt.
The customer who/that gave in the receipt brought back her microwave.
8 We have to contact those board members who/that were unable to attend the meeting.

5

2 the project that / which she's been working on
on which she's been working
3 the hotel that / which she wanted to stay in
the hotel in which she wanted to stay
4 the positions that /which he's applying for
the positions for which he's applying
5 the movie that we told you about

D Vocabulary

1

2 development 3 revolutionize 4 invents
5 discoveries 6 innovative 7 licensed 8 design

2

2 exclusive rights 3 research and development
4 creative process 5 trial and error

3

2 breakthroughs 3 patent 4 spin-offs
5 trial and error 6 exclusive rights 7 research

Unit 22

A Context listening

1/2

1 c 2 a 3 b

3

2 c 3 e 4 a 5 b 6 d

4

1 provided that, unless, as long as

5

1 **b** approved 2 **a** policy **b** compensation
3 **a** negligent **b** liability

C Grammar exercises

1

2 will get 3 walk 4 will/'ll meet 5 put
6 tell 7 forget 8 try

2

2 I get 3 I'm not / am not 4 you need
5 there is / there's 6 I'll make / I will make
7 you get 8 should I say 9 she wants
10 you will have/you'll have

3

2 if you have paid 3 Unless the traffic is
4 If I can avoid 5 unless you make
6 Unless the door is

4

2 if 3 in case 4 If 5 on condition that
6 As long as

5

2 g 3 a 4 f 5 d 6 b 7 e 8 c

6 Sample answers

2 I have finished my work
3 I always take my laptop along
4 he always listens to my opinions
5 your computer crashes
6 I have nice colleagues
7 they offer it
8 the information on the form is correct
9 we might improve our image
10 if you completed that deal

D Vocabulary

1

2 d 3 b 4 g 5 c 6 a 7 e

2

2 cover, file, claim 3 risk, claim 4 damaged, files

3

2 negligent 3 compensate 4 deductible
5 assessment 6 approval 7 coverage 8 claimant

Unit 23

A Context listening

1

Possible answer: In one picture, they look organized and successful and in the other picture, they are disorganized and the people are going to other stands.

2

Picture 2

3

2 As a result 3 Because 4 after that 5 in addition

4

1 Because 2 so, As a result
3 after that 4 in addition

5

2 c 3 a 4 b

C Grammar exercises

1

2 D 3 S 4 S 5 D 6 D 7 S 8 D

2

2 d 3 f 4 a 5 c 6 e

3

2 Consequently 3 Fortunately 4 However
5 because 6 since 7 However 8 Furthermore
9 although 10 most importantly

4

2 Consequently 3 because 4 due to
5 On the other hand 6 first

5 Sample answers

2 we haven't received the parts
3 some of our staff are absent
4 we should give him a refund
5 we should seriously consider him for the position
6 the entrance area will be extended

D Vocabulary

1

2 f 3 a 4 b 5 g 6 e 7 c

2

2 exhibition 3 distribute 4 sponsoring
5 demonstrations

3

2 contacts 3 launch 4 competitor

Unit 24

A Context listening

2

The new product is hiking boots /shoes. People who like to go hiking would be most interested in buying them.

3

2 to develop 3 to wear 4 targeting
5 concentrating

4

1 verbs
2 *to* infinitive; *-ing;* preposition + *-ing*.

5

2 d 3 a 4 b

C Grammar exercises

1

2 to break 3 to produce 4 doing
5 to complete 6 to use 7 working/to work
8 to start 9 to use 10 making/to make

2

2 using 3 decide 4 to visit 5 understand
6 to catch 7 smoking 8 to buy 9 closing
10 spending 11 to give 12 eating

3

2 a 3 a and b 4 b 5 a and b

4

2 waiting until after next week
3 to come at five o'clock
4 to meet you soon
5 finishing the market analysis

5 Sample answers

2 You should quit playing computer games at work.
3 I recommend you get help with difficult projects.
4 Why don't you stop wasting time and get on with the tasks you have to do?
5 You should learn to communicate better.
6 Don't forget to arrive on time every day.
7 You can try completing projects before the deadlines.
8 You could offer to help colleagues when they are having problems.

D Vocabulary

1

2 j 3 c 4 h 5 i 6 a
7 g 8 d 9 f 10 e

2

2 potentially 3 loyal 4 analyst 5 market
6 image 7 promotion 8 product

3

2 in-house 3 special offers 4 consumption habits
5 free samples 6 tough competition

Unit 25

A Context listening

1/2

1 subsidized gym membership
2 telecommuting (working from home)
3 flexible working hours
4 company car
5 possible answers: bonus, paid vacations, promotions, personal leave, health insurance, pension plan

3

2 fill in 3 find out 4 brought in 5 hold on to

4

2 a 3 d 4 e 5 c

C Grammar exercises

1

2 on making 3 to find 4 to see 5 in testing
6 to be 7 to get 8 of losing

2

2 You can't back out of it.
3 We'll have to cut them back.
4 I would have backed her up.
5 We have to put up with them.
6 I want to get out of it. 7 Can we throw it out?
8 He really doesn't get along with us/them.
9 They've called it off. 10 She turned it down.

3

2 ask for a raise 3 to draw up 4 deal with working
5 catch up with things 6 asking for 7 giving up
8 bring this up 9 turned down

4 Sample answers

2 Yes, I'm looking forward to it very much.
3 No, but I have to put up with noises after leaving the office building.
4 Of course, you can pay for my lunch.
5 Sometimes after a busy week, I run out of motivation.
6 I can bring them back tomorrow.
7 I never turn down a good opportunity.
8 Don't worry. I won't back out of it.
9 No, I have gone through it twice already.
10 To be truthful, I'll never catch up with all my work.

D Vocabulary

1

2 d 3 a 4 f 5 b 6 c
2 expense account 3 discount prices
4 incentive rewards 5 flexible working hours
6 paid vacations

2

Noun	Verb	Adjective
	attract	attractive
benefit	benefit	
motivation		motivated / motivating
trainer	train	trained / training
training		
recruiter	recruit	recruited / recruiting

2 attractive 3 motivated 4 benefits 5 training

3

2 f 3 e 4 a 5 h 6 c 7 d 8 g

4

Benefits package: paid vacations, retirement plans, health insurance
Perks: subsidized gym facilities, training programs

Practice test 5

Reading Section

Part 5

1	B	8	C	15	C	22	B	29	C
2	D	9	B	16	C	23	A	30	C
3	A	10	D	17	B	24	A	31	B
4	C	11	A	18	C	25	B		
5	C	12	D	19	B	26	C		
6	A	13	D	20	A	27	A		
7	A	14	B	21	C	28	B		

Writing

Sample answers

Question 1:

The accident caused serious damage to my car.
Our car was damaged in the accident.
I had an accident and my insurance paid for the damage.

Question 2:

He went to his office but couldn't get the computer to work.
He was working in his office, but the phone interrupted him.
His office telephone is out of order, but he has his cell phone.

Question 3:

He will slip on the banana unless he is careful.
Garbage, like this banana, will keep falling onto the floor unless we get a new trash can.
Don't slip on a banana unless you have good insurance.

Question 4:

I always buy something whenever I go to an auction.
It is fun to go to an auction to see what people buy.
Sometimes you can buy things at a bargain price at an auction.

Question 6:

Dear Mr. Jonson,
Thank you for your letter. I was surprised to hear about the situation regarding my life policy. According to the contract, I was supposed to make monthly payments, which I understood would be unchanged for the term of the policy.
I would like to continue the policy, but before I make a decision, would you please answer my two questions below?

1 Why does the insurance company want to increase the monthly premiums?

2 What is the proposed monthly increase in the premium?

Would it be possible to meet at your office to discuss this in more detail?
Best regards,
Judy McAnsh

Question 8:

Many kinds of insurance are available in the market today and choosing the kind to suit your circumstances is essential. It is important to buy insurance in order to be covered for all kinds of accidents that might happen in your life. Of course, just because you are covered doesn't mean that an accident won't happen. But if you own an insurance policy, you will at least be given financial compensation in the event of loss. Three kinds of insurance that should be considered are car insurance, house insurance and life insurance.
Everyone who owns a car must be covered in case they have an accident. Usually, if you have an accident, your insurance company will pay to have the damage repaired. If the accident is your fault, then your insurance company will have to pay for any damage caused to another driver's car. Fortunately, I have never had an accident, but I always make sure I am insured. Every year I renew my policy. Also, I know several people who have had accidents, and in those cases the insurance company paid for the damage.
Even though I don't own a house myself, I would strongly recommend all house owners to purchase house insurance. You can get coverage for the property itself, and you can also get a policy for the furniture and other items within the house. I saw the value of this when I was growing up; my parents' house was burglarized on more than one occasion. They filed a police report and sent it to the insurance company and they were compensated for the stolen items. If something really bad happens, like a fire, for example, the company may pay you a sum equal to the value of the destroyed property.
It may also be a good idea to insure your life. The reason for this is that if you die and you have a life insurance policy then the company will pay your family an agreed amount. This is especially important if you have young children. The money will allow your surviving spouse and children to have a comfortable life without your regular salary.
So, in conclusion, I think that in the modern world it is essential to have some insurance cover. The three kinds of insurance I have described will protect you and your family against many risks

Grammar Focus Task

1 e **2** d **3** b **4** c **5** a

Vocabulary Focus Task

1 insurance **2** inventors **3** consumer
4 distributed **5** attract

Recording script

Recording 1

Kevin: Good morning. My name is Kevin Bates. I'm the personnel manager here at MacNulty's Chocolates. You're the applicant for the secretarial job, right?

Laila: That's right. My name's Laila Joseph. The employment agency said you have a temporary vacancy.

Kevin: Yes, that's right. Mr. Murphy's regular secretary, Emma, is taking maternity leave.

Laila: Oh, OK. How long will she be away?

Kevin: About two months. Emma's famous in our office for her efficiency, and she'll organize her work to make it as easy as possible for someone to step into her place.

Laila: OK.

Kevin: So, tell me about yourself, Laila. I see from your cover letter that you've done this kind of work before.

Laila: Yes, I've held several temporary jobs for companies in the area. I like it because it gives me a lot of freedom and I can broaden my experience at the same time.

Kevin: Your résumé certainly is impressive. And your references are excellent. Your last employer was very impressed with you. He says that you are enthusiastic, hard working, and efficient.

Laila: That's very kind of him.

Kevin: You know, I'm a little surprised you haven't applied for a permanent job. Secretaries with your experience and skills can make a good salary nowadays.

Laila: Well, doing temporary work suits me since it gives me a lot of time to practice my other job.

Kevin: Your other job?

Laila: Yes. You see, my background and qualifications are in theater. I really want a career in acting. When I don't have a part in a play, I enjoy working as a secretary.

Kevin: You're an actress? I thought that you looked familiar.

Laila: Well, maybe you saw me on stage. I was recently in a comedy at the Globe Playhouse. Maybe you saw it. It was called "The Over-Qualified Graduate."

Kevin: Yes, of course! I did see it. I enjoyed it very much. I knew I recognized you. You played the part of the secretary with such enthusiasm.

Laila: Yes, that was me. I think that all my temp work prepared me for that particular role.

Recording 2

Emma: Hello.

John: Emma. John here.

Emma: Oh, hello John. How's everything going at the conference?

John: OK. Uh, I realize it's 10:00 and that's when you usually have your coffee break. Are you busy?

Emma: Well, I'm just having my coffee now, but that's OK. What is it?

John: I'm in my hotel room, looking through my papers and I have lost the Newhaven report. I want it for my presentation today. Do you have a copy?

Emma: Yes, I do, but I'm afraid I can't fax it to your hotel. The fax machine is still broken.

John: Still?

Emma: Don't worry, John. I called the Friendly Business Machines and they sent someone over. He's working on it now, but he says he has to come back tomorrow with a replacement part. The guarantee still covers the repair costs. It's good for another year.

John: Thank you, Emma. That's great, but the report . . .

Emma: I'm sending you an email with an attachment now. You did take your laptop, didn't you?

John: Yes, I have my laptop, but I need a printer.

Emma: Oh, I'm sure your hotel has one.

John: Oh, yes, probably. Another thing, I'm looking at the file of the Stanford account, but the page with the figures we agreed on is missing. I know the original copy of those papers is in the office. Do you have the folder with that file?

Emma: Just a minute. I'm looking through the folder right now. What do you want me to do with the file when I find it?

John: Call me back with the figures and also, could you make a photocopy of the original and put it in my in-box on my desk?

Emma: Sure. I'll get right back to you. Anything else?

John: No, I don't think so. How's everything in the office?

Emma: Fine. I've just sent around the memo about the team meeting next week. Also, you do realize you left your cell phone in the office, right? I think the battery is dead because it isn't ringing anymore.

Recording 3

Jenny: Hello, Bill. Welcome to Seattle.

Bill: Thanks, Jenny. It's good to see you.

Jenny: You too. And how was your flight? You're very late!

Bill: Yes, sorry about that. I hope you weren't waiting too long.

Jenny: It was fine. I looked at a couple of magazines and I was just catching up on my email when your flight arrived. So what happened?

Bill: Well, it started off OK. Check-in used to take a long time, but I had an e-ticket, so it was much easier.

Jenny: Oh yes, they're great, aren't they?

Bill: And then, as usual, a security guard pulled me aside when I set off the alarms with the metal pin in my foot.

Jenny: That must happen all the time.

Bill: Yes, I was expecting it. I'm used to setting off alarms these days! Even though I showed the security guard my medical documents, he still checked me with his metal detector.

Jenny: Is that why you were delayed?

Bill: No, I didn't get my connecting flight in Minneapolis. Bad weather was causing a lot of problems and my flight was canceled. They put me on another flight, but I had to take the airport shuttle to a different terminal and in the confusion, I misplaced my boarding pass.

Jenny: Oh dear. But they must have let you on eventually.

Bill: Yes, they did, in the end. One of the cabin crew was working at the boarding gate and he helped me. He found a record of my booking on the computer system and so they let me on the flight. And when I finally got here, my luggage didn't turn up on the carousel at the baggage pick-up.

Jenny: And I bet a lot of people were waiting at the lost luggage counter!

Bill: Oh yes. But as I was filling out the forms to get my bags back, one of the baggage handlers found them and brought them over. And after that everything went smoothly.

Jenny: Well, you're here at last! You must be suffering from jetlag after such a long trip and crossing so many time zones. The hotel we've booked for you isn't far away.

Bill: Oh good, I am rather tired. And I almost forgot, Jenny. Here is a little duty free present for you. I picked it up during one of my layovers.

Jenny: Thank you, Bill. How thoughtful of you.

Recording 4

Anita: Hi Mary! How are you?

Mary: Well, I'm a bit tired. I've just returned from my trip to the New York City book fair.

Anita: Of course! When did you get back?

Mary: I arrived late last night.

Anita: You were looking forward to that trip, weren't you? How was it?

Mary: It was really good and I've placed lots of orders for some really interesting books and also lots of popular science titles.

Anita: Great. You've been going to that book fair for a while now, haven't you?

Mary: Yes, every year for about 10 years. Anyway, this morning I came in early to catch up on some paperwork before everyone arrives. But I've been wondering why no one was on the streets and there was no traffic. Is there any special reason why everything is closed? I haven't seen anyone all morning—until you arrived.

Anita: But it's still really early.

Mary: Early! It's already 9:30.

Anita: No, it's not. It's only 7:30.

Mary: 7:30! It can't be! Oh, I know. I forgot to change the time on my watch after my trip! So, I've been thinking that everyone was really late, but in fact, I was really early. That means I've been here since 5 a.m.!

Anita: Well, did you get a lot done?

Mary: Yes. In fact, I've been working really hard all morning. I've already put the money in the cash register, arranged some merchandise on the counter and put some new books on the shelves. I've also put the summer clearance sale sign up in the window and changed the display.

Anita: Wow, that's great. Maybe you should go home and take a nap. I can look after the store for the rest of the morning.

Mary: Yes, good idea. I've been feeling a little sleepy!

Recording 5

Inez: So, is my itinerary for the trip to Helsinki ready, Nan?

Nan: Sure. You leave Tuesday evening at 6:00. You have a short stop in Zurich and arrive in Helsinki at 11:00 P.M. local time.

Inez: Great. Will the courtesy bus from the Kivilinnan Guesthouse be available at that time of night? You did reserve a room for me there, didn't you?

Nan: Well, no, I didn't. It's going to be closed for repairs when you're there.

Inez: So where am I staying?

Nan: I haven't booked you a room yet. I'm still looking into the different possibilities. The trade fair is being held in the exhibition center close to the train station. There's a chain hotel just next to the exhibition hall but it doesn't have any vacancies the night you arrive. I asked the receptionist to put your name on a waiting list in case there's a cancellation.

Inez: Well I really would like accommodations within walking distance to the exhibition hall.

Nan: Yes, that would be easier. I'm also looking for a hotel that has a courtesy bus from the airport. I'll let you know what I find out.

Inez: OK.

Nan: It's possible that you'll have to take the airport shuttle bus or a taxi into the city. If you use the bus, it will bring you to the train station in the city center. From there...

Inez: What about car rentals?

Nan: I didn't look into that. Would you like me to book a rental car for you at the airport?

Inez: Never mind. I'll just take a taxi. That will be the easiest thing to do. And when you're looking at other hotels, could you check the facilities, uh, free internet service, complimentary breakfast, and amenities like that before you make the reservation?

Nan: Sure.

Inez: So, when will I be meeting with the people at our Helsinki branch?

Nan: You meet with them at 10:00 A.M. on Wednesday morning. They're sending someone to your hotel to pick you up at 9:30. I'll email them about the hotel arrangements as soon as I make the booking.

Inez: Great, thanks, Nan. I'm looking forward to this exhibition. It looks great in the brochure.

Nan: The exhibits should be interesting.

Inez: By the way, did you ask about the weather?

Nan: Yes, I did. They are expecting snow.

Inez: Really? At this time of year?

Nan: Yes. Quite a lot, I think.

Inez: Oh dear. I'll have to rethink what I'm going to pack.

Practice Test 1

1 Now listen to the four statements.
(A) She is leaning over the balcony.
(B) She is looking out the window.
(C) She is standing in the doorway.
(D) She is staying at a guesthouse.

2 Now listen to the four statements.
(A) He is reading the instructions.
(B) He is filing documents.
(C) He is typing a report.
(D) He is making a photocopy.

Part 2

3 Is it possible to hire more staff?
(A) I didn't think it was so funny.
(B) We can look into it.
(C) We have enough cakes already.

4 When did Anita say the train was due to leave?
(A) Grand Central Station
(B) Four thirty
(C) Every Wednesday

5 Have you considered what your expenses will be?
(A) I don't expect so.
(B) I haven't really thought about it.
(C) I haven't spent any money at all.

6 Will you confirm my reservation at Groppi's Hotel?
(A) Yes, I'll make a reservation.
(B) No, I'm going to serve apple pie.
(C) I've already done that.

7 Which tray does this file go into?
(A) The out-tray.
(B) Turn right onto Grand Avenue.
(C) Yes, the parade is filing past now.

8 Where is the guesthouse?
(A) On Friday night
(B) It's just behind the exhibition hall.
(C) The porter will take your bags.

Part 3

Questions 9 through 11 refer to the following conversation:

Woman: Here is your itinerary, sir. Will you check it and see that everything is in order?
Man: Yes, of course. Let me see ... I'll have to change planes in Athens. Is that right? Or do I stay on the flight?
W: I'm afraid you'll have to stay the night in Athens. There is no onward flight to Copenhagen that evening. Is that OK?
M: Yes. I'm going to need to break up the journey anyway. Is there a hotel within walking distance of the airport?
W: No, but we can get a discount price for you at a hotel that has a courtesy bus.

9 Where does this conversation take place?
10 What will the man do?
11 What does the woman offer to do?

Questions 12 through 14 refer to the following conversation:

Man: The office smells terrible.
Woman: I know. It's the tar they're using for the new roof on the building next door. That's why I closed the window.
Man: I don't think I can work here. The odor is already giving me a headache and I need to concentrate on updating the figures on this account.
Woman: Why don't you use Tim Hayworth's office? He's working in Paris this week and I know he has offered people his office before. So, I don't think he minds if colleagues work there. I can transfer your calls.
Man: Thank you. I appreciate that. Are you sure you will be OK?
Woman: Well, I have to make a photocopy of each of these reports and file them. I can't do that in Tim's office.

12 Where does this conversation take place?
13 Where is the man going?
14 What does the woman offer to do?

Part 4

Questions 15 through 17 refer to the following talk:

Clarke Airport is currently being refurbished, and we apologize for any inconvenience this may cause you. We are working hard to improve the airport and make life easier for travelers. In particular, business travel will soon be much easier than it has been. We are going to introduce new executive business lounges which will make your journey much more comfortable. We will offer complimentary snacks and drinks and you will be able to buy newspapers and magazines from around the world. In addition, you will soon have constant communication with your headquarters and your clients when we introduce free wireless internet throughout the airport. We are also going to offer six new meeting rooms, with video and telephone conference facilities.

15 Who is speaking?
16 What does the speaker say about the business lounges?
17 What is the purpose of this announcement?

Questions 18 through 20 refer to the following talk:

The workplace for many people is in an open-plan office where everyone is visible and available, a place that makes communication easier. The space is used more efficiently and shared facilities such as fax machines, photocopiers and printers are easily accessible to everyone. However, our survey company has found that a large percentage of employees are dissatisfied. These open-plan offices tend to have rows of impersonal workstations and overhead lighting which may or may not serve the needs of all the staff. They are not inviting places to work. Employees want their private space where they can get their work done undisturbed, personalize their surroundings, and hold private discussions.

18 Who is speaking?
19 What is the speaker comparing?
20 Which piece of equipment is not mentioned?

Recording 6

Man: Hello. How can I help you?
Woman: I would like to make a complaint. I bought this cell phone from this store last August and the screen has broken.
Man: I am sorry to hear that ma'am. Has it been mistreated in any way?
Woman. No, it hasn't. It was on my desk at the office in perfect condition. I put it into my pocket and walked home, took it out of my pocket and it was broken. I did not drop it or mistreat it in any way.
Man: I'm sorry, ma'am, but we cannot replace or fix the screen. You can take it to the Phone Fix-It shop. They repair those kinds of problems, but I don't know how much they charge.

Woman: What do you mean? Do I have to pay to have it fixed?
Man: Yes, you do.
Woman: But this is the guarantee, isn't it? Don't you have a commitment to fix it?
Man: I'm sorry, but the guarantee only covers the software.
Woman: What do you mean the guarantee only covers the software?
Man: The guarantee is that the phone will do all the functions that it should.
Woman: You mean you guarantee the reliability of the software, but the phone itself can be poor quality, cost a lot, and break in less than a year?
Man: If you would like to make a complaint . . .
Woman: That is what I'm doing here at customer service. I am not satisfied with the product.
Man: Ma'am, we only sell the phone. You can complain to the company that makes them. Go to their website and click on the 'contact us' link and send them your complaint.
Woman: Well, if they don't meet customer expectations by providing quality products, then in the future I will buy their competitor's products. Thank you and good-bye.

Recording 7

Frank and Lydia

Lydia: Excuse me. Could you tell me where I can find Mr. Jacobs?
Frank: Oh, I'm Mr. Jacobs.
Lydia: Hi, I'm Lydia, Lydia Fenway. I made an appointment for you to show me some apartments this morning. I'm sorry I'm a bit early.
Frank: Oh, no problem. Call me Frank, by the way. Before we start, I need to know whether you're looking for a place to buy or rent.
Lydia: Well, I'd really like to buy a one-bedroom apartment in the city center, but I haven't found out whether the bank will give me a mortgage or not.
Frank: OK. Well, come this way and we can look at the listed properties for sale and rent.

Frank and Robert

Robert: Are you Frank Jacobs?
Frank: Yes, I am. Can I help you?
Robert: Yes. My name's Robert Goldberg and I'm looking for a realtor to take care of selling my home.
Frank: OK. Could you tell me where your residence is?
Robert: It's in the Elegant Views housing development. It's a lovely family home with a large yard and double garage. Are you familiar with the area?
Frank: Yes, I am. House prices have fallen recently, but I'm sure we can still get you a good price. Can you give me an idea of how quickly you need to sell it?
Robert: Well, I'm being transferred to a different state, but we can't move until the children are finished with school this year.
Frank: So, the house won't be empty for another three months.
Robert: Yes, that's right.

Frank and Alex

Frank: Good morning, Alex. How's the chocolate business going?
Alex: Just fine, Frank. I'm sure you've been wondering what I've decided about that building complex you took me to see.
Frank: The property is still available.
Alex: Good. I really like the place, but I'm not sure what to do. Before I make a decision, I need to know how much renovation the owner will allow me to do.
Frank: OK. Could you tell me what changes you have in mind?
Alex: Well, I'd like to know if I can extend the back room to accommodate a larger cold storage area.
Frank: OK. Is there anything else?
Alex: Yes. Could you find out if the owner would consider a lease that gives me the option to buy the building later if my business continues to grow?
Frank: Sure. I can do that for you.

Recording 8

Teller: Good afternoon. Can I help you? . . . Excuse me, sir. Good afternoon.
Mike: Oh, good afternoon. I'm sorry. I was looking at this brochure about business loans.
Teller: Are you interested in a loan? Would you like me to see if a loan officer is available to speak to you?
Mike: Yes, please. But first, I'd like to deposit these checks.
Teller: Of course. Could you sign the deposit slip here, please? Thank you. Now, if you wouldn't mind waiting a few minutes, I can get a loan officer to come and speak to you.
Mike: No problem. Thank you.

Loan Officer: Good afternoon, Mr. Martin. Sorry to keep you waiting. I'm Samantha Schmitt, and I understand you are interested in getting a loan.
Mike: Yes, that's right. My wife and I want to invest in a franchise. We want to open an outlet of the Oskari's Tasty Snacks food chain.
Loan Officer: Do you have experience in running a restaurant?
Mike: Well, we're both managers of Oskari's Tasty Snacks. In fact, we met at a managerial training program. Now my wife manages the outlet in the Grand Forks shopping mall and I'm at a branch downtown.
Loan Officer: So you both know the business quite well?
Mike: Yes. We started out at the bottom and worked our way up. And now that we've been in the business for quite a while, we thought that we would like to have our own business.
Loan Officer: How much are you thinking about as a down payment?
Mike: We haven't really discussed that yet.
Wilma: What took you so long? You said that you were just going to the post office and you've been gone a long time. I was getting worried.
Mike: I'm sorry. I wanted to call, but my phone needed recharging. I stopped off at the bank to deposit our paychecks.

Wilma: Oh, great. You remembered them.

Mike: And when I was waiting in the line, I saw a brochure about business loans with good interest rates. The teller offered to see if a loan officer was available to talk to me. I said yes, and she asked me if I minded waiting for a few minutes. It was a while before a loan officer called me into her office.

Wilma: Did you say why we wanted to get a loan?

Mike: Well, I told the loan officer that we wanted to invest in a franchise. She asked if we had any experience in this business and I said that we were both managers at different branches of Oskari's Tasty Snacks. Oh, and she asked how much we were thinking about as a down payment.

Wilma: Did she mention that the bank would run a credit check on us?

Mike: She said that we'd have to complete this form and the bank would have to check our credit rating.

Wilma: Did you check our balance today?

Mike: No, I didn't. Why?

Wilma: Umm, well, dear, I thought you deposited our checks last week. On Saturday I wrote a check for a large amount, so there was not enough money in our account to cover it.

Recording 9

Jack: I'm Jack and I take the subway to work. Every morning I walk from my apartment to the station. My stop is not usually very crowded, but the station where I get off in the city can be unpleasantly busy. At each stop, there are always more and more people impatiently trying to get on. Sometimes coming home, people rudely push and shove to get into a car. I try not to get annoyed but sometimes it's difficult!

Cindy: My name is Cindy. I take the bus to work. I could take the train, which is, in fact, faster, but I would have to change trains. The stop where I would have to change is often crowded. The bus takes a bit longer and sometimes the traffic jams cause extremely long delays, but I don't have to change buses, so I prefer it. Also, the number 19 stop is conveniently located just around the corner from my house and I can get off almost at the front door of the building I work in. And I can buy a commuter pass that gives me unlimited travel for three months, which works out much cheaper.

Ivana: My name is Ivana and I live in the heart of the city. I rent a tiny apartment because a big place in the area is really expensive. But there are many advantages to living in the city. I walk to work, so I don't have to wait in long lines to buy a ticket for a bus or the subway or worry about missing the last train home, which is great. It takes me about 20 minutes to walk to work. While walking, I can look in the store windows and think how I will organize my day. By the time I get to work, I have had my exercise and my mind is clear for the day's work.

Francisco: Hi, my name is Francisco. I drive to work everyday. I live in a quiet suburb and there is no public transportation in the area. I wanted my children to grow up in a peaceful neighborhood, but it means that I have to commute quite a distance to get into the city. There's always a lot of congestion on the highway because I come and go during rush hour. I could take the fast lane if I were in a carpool. I'd like to carpool because I get bored being in the car alone for an hour or so every day. However, none of my neighbors work in the same area as I do, and so I have no one to carpool with.

Recording 10

Clara: Hi, Enzo. What did you want to talk to me about?

Enzo: Well, Clara, Wrinkleless Wardrobes have asked us to plan a promotional campaign for their steamers.

Clara: Steamers? What's a steamer?

Enzo: Well, apparently, it's a machine like an iron, but better!

Clara: Oh, I like the sound of that. Tell me more.

Enzo: Well, the smallest of their steamers is a hand steamer, which is good for travelers. It's small and compact, so it will fit into your luggage, and you can use it in a hotel to get the wrinkles out of your clothes before you go to an important meeting.

Clara: OK. That's cheaper than paying the hotel laundry services to iron your clothes, although some hotels do provide an iron in the room.

Enzo: True. Then there's a personal steamer, which you use in your home. It's larger than the travel steamer and they say you can steam your clothes much faster with this one. The largest size is an industrial steamer for retail stores that have a lot of clothes that are wrinkled when they are taken out of the box and need to be steamed before they are put out for sale.

Clara: So why use a steamer instead of an iron? What are its selling points?

Enzo: Well, a steamer's actually better than an iron at getting wrinkles out of your clothes. It's also gentler and causes less damage to the fibers.

Clara: Anything else?

Enzo: Oh yes. Apparently, when you use it on carpets and rugs, it kills the insects that can cause allergies.

Clara: OK. Those are good advertising points. So, what kind of ad campaign are we talking about?

Enzo: Well, we have three groups: the retail business, the homemaker and the traveler.

Clara: Should we have three different commercials aimed at the different target audiences or just one aimed at the entire community?

Enzo: Well, we can think about that. I was thinking about some sort of a promotion in shopping malls. We can make up some brochures or flyers to hand out and get someone to give demonstrations.

Clara: I can get Laurence onto writing a catchy jingle for an ad on the radio and perhaps we can produce a TV commercial.

Enzo: I think if we drum up just a little publicity we can increase brand recognition quite quickly. I think there's a big market for this kind of product.

Clara: How about a slogan?
Enzo: I was thinking of that. What do you think of "Wrinkles Away?"
Clara: Uh, I think that sounds more like an anti-aging cream.
Enzo: Oh. You're right. Well, we can work on it.

Practice test 2

Part 1:

1 Now listen to the four statements.
(A) The woman is arguing with her boss.
(B) The man is laughing at the woman.
(C) The woman is holding a slip of paper.
(D) The man is working in a big department store.

2 Now listen to the four statements.
(A) They are running for the bus.
(B) They are waiting for the bus.
(C) They are crossing in front of a bus.
(D) They are going home by bus.

3 Now listen to the four statements.
(A) They are reading a paper.
(B) They are talking about cars.
(C) He is signing a document.
(D) He is writing about cars.

4 Now listen to the four statements.
(A) They are returning items to the shelves.
(B) They are comparing packages.
(C) They are waiting in the grocery line.
(D) They are going to the check-out counter.

5 Now listen to the four statements.
(A) They are buying houses.
(B) They are looking at pictures in the windows.
(C) They are walking their dog.
(D) They are waiting for some friends.

Part 2

6 They turned us down for a mortgage.
(A) It turned up yesterday.
(B) The mortgage company is downtown.
(C) I'm sorry to hear that.

7 Did you ask him if the tenants accepted the offer?
(A) I asked him for five, not ten.
(B) There were no exceptions.
(C) I forgot.

8 Are you sure it is broken?
(A) I spoke confidently.
(B) Well, it won't turn on.
(C) You brought it yesterday.

9 Would you sign on this line, please?
(A) Sure. Do you want me to date it?
(B) Well, I forgot it.
(C) Please, follow the line.

10 Could you tell me where we are supposed to meet?
(A) At six o'clock
(B) Exactly five
(C) In the committee room

11 Why did the bank return the check?
(A) It wasn't signed.
(B) They checked it back in.
(C) I had to return to the bank.

12 What exactly is the problem, sir?
(A) I am not acting.
(B) The engine won't start.
(C) Yes, I was robbed.

13 You need the sales receipt to make an exchange, don't you?
(A) Yes, and I forgot to bring it.
(B) Yes, I made the exchange.
(C) No, I changed it for a new one.

14 Do you plan to attend the conference?
(A) I have to check the dates.
(B) I won't depend on the plan.
(C) Right away, sir.

15 What is that advertising agency called?
(A) Yes, that's the agent's name.
(B) That's a long distance number.
(C) It's something like Media Marketing.

16 Are you planning to stay late today?
(A) No, I'm taking off early.
(B) No, I won't be successful.
(C) No, I scanned it yesterday.

17 Could you try to get here earlier tomorrow?
(A) I'll do my best.
(B) That's not good enough.
(C) I'll try now.

Part 3:

Questions 18 through 20 refer to the following conversation:

Woman: Good morning. This is Hansford's Garden Center Customer Service. Sandra speaking. How can I help you?
Man: Good morning. My name is Ed Smiley. I'm calling about the backyard inflatable swimming pool I bought from you last week.
Woman: Is there a problem, sir?
Man: Yes, there is. The assembly instructions are not clear and I can't seem to inflate it. I have tried using the pump that came with my purchase but it doesn't work. I thought maybe there is a leak in the plastic that is letting the air out. Can you help me?
Woman: Have you checked that the pump is attached properly, sir? That could be the cause of the problem. The pump has to be securely attached to the valve on the side of the pool. If it still doesn't inflate, we would be happy to send over a technician to help with the assembly.

18 What product did the man purchase?

19 What is the man's problem?

20 What does the woman offer to do?

Questions 21 through 23 refer to the following conversation:

Man 2: Sorry I'm late for the second time this week. I tried to be on time but the traffic jams were worse than ever. Street repairs are causing delays, especially around rush hour.

Woman 2: That's OK. We can't start the meeting yet because Sam's late, too. So, help yourself to some coffee while we wait.

Man 2: Oh, I don't feel so bad then. I think I could get here more quickly by bicycle, at least until the repair work is finished.

Woman 2: And bicycling is healthier and a lot easier. Although, honestly, I don't feel so safe on a bike. I'm glad that the new bicycle route will be opening soon.

Man 2: I'm looking forward to that too. I'll definitely use the new bike route for my daily commuting. Just think, no more rush hour traffic jams and no more road rage problems.

Woman 2: And then, we'll always be able to start our meetings exactly on time!

21 Where does this conversation take place?

22 Why does the man apologize?

23 What does the woman think?

Questions 24 through 26 refer to the following conversation:

Woman: Good morning, John. Could you have a look at the report on Greenaway Gadgets and let me know what you think about their plans for expansion?

Man: Well, Lisa. I've already looked. Right now there isn't much scope for increased sales on luxury items and what you might call unnecessary items. I think we should advise them to wait before taking on any loans.

Woman: I agree. They should wait till the economic conditions improve. Maybe in a year or so we could take another look and see how their goals fit in with the business situation.

Man: OK. We meet them next week for a consultation. I'll have a summary and recommendations report ready to present by then.

24 What is the company Greenaway Gadgets planning?

25 What do the speakers think about the Greenaway Gadgets plan?

26 What will the man do by next week?

Questions 27 through 29 refer to the following conversation:

Man: You know what? The supermarket cashier just told me that if you write a check in red ink, the bank will take longer to process the check. So if you don't have enough money in your bank account and you're expecting your salary to be added soon, the check will clear *after* the money is deposited.

Woman: Don't believe everything you're told. Bank scanning machines can read any color of ink. Your check would bounce.

Man: How do you know that for sure?

Woman: Well, I used to work in a bank and one of my jobs was to electronically scan checks that came in. Believe me, red ink is as readable as any other color. I'd advise you to write a check only when you have the money to cover it.

27 What was the man told about checks?

28 Where did the woman work in the past?

29 What advice does the woman give?

Questions 30 through 32 refer to the following conversation:

Man: Good morning. I've come to discuss investing in time deposits.

Woman: Welcome. Let me show you the time deposits we have on offer at the moment. Here is our list where you can see several different rates.

Man: Yes, I see. This one is only for 3 percent. That's not a very high rate. And it's only for six months, so it'll have to be reinvested after six months. Can I get a better rate if I deposit my money for, umm, let's say for a year?

Woman: Yes. At the moment we have a one year special deposit which must be kept for one year. At the end of the year, you'll receive 4 percent interest on your initial deposit.

Man: That's a better rate, and I think I could leave my money with you for at least a year. I think I'll choose that one. The funds can be transferred from my account tomorrow when my salary comes in.

30 What does the man want?

31 What does the man decide to do?

32 When will the funds be transferred?

Part 4

Questions 33 through 35 refer to the following talk:

Good morning, everyone and welcome to the Property Hour Show. I'm Eduardo Gonzales, your talk-radio real estate agent, and today I'll be giving advice to prospective tenants. OK, so before you sign a contract as a tenant there are several things you should carefully check. First, look at the location of the property. Are you close to public transportation and stores? Second, you must be sure that there is adequate heating for cold winter weather. Check if the heating system works well. Also, you should make sure the toilets and sinks are in good working order. Finally, you need to think about your insurance situation. Are your personal possessions insured by the landlord's policy? To get our brochure with a fully comprehensive list of what you should look for, drop in at our agency on the corner of 23rd and 2nd Streets. And now for a word from our sponsor.

33 Who is Eduardo Gonzales?

34 Why is Eduardo giving this talk?

35 Where can interested people get the brochure?

Questions 36 through 38 refer to the following talk:

You can stay ahead of your competitors in the way you handle complaints. If a customer complains about a product or service, don't react negatively. Think positively. How can you turn the situation into an opportunity for your business? Remember a complaint that is solved successfully will lead to more customer loyalty. You should also remember that a customer who alerts you to a problem is doing your business a favor since many customers with problems may have just taken their business elsewhere without bothering to mention it. Above all, remember that complaints must be dealt with as courteously, swiftly, and sympathetically as possible.

36 What is the main point of the talk?

37 What may be true if customers do not complain?

38 Who is the talk probably aimed at?

Questions 39 through 41 refer to the following talk:
Remember, if you are sent a job offer you must read the letter carefully. The offer letter should include several key pieces of information. For example, it should state the date when your new work starts, the starting salary and benefits and a clear description of your expected duties. Does the offer agree with what you discussed at the interview with your new employer? If there are differences between the details of the letter and what was discussed, you need to be certain that these differences are acceptable to you. Finally, you should check whether you have to fulfill certain conditions before the contract can be signed. For example, you may be required to have a health checkup or to send in references or educational certificates.

39 What is the main point of the talk?

40 Who is the talk directed at?

41 What is NOT mentioned as a key piece of information to look for?

Questions 42 through 44 refer to the following talk:
I'd like to introduce my new chewing-gum removal machine which I invented to take care of a big problem for cities everywhere: chewing gum carelessly dropped on the streets. You can see on this sidewalk that the used gum looks bad, and of course, is a nuisance if it sticks to your shoe. Most traditional gum-removal devices use huge amounts of water, high pressure hoses and dangerous chemicals to force the stuck gum off the sidewalks. But my new gum-removal device uses much less water at a low pressure. Unlike other devices, this one can be rolled along by one person and causes no environmental damage. Also it makes less noise and doesn't damage the surfaces like other systems do. Here, try this excellent machine out, now, but watch out for those pedestrians.

42 Who is speaking?

43 What is the speaker comparing?

44 Where is the speaker?

Questions 45 through 47 refer to the following talk:
Our guide to buying a home has been fully updated to take account of the recent difficult market conditions. It has been written by experts in the field of house purchasing who will help you to figure out what kind of home you should buy, how to estimate your price range and how to negotiate the whole business of obtaining a mortgage and making a sale or purchase. Whether you are a first time buyer or an experienced professional, this guide will tell you all you need to know about making this important step.

45 What is being presented?

46 Who wrote the document?

47 Who is the document aimed at?

Recording 11

Alberto: I've just looked at the figures and our profits are still falling. We must do something soon. Any suggestions?

Rosemarie: Well, I was thinking that we could start selling toys for older children as well as toddlers.

Alberto: But how can we think about expanding right now? I don't think we could get a loan to buy more stock when our profits are dropping.

Rosemarie: We can make a good argument on how this change could improve our business. If we want to ask for a loan, we must study the market, the costs and the possible profits, so that we can have all that information ready for the bank.

Alberto: Well, don't forget that the sales representative from Wooden Toyz Company. is coming today.

Rosemarie: That's right, she is, and I just might ask her about toys for older children.

Alberto: OK. Good idea. She may have some good suggestions.

Rosemarie: Yes, and we could start out by expanding slowly.

Alberto: But what about our name? We can't attract older children with a name like Toys for Toddlers. We would have to change our name, which would be expensive. We'd have to change all of our stationary, our logo, even the registration of the company. Can we really afford to do that?

Rosemarie: Well, how about keeping this store as it is? We could rent the empty store next door and start another toy store for older children there. An inside door could join the two stores.

Alberto: What? We couldn't expand that much!

Rosemarie: OK, well, what do you think of taking on a partner?

Alberto: A partner? Oh, I don't know. It might mean we'd have to totally restructure the business.

Rosemarie: Well, a partner could bring in the money needed for expansion and then we wouldn't have to take out a big loan. It might not be that difficult to find a new partner.

Alberto: Next you'll be talking about becoming a big corporation with stockholders!

Rosemarie: Maybe in the future, I will. But right now I need your help in hanging these balloons. I can't reach that high.

Alberto: OK. I can do that for you.

Rosemarie: And while you are at it, think about what I suggested. I agree that we mustn't rush into anything, but it can't hurt to think about expanding, and once we have all the information, we can make an informed decision.

Recording 12

Maria: So, Alex, have you got any questions so far?

Alex: Yes, actually. I need to clear up some questions before I sign it. Could you help?

Maria: Yes, of course. You should make sure you understand all the terms and conditions before you sign.
Alex: Well, first of all, I can't find where it mentions vacation time. It should say that here somewhere.
Maria: Let me see. Here it is, at the bottom of the second page. You're entitled to 20 days vacation time per annum. After five years, the company must give you an extra day of vacation time for every year you stay with us – it's a legal requirement. That increases up to a maximum of 30 days.
Alex: Oh, that's good. And what happens if I'm sick?
Maria: We'll pay you for up to 28 days sick leave within a one year period. But you must bring in a doctor's certificate if you're sick for more than two consecutive days. If you're off for just a day or two, you don't have to bother about one. But obviously you should let your manager know if you're going to be off work.
Alex: OK. And what about if I want to leave the company? When do I have to let you know?
Maria: During the first month you can leave at any time and you don't need to tell us in advance. Similarly, we don't have to give you any notice. After you have been with us one month, you have to tell us at least three weeks in advance if you plan to terminate the contract.
Alex: And what if you want to fire me?
Maria: Well, we also have to give you three weeks notice if we decide to lay you off. However, if an employee is involved in some kind of misconduct, we don't have to give any notice to terminate a contract. We can fire you immediately and without pay. Employees mustn't assume that this never happens. Is there anything else you need to know?
Alex: No, I think that's it.
Maria: OK, well, I think you'd better go away and read it though once more before signing it.
Alex: Good idea. Thank you for your help.
Maria: You're very welcome.

Recording 13

Waiter: Good afternoon, sir, madam. A table for two?
Lauren: Oh, we made a reservation. The name is Richards.
Waiter: Ah yes, could you follow me, please?
Brandon: Oh, there isn't much of a view here. Could we have that table over there by the window?
Waiter: Certainly sir.
Lauren: Yes. This is a wonderful view.
Waiter: Here are menus for you.
Brandon: Thank you.
Waiter: And may I suggest today's special? It includes appetizer, entrée and dessert.
Brandon: What is the special today?
Waiter: A choice of vegetable soup or tossed salad as an appetizer and an entrée of asparagus with grilled salmon....
Lauren: Oh, I really like salmon, but I'm not that hungry.
Waiter: Well, we have a very nice salmon salad on our regular menu.
Lauren: Yes, that would be fine.
Waiter: And you, sir?
Brandon: Well, I *am* hungry so I would like the special, please.
Waiter: Certainly, sir. And for the appetizer?
Brandon: I'll have the tossed salad.
Waiter: The tossed salad. And can I get you something to drink, madam?
Lauren: Oh, just water is fine, thank you.
Waiter: And for you, sir?
Brandon: Umm, would you mind bringing the drinks menu?
Waiter: Yes, of course, sir. Would you like anything else?
Brandon: Not that I can think of.
Waiter: OK. May I take your menus? And I'll be right back with the drinks menu, sir.

Recording 14

Tony: Hello Marie. You look lost in thought.
Marie: Oh, hi Tony. Yes, I was just thinking about the Health and Safety committee meeting this morning. We had to discuss the update we'll give everyone at the meeting on Wednesday morning.
Tony: Why do we need another update? We've just passed the fire safety inspection after getting lots of new factory safety equipment. We now have a fire escape, fire extinguishers and fireproof doors.
Marie: I know. But according to the new guidelines on hazards at work, we still have some potential dangers in this office.
Tony: But we all have hard hats and safety goggles for going into the factory area. And of course, we've posted warnings about certain hazards. Just yesterday, I put up a warning sign beside the water cooler about the dangers of falling on wet and slippery floors. What more do we need?
Marie: We've taken care of all the government safety regulations, but we haven't considered the noise-related problems.
Tony: But this office isn't particularly noisy. The noise from machinery on the factory floor doesn't usually reach here unless someone leaves the door open.
Marie: True. But apparently there is 'low-level noise' in open plan offices like this one. Jane was telling us at the meeting that low level noise is also considered harmful. She said it increases levels of stress and in the long term that leads to heart disease.
Tony: I find that hard to believe. All I hear at the moment is the sound of people talking in the background, and typing. Ah, and Sam's whistling as usual. That's not going to hurt anyone, is it?
Marie: Well, you forgot to mention the sound of the printers and photocopiers, the doors opening and closing and the ventilation system. And there is some traffic noise coming from beyond the front gate. Oh, and of course, the phones are forever ringing.
Tony: I suppose there is a lot of background noise in this office. It's never really bothered me though.

Recording 15

Elisa: Welcome everyone. Let's get straight to the items on the agenda. Can someone volunteer to take minutes today?
John: I'll take the minutes, Elisa.

Elisa: Thank you, John. Can we approve the minutes of the last meeting?

Alberto: I just want to ask – did we do anything about the broken automatic gate at the entrance to the main parking area?

John: My understanding of the situation is that the maintenance department has ordered the parts and will fix it by the end of the month.

Elisa: Are there any other comments about last week's minutes? . . . . OK, then last week's minutes are adopted. Now, looking at today's agenda, the first item is the fundraising event the city has scheduled. The money will be used for repairing the damage after the fire in the city library last summer.

Alberto: Sorry, I was away last week. So, you definitely agreed on our taking part in the fundraiser, did you?

Elisa: Oh, sorry, Alberto. Yes, the vote was unanimous. We discussed providing homemade cookies and cakes for the stand that sells baked goods. We also discussed selling balloons for children. But no one was really interested in either idea.

Andrea: Well, over the weekend, I was thinking about the idea of holding an auction instead of baking things or selling balloons. We could sell some of our old merchandise.

John: I think that's a great idea, Andrea. Alberto has done a charity auction before, right, Alberto?

Alberto: Yes. I have. The great thing is we could get rid of old merchandise as well as auction products which other businesses donate. We might get a really good response.

Elisa: Well, let's put it to a vote. Could I see a show of hands? OK. Everyone's in favor of an auction. Alberto, will you take responsibility for planning that?

Alberto: Of course. I'll arrange a meeting with other local businesses. I know several people who might be interested in participating.

Elisa: OK. Well if you're happy to do that, let's move onto the next item on the agenda.

Practice Test 3

Part 1

1 Now listen to the four statements.

(A) They are working on their computers.
(B) They are seated at a table.
(C) They are enjoying the main course.
(D) They've finished the meeting.

2 Now listen to the four statements.

(A) He is looking at the screen.
(B) He is checking his papers.
(C) He is talking on the telephone.
(D) He is playing a computer game.

Part 2

3 Could you check the wording on the contract?

(A) I've already written the check.
(B) I could work afterwards.
(C) I did that already.

4 Can I have the afternoon off?

(A) Didn't I already say yes?
(B) I can't possibly.
(C) We can remove it.

5 Will we need a loan to expand?

(A) We'll have to check our finances.
(B) I'll send one home next week.
(C) We have our own one.

6 Did you invite the new bookkeeper to have lunch with us?

(A) Yes, I gave him a book to keep for us.
(B) I heard you had lunch with our accountant.
(C) No, I didn't even think about it.

7 Could you fax Mr. Chang the corrected contract?

(A) I'm making the corrections.
(B) I've already faxed it.
(C) I'll contact him now.

8 Do the staff meetings here usually start on time?

(A) Yes, we have weekly meetings.
(B) Not always.
(C) Start the meeting without me.

Part 3

Questions 9 through 11 refer to the following conversation:

Man: Hi Maria. How did it go at the interview?

Woman: Great. I got the job. They are going to send me a contract next week.

Man: Congratulations. But remember you need to check the contract carefully before you sign it.

Woman: Oh, I will, don't worry. At least, I know what the salary will be.

Man: Ok, but you'd better find out about things like sick leave and how much vacation time you will have.

Woman: Yes, that's true. Thanks, I will. By the way, Mike, why are you grocery shopping at this time of day? Shouldn't you be at work?

Man: Oh, umm. I don't have a job now. My last job didn't work out. I didn't read the contract carefully.

9 What is the woman expecting to receive?

10 What advice does the man give the woman?

11 Why is the man in the supermarket at this time of day?

Questions 12 through 14 refer to the following conversation:

Woman: The restaurant I booked was recommended by a good friend at the office. It specializes in food from Thailand.

Man: Oh, good. I like Thai cuisine. . . I wonder why the taxi is taking so long. We called for it to come at 7 o'clock, didn't we? And it's now 7:30. Should I call them to find out what has happened?

Woman: Yes, and would you tell them to hurry up? I made the table reservation for 7:15.

Man: You know what? I've got a better idea. Let's just stay home. The Chinese restaurant around the corner does home deliveries. Should I call the Thai restaurant and cancel the reservation?

Woman: Yes, you should tell them we're not coming and apologize. And um, could you also cancel the taxi?

12 Where did the people plan to go?

13 What problem do the people have?

14 What do the people decide to do?

Part 4

Questions 15 through 17 refer to the following talk:
Today I'm going to tell you about falling asleep in the afternoon. I'm sure you've noticed that most people feel sleepy after a big meal. But do you know why that is? Well, after eating a lot of food, most of the oxygen in your body is being used by your digestive system in order to help process the meal. Consequently, your brain doesn't get as much oxygen as it needs to work efficiently. So with less oxygen getting to the brain it is difficult to stay mentally active. Because of this you tend to feel sleepy after a big meal. This is why lots of people who work in offices, as you all do, are less productive in the afternoon. As an expert in nutrition, I suggest that you eat smaller meals for lunch and eat healthy snacks in between meals.

15 Who is speaking?

16 What does the speaker say office workers should do?

17 According to the speaker, why do we feel sleepy in the afternoon?

Questions 18 through 20 refer to the following talk:
Welcome to the Planning your Business show at KCD radio. On today's program, I will give some instructions on how to expand your business. There are two basic ways your business can grow. First, you can increase the number of customers. To be able to do this successfully, you must research the market to find out who needs your products and where those people are located. Second, you can increase the frequency of purchase by customers who already exist. This means giving good value to those people who make purchases from you so that they develop loyalty to your company. These should be your two top priorities if you really want to expand your company.

18 Who is this talk for?

19 What is the topic of the program?

20 According to the speaker, how can you get people to return to your business?

Speaking Questions 7–9:

Good morning. I'm calling about the convention today. I seem to have misplaced my invitation that includes the information about the convention. I was hoping you could answer some of my questions.

7 Could you tell me where the convention will take place?

8 How much is the registration fee for the convention?

9 I cannot attend the entire day. Could you tell me the times and titles of the afternoon talks?

Speaking Question 10:

Oh good afternoon. My name is Greta Blomqvist. I have just received the order for office supplies that I placed with you last week. When we unpacked the order there were a few mistakes. First of all we did not order three desk lamps, we only ordered two. And the color is wrong. We wanted light green to match our office décor. These lamps are bright orange. The office stationery arrived but the headed notepaper is misspelled. It should say Vanguard Trading and not Vanguard Shading. I'm afraid you will have to redo this order. Please could you offer an explanation? Our number at Vanguard is 324 9786. Thank you.

Question 11:

What are some important features of your job?

Recording 16

Anna: And now to our Focus on Success segment. Each week we look at a different business that is doing well and look at exactly what it is they do. This week we are talking to Harry Stubbs, whose freight packaging business is expanding rapidly. Is that correct, Mr. Stubbs?

Harry: Oh, call me Harry, please. Yes, my company produces special shipping containers for the export/import industry.

Anna: OK. But tell me, why can't a factory just ship their products in a normal cardboard box? Why do they need your containers?

Harry: Well, you can't put a product in just any box. You know, some are just not strong enough. We deal with freight that has some special requirements for containers and these have to be specially made.

Anna: OK. So what kind of containers do you make?

Harry: Well, it depends on the cargo. For example, large, heavy products may need a box with reinforcement, but we want to reduce the weight, so the packaging needs to be strong enough to protect the cargo but light enough so that it doesn't increase costs too much.

Anna: So Harry, show us the packaging you've brought in.

Harry: OK, well, this is a small box that is suitable for very fragile items. Both the inside and the outside of the box are cushioned. As neither cardboard nor plastic offer enough protection, we use a material that was specially developed for this type of packaging.

Anna: Yes, that must be important. Besides dangerous cargos and heavy products, what else do you need to consider?

Harry: Well, every manufacturer has different requirements. One may be exporting a product that is fragile and needs protective packaging – that is some type of cushioning, to prevent the cargo from breaking. Those are very popular. Or a manufacturer may need a container that protects the commodity from changes in the outside temperature as it travels through different climates. Some products may be stored in a warehouse for several months before being shipped.

Anna: Before we take a break, I would like you to show our studio audience some of the other, more unusual packaging you have to show us. What about this one? It looks like a regular egg carton.

Harry: It may look like one, but it is special. Go ahead and throw it against the wall. I can assure you neither the eggs nor the package will break.

Recording 17

PA: Hello. Mr. Nesbitt's office. How can I help you?

Customer: Could I speak to Mr. Nesbitt, please?

PA: Well, I'm afraid he's busy right now. Can I take a message?

Customer: I really need to speak to him,... now. Is there any way you can put me through?

PA: Well, I'm afraid he's in a meeting, and he's very strict about not being disturbed in meetings.

Customer: Well, this is Charles Harrison speaking. I called your company yesterday, and the day before that. And the day before that. The line was always busy or the phone would ring and ring and no one answered. When someone finally did answer, I was put on hold and then the line went dead. I was disconnected. I never managed to get anyone to listen to my problem. Anyway, eventually I got through to the customer service. The person there told me to contact Mr. Nesbitt and that he would sort out the problem.

PA: What exactly is your problem, Mr. Harrison?

Customer: Well, about a month ago I placed an order with your company. You told me it would arrive in about a week. I haven't received the order yet, and when I called your office I couldn't get through. So now I'm calling the headquarters.

PA: Well, can I get Mr. Nesbitt to call you back after his meeting? It will finish in about 15 minutes. Can I take your number please?

Customer: Of course. It is 283-9528.

PA: 283-9528.

Customer: Yes. That's correct.

PA: OK. I'll tell him myself and see that he contacts you.

Customer: Thank you. I'm very anxious to speak to him so please make sure he calls me. Goodbye.

PA: Wait. Don't hang up yet. I think I hear him coming now. ..... Oh, dear. He hung up. ......Hello Mr. Nesbitt. How was the meeting?

Mr. Nesbitt: Well, the main item on the agenda was how to inform people that the name of our company is EDF and not EDS. Lots of people are calling us to complain, but we can't help them since EDS is a completely different company. If anyone calls for me with a complaint, could you ask them which company they are trying to contact?

Recording 18

Mr. Boswell: Good morning, Bill. Are you ready to interview the new applicants?

Bill: Well, yes, Mr. Boswell, Uhhh. . . . although I 'd like to make a few changes to the room before we start.

Mr. Boswell: OK, fine. What do you think we should do?

Bill: Well, for a start – what about the layout of the furniture here? Don't you think we should spread it out a bit? There is plenty of space here. We could move the table away from the wall a bit and put those plastic chairs in the storeroom. The leather chairs would be more comfortable and make the room look better. Ahh, and we should also set that lamp on the side table.

Mr. Boswell: Yes, that's a good idea, Bill. Let's do that. Anything else?

Bill: Well, yes, there is. Don't you think we should clear off this table and throw away the trash?

Mr. Boswell: Don't worry about that. The cleaner will come and clean up after lunch and our interviews don't start until three.

Bill: OK, that's good. Also the applicants' files are not here. Shouldn't we have them on hand to look at before each candidate comes in?

Mr. Boswell: Yes, we should. I think I saw them on Annie's desk. I'll go and get them right away. And I'll ask Annie to get us some pens, note pads and paper clips. Can you think of any other supplies we need?

Bill: Well, a stapler and some scissors would be useful. Oh, and if you are going to see Annie about that, could you ask her to turn her music down? The noise is very distracting, especially when we're doing interviews.

Mr. Boswell: I'll do that, Bill, and thanks for all your advice.

Recording 19

Leroy: I heard that the product presentation that the Metal Works representative gave was a disaster.

Cheryl: It wasn't a disaster at all. Although I felt sorry for the speaker. He arrived with his presentation on his computer but our projector wouldn't work.

Leroy: You mean the projector hasn't been fixed yet?

Cheryl: It was just the light bulb, but we didn't figure that out until after the presentation. By the way, we still need to replace it.

Leroy: So the speaker, Mr. Chertok, didn't have any transparencies that he could use on our overhead projector?

Cheryl: No, he didn't and he didn't have any handouts either.

Leroy: So what happened next?

Cheryl: Well, he was going to use the whiteboard, and guess what? All the whiteboard pens were dry. Lucy ran to the supply room to get new ones, but she discovered that we only had permanent markers. And as you know, you can't use permanent markers on a whiteboard.

Leroy: You're right about that.

Cheryl: So, I got out a flip chart and Lucy had already brought a set of colored permanent markers back from the supply room and the presentation went ahead.

Leroy: Wouldn't it have been better to postpone the presentation or send someone out to buy some whiteboard pens?

Cheryl: Well, Bernie was already here, wasn't he? And, after all that, it didn't matter. He quickly drew pictures of the product, but to be honest the pictures didn't look much like the real thing. Then he added information such as figures on a chart or graph and told us the exact statistics. These pictures were drawn so quickly, and Bernie's comments as he was drawing them were so funny that we couldn't stop laughing. In fact, I was glad the projector wasn't working. The speech was spontaneous enough to keep our interest and not too conventional. It was great.

Leroy: It sounds like Mr. Chertok was very well prepared.
Cheryl: Yes. And even though his drawings were bad, he presented credible information and support for the products. His key points and summary were well presented. In fact, instead of being a disaster, I would say it was the best presentation I have seen recently.

Recording 20

Jackie: So, Maruka, we heard that you have been left a large sum of money. Have you got any big plans for it yet?
Maruka: Oh no, not really. I need to find a financial advisor to help me.
Isaac: Yes, you should be careful. I've just been reading about people who suddenly become rich. They often buy a lot of things and soon it's all spent.
Maruka: Well, I'm not that rich! But I do have to think carefully about what to do. Have you guys got any suggestions?
Jackie: Don't you think that any money you owe should be paid back first?
Maruka: Yes. I think you're right. First, there will be taxes. And I also have a student loan. It'd be nice to pay that off.
Isaac: I don't entirely agree that you should pay it off. If the interest rate for your loan is low, your money should be invested in a bank fund that has a higher interest rate.
Jackie: Or you could put your money into stocks.
Maruka: Isn't that taking a chance, considering the way the market goes up and down?
Isaac: Well, you don't put it all into the stock market. It is important to diversify your investments. I think the experts advise dividing your money. First, you need some money that is liquid; in other words, invested in a way that you have immediate access to it, like in a bank account where the money can be withdrawn in case of an emergency. And then, you should have some for something like starting up a business.
Jackie: Or buying a house instead of paying rent. You probably have enough capital for a deposit.
Maruka: Well both of you have lots of good ideas.
Jackie: So, what do you think, Maruka?
Maruka: Well, you know what? I think I'll put half of it under my mattress since I don't trust banks, and the other half, I'll use to buy some lottery tickets and see if I can win more.
Jackie and Isaac: What?!
Maruka: Hey, you two don't really think I'm being serious, do you?

Practice test 4

Part 1

1 (A) They are pointing to a chart.
(B) They are calling a friend.
(C) They are watching a presentation.
(D) They are waiting for a response.

Part 2

2 Let's call a taxi.
(A) It's a big tax.
(B) It's not in the hallway.
(C) Do you have the number?

3 Should I pay for the meal with my credit card?
(A) I don't have a credit card.
(B) No, I'll take care of the bill.
(C) Yes, I'll give you credit for the dinner.

4 I wonder what time the agent will arrive.
(A) Sometime after lunch.
(B) The show will be broadcast live.
(C) I don't know the agent.

5 Could you recommend something?
(A) The set menu is excellent today.
(B) I already had it mended.
(C) I didn't say anything.

6 Has the exchange rate changed?
(A) I got here on time.
(B) It's gone up.
(C) It's at a different time.

7 Have you spoken to your financial advisor?
(A) He wasn't in.
(B) I don't give advice.
(C) It's not broken yet.

Part 3

Questions 8 through 10 refer to the following conversation:
W: I like this property. Do you think we should make an offer for it?
M: Yes I do. But first we have to be sure we can get a mortgage. The bank hasn't agreed to give us anything yet. I'll call them tomorrow and ask if the loan has been accepted.
W: I hope they do – I really like this neighborhood. To me this one seems a perfect place to raise children. And there's a school and a good supermarket within walking distance.
M: And there's nice park just around the corner. Let's go home and try to work out how much we should offer and how much we're prepared to increase the offer if the seller doesn't accept it.

8 Why is the couple unsure about whether to make an offer?
9 What does the man say he will do tomorrow?
10 What facilities are NOT mentioned as being near the house?

Part 4: Talks

Questions 11 through 13 refer to the following talk:
Does your family want you to buy a flat screen TV? Do your children keep asking to go to Disney World this summer? Have you charged the maximum on your credit card? Do you have a negative bank balance? Are you lost in a world of easy credit and internet banking? It's time to take control of your spending habits. And how can you do that? Well, come to our free workshop on restructuring your finances and getting out of debt at the Rawlings Public Library meeting room Monday at 7:30 pm. This KID radio announcement has been sponsored by Rawlings Investment Association.

11 Where was this announcement heard?
12 What does the speaker suggest to the listener?
13 What problem does the speaker not mention?

Speaking questions 7–9
(Narrator) Hello, I'm calling about a position for employment that I heard was advertised in the newspaper. It is for an assistant manager. Could you give me some information about the position?

7 Could you tell me where the Movefast Shipping Company operates?
8 How do I apply for the position?
9 What kind of candidate is the company looking for?

Speaking question 10
Oh, good morning. I came to the office over the weekend and found that the lightning storm has caused a tree to fall down and it is blocking some of the parking places in the main parking area. The electronic barrier was also damaged so I couldn't get in.

Speaking question 11
What is more important for success: hard work or good luck?

Recording 21

Linda: Good morning. My name is Linda Evans, and on today's program, we have a guest who is going to tell us about his inventions for everyday use in the kitchen. Terry Davies, you've brought us a lot of inventions today. Can you describe them for us?

Terry: Well, first of all, Linda, I have the ForeverHot mug. This is actually a mug that I invented when I was working in my garage on my other inventions. I kept forgetting about my coffee and it would get cold. But now, because of my invention, the days when I have to drink cold coffee are over. My ForeverHot mug has a small hot plate in the bottom which keeps your coffee hot for over an hour. You can even adjust the temperature with this red button here on the side.

Linda: That sounds like a great idea. What about this next one, which is, well, it looks like a sink?

Terry: Yes, Linda, it is a sink, an adjustable one. I call it my UpDownSink. Different people in the same house can change the height of the sink to the position where they feel most comfortable. This has real health benefits. If you use a sink which is too high or too low for you, you can hurt your back.

Linda: Yes, your sink is one invention that people with back trouble will really appreciate, I'm sure. And finally, we have one more idea that Terry hopes will revolutionize our kitchens. Terry, what's this? It looks like a pretty ordinary set of dishes to me.

Terry: Ah, that is where you are wrong, Linda. In fact, my SqueekyClean dishes are dishes that clean themselves. Self-cleaning glass, which is sometimes used in skyscraper windows, was a real breakthrough. But I think that there are quite a few more possibilities for this technology. So these plates are just one spin-off. I actually have one or two more in development.

Linda: I'm afraid we've run out of time, Terry but thank you very much for coming in. It's been fascinating. And good luck with all your inventions.

Recording 22

1

Tom: Red Tree Insurance. This is Tom speaking. How can I help you?

Kate: Hi, I'd like to make a claim. I had a car accident yesterday. Someone backed into me in the parking lot.

Tom: Have you reported the incident to the police? If you haven't done that yet, we can't file the claim.

Kate: Yes, I've talked to them already and I have a copy of the police report.

Tom: Good. And whose fault was the accident? As long as it was the other driver's fault, his insurance company should pay for the damage. You may have to pay the deductible, but your premiums won't increase.

Kate: It was definitely the other driver's fault. My car was parked and he backed into it.

Tom: OK then. Your claim should be approved quite quickly provided that you send us all the paperwork as soon as possible. Now, if I could just take your details...

2

Tom: Red Tree Insurance. This is Tom speaking. How can I help you?

Jim: This is Jim Snow of Pineapple Technology. We have a policy with you. I'd like to report a fire at our premises last night.

Tom: Just a minute. Let me take a look at your policy. Ah yes. I see that your premiums are up to date. We'll send someone over to assess the damage as soon as possible. There shouldn't be a problem with compensation unless there are unusual circumstances. Do you know the cause of the fire?

Jim: We're not sure. It started in the kitchen area. But no one was working on the premises last night. Since no one was in the building, it must have been an electrical problem.

Tom: Well, if you suspect it was done intentionally, you'll need to file a police report. Anyway, our assessor will visit you and help you fill in the claim form. When would be a convenient time for him to come?

3

Tom: Red Tree Insurance. This is Tom speaking. How can I help you?

Fran: My name's Fran Harvey and I'm phoning from Winston's Supermart. I wanted to speak to someone about a legal action against us.

Tom: OK, if you give me some details, I'll be able to put you through to a claims advisor. What is the reason for the legal action?

Fran: Well a woman tripped over a box in the parking area last week and broke her arm. She says we were negligent. But it wasn't our box. The wind blew it into the parking area just before she tripped over it. She simply wasn't paying attention.

Tom: OK. I should warn you though that your liability insurance premiums will increase if she wins her claim and we have to pay compensation.

Fran: Yes, I know. But I don't think that'll happen. It really wasn't our fault.

Recording 23

A: You look tired, Juanita.

J: Yeah, I am, Akira. I've been working overtime to get everything ready for the Midwest Food and Drink Fair next week. Last year we didn't do a very good job of representing the company, so we started planning early this year.

A: Oh yes, I remember last year's fair. It was the launch of the *Gold Flakes* cereal, wasn't it? What went wrong exactly?

J: Well, we waited until the last minute to book a space in the exhibition hall. As a result, the space they gave us was very small and far away from the main exhibition hall. When we arrived to set up our exhibit, we discovered that the stand we brought with us was too large. So, we had to rebuild it once we got there.

A: Oh no! I didn't realize you had so many problems.

J: Well, that wasn't all. Because our rebuilt stand was so much smaller than we had planned, we didn't have space to showcase our products properly. And after that, we noticed that our promotional leaflets had lots of spelling mistakes in them.

A: Oh dear! But was it a total disaster? Normally you can at least check out what competitors are doing and look out for new trends in the industry.

J: Oh yes. In fact, we did quite a lot of useful research and were also able to liaise with some potential buyers as well as do a bit of networking. It's just a shame the launch wasn't very successful.

A: So what are you doing differently this time?

J: Well, for a start, we have paid more attention to the venue layout so that we were able to book a space in the center of the exhibition hall. We have designed a stand specifically for that space, so there should be no problems with the size. And in addition, we are sponsoring a couple of social events and will be handing out cups and bags showing our logo, so we should be pretty visible this year!

A: Well, it sounds like you've organized it really well. I'm sure things will go better for you this year. I might be able to come along and give you a hand.

Recording 24

Jan: OK, let's start by looking at the Scott's market research report. Scott, would you like to talk us through it?

Scott: No problem. As you all know, we are looking at two target markets: people who hike all year round and people who go on one or two hiking holidays a year. We know that people who enjoy going out all year round are looking for a hiking boot that is long lasting. They like to study consumer reports and catalogs carefully and they are prepared to pay higher prices for footwear that is dependable and comfortable. These people also tend to develop a loyalty for a particular brand.

Jan: So would you say that this group recognizes our name as one of the market leaders?

Scott: Yes, definitely, and because of this, they are less likely to respond to the kind of promotion we have been considering.

Jan: And what about the other group of purchasers – the occasional users? How do they decide what to buy?

Scott: Potential customers in this segment are less concerned about the smaller details of footwear, but also are less prepared to pay a higher price for brand names. They also like to wear comfortable shoes, but they aren't prepared to spend time comparing features, so they are less aware of our logo and more likely to respond to our company's special offers and competitions. It is here that we have most potential for increasing our market share, so I'd suggest targeting most of our advertising at these consumers.

Jan: Well, at least we should think about concentrating on the occasional hikers. Bridget, have you had any thoughts about an advertising campaign?

Recording 25

Doug: Iris, have you got a moment? I wanted to ask for your opinion about the company *SmartThink*. Your husband works there, doesn't he?

Iris: Yes, he does.

Doug: Well, I'm thinking of applying for a job there and before I fill in the forms, I'd like to ask you a couple of questions.

Iris: Well, I'd be happy to tell you anything I can. What would you like to know?

Doug: Well, I've looked at the job ad, so I know about the salary and the requirements, but I wanted to find out what it's like working there. What kind of perks does your husband get?

Iris: Actually, they've just brought in a new one. They now get discount prices on meals every Friday at the Garden Restaurant.

Doug: Really? Well, that's something. I guess he goes there every week now.

Iris: No, actually he doesn't benefit much from it. He usually doesn't go into work on Fridays since he does a lot of his work from home now. He telecommutes at least two days a week.

Doug: He has a lot of control over his working hours, then?

Iris: Yes, that's true. He also has flexible working hours so he can take off for work later in the morning on the days he does go into the office. And, of course, I forgot to mention, he has the use of a company car since the job involves some traveling. I think that is one of the perks that first attracted him to the job.

Doug: It sounds like an attractive package. Is there anything else?

Iris: Well, they are going to open an on-site gym which employees can use. It will be equipped with all the latest exercise machines, apparently. Steve is really looking forward to using it.

Doug: So, would you say Steve is happy working at SmartThink?

Iris: Oh yes. It's a great company to work for. They try really hard to attract and hold on to good workers. You really should apply.

Appendix 1: Common phrasal verbs

Some phrasal verbs are common in TOEIC. The meaning given is the one we often use in the workplace.

ask for = request
back out of = to decide not to do something you had planned or agreed to do
bring out = launch
bring up = introduce topic
build up = increase or develop
carry out = accomplish, perform
check in/out = register arrival/departure at a hotel/airport
cut back = reduce
deal with = discuss, negotiate or cope with
do away with = remove
draw up = compose plan
fill in/out = complete a form
find out = discover
get on with = continue
go out of (business) = lose the business
go through = follow procedures
hang up = end a phone call
hold on = keep, wait
hold up = delay
keep up with = be up to date
look for = search
look forward to = feel happy about something that is going to happen
pay for = give money to buy
pay off = end debt
run out of = finish the supply
set up = start
take off = leave
take over = take the responsibility
turn down = refuse
write up = record

Appendix 2: Common irregular verbs

Verb	Past simple	Past participle
arise	arose	arisen
be	was/were	been
beat	beat	beaten
become	became	become
begin	began	begun
break	broke	broken
bring	brought	brought
broadcast	broadcast	broadcast
build	built	built
burn	burnt	burnt
buy	bought	bought
catch	caught	caught
choose	chose	chosen
come	came	come
cost	cost	cost
cut	cut	cut
deal	dealt	dealt
do	did	done
draw	drew	drawn
drink	drank	drunk
drive	drove	driven
eat	ate	eaten
fall	fell	fallen
feel	felt	felt
fight	fought	fought
find	found	found
fly	flew	flown
forgot	forgot	forgotten
freeze	froze	frozen
get	got	got
give	gave	given
go	went	gone
grow	grew	grown
hang	hung	hung
have	had	had
hear	heard	heard
hide	hid	hidden
hit	hit	hit
hold	held	held
hurt	hurt	hurt
keep	kept	kept
know	knew	known
lay	laid	laid
lead	led	led
lean	leant	leant
learn	learnt	learnt
leave	left	left
lend	lent	lent
let	let	let

Verb	Past simple	Past participle
lose	lost	lost
make	made	made
mean	meant	meant
meet	met	met
pay	paid	paid
put	put	put
quit	quit	quit
read	read	read
ride	rode	ridden
ring	rang	rung
rise	rose	risen
run	ran	run
say	said	said
see	saw	seen
seek	sought	sought
sell	sold	sold
send	sent	sent
set	set	set
shake	shook	shaken
shine	shone	shone
show	showed	shown
shrink	shrank	shrunk
shut	shut	shut
sink	sank	sunk
sit	sat	sat
slide	slid	slid
speak	spoke	spoken
spend	spent	spent
split	split	split
spread	spread	spread
spring	sprang	sprung
stand	stood	stood
steal	stole	stolen
stick	stuck	stuck
strike	struck	struck
strive	stove	striven
sweep	swept	swept
swing	swung	swung
take	took	taken
teach	taught	taught
tear	torn	torn
tell	told	told
think	thought	thought
throw	threw	thrown
understand	understood	understood
wake	woke	woken
wear	wore	worn
win	won	won
write	wrote	written